The Inmates of Willard

of

1870 to 1900

A GENEALOGY RESOURCE

Linda S. Stuhler

This Book Is Dedicated To:

The Inmates Of Willard State Hospital

Formerly, The Willard Asylum For The Insane

In Memory Of:

Charity A. Griswold née Chambers

(1826 - February 3, 1886)

and

Margaret A. Putnam (Putman) née Orr

(August 1852 – August 13, 1928)

TABLE OF CONTENTS

Please visit my website at: inmatesofwillard.com.

"Experience has demonstrated, that the counties are not competent to do this work. The alms-house is not the proper place - indeed, it is a most unfit place for this disordered and dependent class. They require more than a simple home, for, though chronic, they are not all incurable cases, hence they should have hospital accommodations and treatment and care, as well as an asylum or home, and the 'Willard Asylum for the Insane' is just such an institution. It is more than a hospital or than an asylum; indeed, it is both, and meets the exact condition of the class for which it was founded, and was a want long felt. It marks a new era in the care of the chronic pauper insane; it has awakened a wide spread interest and inquiry."

—The Trustees Of The Willard Asylum For The Insane 1872

PREFACE - GENEALOGY GEEK

I am a genealogy geek. It started out simply enough, wanting to find from where my grandparents hailed. I found their parents and all of their children and before I knew it, I had a database of over 20,000 people. Early in my quest to connect the family dots I found other genealogy geeks who had the information for which I had long been searching. Thinking this would be an easy way to collect and compile important information, I downloaded and merged their GEnealogical Data COMmunication (GEDCOM) files with mine only to find out later that the information was incorrect. I spent many days deleting errors from my GEDCOM file all the while cursing myself for being so lazy. This mistake taught me a few valuable lessons: research is time consuming, always verify your sources, and don't ever merge another geek's GEDCOM file with your own.

When I started collecting information on my ancestors, I wondered what they were like and tried to imagine what it would be like to live in their day. We all believe our ancestors were good people, upstanding citizens, very good looking, and even heroes. We hope that somewhere in history one ancestor was wealthy or contributed significantly to the advancement of the human race. I found two U.S. Presidents, my second and fifth cousins so many times removed; a prominent American fashion designer, my ninth cousin; a man I believe is my great-great-uncle, a famous entrepreneur during development of Rochester, New York. Two of my great-grandfathers and a great-great-grandfather served in the Civil War; my third great-grandfather served in the War of 1812; countless ancestors fought in the Revolution and World War II. My seventh great-grandparents were slain at the Schenectady Massacre in 1690. I even found that one of my eighth great-grandmothers was hanged as a witch in Hartford, Connecticut in 1662; one of my ninth great-grandfathers served on the jury that convicted and sentenced her to death. Another ninth great-grandmother was an alleged princess of the Mohawk Nation. I collected this information over a twelve year period, making the search for my ancestors an exciting historical journey into the past.

Finding famous historical figures in a family tree is exciting but most of our ancestors were neither famous nor wealthy; if they were, the fame and wealth didn't trickle down to us. The majority of our ancestors were ordinary folk who didn't make any significant contributions to the advancement of the human race, but they did the best they could; they were common people who followed the social norms of the time in which they lived. With a cordial dream of a better life, they immigrated to America. That alone took tremendous courage, considering the voyage often took two months or more. Our ancestors worked farms, owned businesses, provided for their families, and hoped their children would have a better life.

The quest for the truth into the lives of my ancestors included some sad discoveries. We believe unrealistically that our ancestors were good, kind, educated people who were literate, owned their own homes, and held steady employment but what we find in our family tree is reality. Some of our ancestors were paupers, criminals, prostitutes, drug addicts, alcoholics, and the best kept family secret of all is that some of them were insane. With illiterate ancestors, you often cannot locate family bibles; your grandparents are long deceased and the quest to find the truth involves mountains of newspaper articles, obituaries, city directories, and federal censuses. Much of these exist in digital form on the Internet, especially on free genealogy websites. Some of these websites are for members only; they cost money, which presents a barrier to more casual inquirers. Be aware that the family tree information on these websites is often made possible by amateur genealogists like you and me; they may not be reliable but they are a great place to start.

There are two women I wish I could have spent some time getting to know. Charity A. Griswold née Chambers was my great-great-grandmother on my mother's maternal side and Margaret A. Putnam (Putman) née Orr was my great-grandmother on my mother's paternal side. The stories of their lives were filled with hardship, tragedy, and sorrow. The reason for my interest in the Willard State Hospital arose when I happened upon the obituary of my great-grandmother, known to her friends as Maggie. According to the Penn Yan Democrat newspaper dated August 17, 1928:

PUTNAM - At the State Hospital in Willard, Monday, August 13, 1928, Mrs. Margaret Putnam, aged 76 years. She is survived by one son, Jarvis Putnam, of Penn Yan. The funeral was held from the Thayer Funeral Home Wednesday afternoon, Rev. W.A. Hendricks officiating. Burial in Lake View cemetery.

I had no idea Maggie was a Willard State Hospital inmate or that she died in that hospital. As I recall, no one in my family had ever spoken about it. My grandmother told me about Maggie; what a sweet little woman she was with her strong Irish accent, how she lived with her for a while after her husband Richard, my great-grandfather, died in 1924. Maggie would stand at the window and say that he would be coming home soon. She rearranged the furniture in the parlor the way she liked it, not the way my grandmother wanted it. My grandmother was thirty-two at the time with five young children. I understand how difficult it must have been for my grandmother to care for an elderly woman likely suffering from dementia. I will never know Maggie's true diagnosis and I will never see her photograph or medical records unless current law changes.

My county poor house curiosity began when I found Charity along with three of her children listed on a U.S. Federal Census as an inmate of the Yates County Poor House. Before I researched Willard, I did not know that its creation was the result of Legislature of the State of New York investigations into the inhumane treatment of the insane kept in seclusion and chains in county poor houses. I have often wondered how Charity was able to keep her sanity living so many years in poor house squalor. Both Willard State Hospital and Yates County Poor House were located near the Finger Lakes, Seneca and Keuka respectively.

Both women's lives are important to me and relevant to this book because both were thrust into similar circumstances beyond their control. I doubt they ever met but their lives are what brought me to research and uncover the names of the Inmates of Willard State Hospital, formerly known as The Willard Asylum for the Insane. It is important to understand that it was much worse for our ancestors when an unexpected illness or loss of income occurred. In the nineteenth and early twentieth centuries, there was no health insurance, Medicare, unemployment insurance, welfare, or social security. Unless you had a relative willing to take you and your family in, you were on your own.

It is difficult to imagine being held against my will under any circumstances, especially being committed to an insane asylum. The only analogy that comes to my mind is being placed in a nursing home. At the end of our earthly journey, we hope and pray that we die quietly in our home, in our bed, without suffering, and without burdening our children and loved ones but only a few are granted these wishes. We know that nursing homes are filled with sick, elderly people suffering from a plethora of illnesses who hoped they would never see the inside of the place where members of our society go to die. We presume our wishes will be respected; in many cases, unscrupulous family members and lawyers change our meticulous plans. Wills, powers of attorney, and health care proxies created when a person possessed full mental capacity are modified for the unsuspecting elderly. So even today, you could find yourself in a place where you don't want to be, all your savings gone and no way out. If you visit a nursing home, you experience only a fraction of what it is like to live there; imagine your days consisting of walking up and down long halls with your walker, listening to the cries and screams of other residents. You may ask yourself, why am I here? Cared for by strangers, you may be bedridden or left outside your room, stuck in a wheelchair and staring at the floor. You never get used to the smell of urine that pervades the air or waiting for a nurse to change your diaper humiliatingly. The medicine they feed you makes you sick and you lose your appetite. You may even become one of them. Depression and loneliness saturate your soul until death is a welcomed visitor. The Inmates of Willard must have suffered similarly. Some patients and attendants assaulted and abused other patients; some died as a result of these injuries, a headline too often seen in today's newspapers concerning nursing homes. Others objected to their incarceration and escaped, and some committed suicide.

Insanity has been romanticized and demonized in literature and film. Some contemporary authors believe it is on the rise and some feel that it doesn't exist at all. I believe it is part of the human condition to which no one is immune. The broad term insanity of the nineteenth century equals the terms mental illness or psychiatric disability of the twenty-first. When I think of insanity, Hollywood imagery comes to mind. An evil madman clad forcibly in a stark white straight jacket, filthy, screaming at no one, walking in circles, talking to himself, and laughing in the darkness of a padded room. And there it is; the stigma that has lasted for centuries, attributed to all who had lost their minds, from the elderly with dementia to epileptics to violent and sadistic murderers.

Mention your ancestor was an Inmate at Willard and most likely the response is derogatory. Mental illness carries a stigma unlike any other because we don't understand what it is and we cannot see the pain and debilitating effects on the body like we do with physical illness. Few hesitate to announce that an ancestor had heart disease, high cholesterol, or diabetes; not many disclose there was mental illness in the family. Why? In my opinion, three basic reasons are responsible: fear, ignorance, and intolerance. If your mother were crazy then you might be crazy too; fear of judgment as mentally unstable because a family member - past or present - suffered or is suffering from a psychiatric disability and our propensity to suffer from the disease as well. We cannot be informed on every subject, especially one as complex as mental illness. We can try to understand the plight of the Inmates of Willard with understanding, greater knowledge, and tolerance.

This genealogy resource book on the Willard Asylum for the Insane and the first generation of Willard Inmates was written with genealogy geeks in mind. It is for those who want to glimpse the past, enjoy reading historical documents with little or no interpretation, and want to acquire basic knowledge about Willard in one resource without having to search the Internet to read hundreds of articles to understand what it was about. I have the utmost respect and compassion for the Inmates of Willard. I am not stating that Willard was a terrible hospital filled with uncaring employees; on the contrary, the majority of doctors, nurses, attendants, and staff that worked at the facility from 1869 until its demise in 1995 were caring people. As in any profession and every large institution, there are always incompetents who give everyone else a bad name. I do not state that I am for or against institutionalization of any human being, nor do I state that none of those people suffered from psychiatric disabilities. I am neither a physician nor psychiatrist and I do not claim to be an expert.

My research includes personal interpretations and transcriptions of the names of the Inmates of Willard from U.S. Federal Censuses for the years 1870, 1880, and 1900 disseminated onto spreadsheets that the reader may find an ancestor more easily. It is a collection of historical documents and laws of the time that tell the most accurate story of the people and politics surrounding the controversial Willard Asylum. Although this book deals with the specifics of Willard and its inmates, the laws, rules, and regulations apply to all county poor houses, city alms houses, and public and private insane asylums in the State of New York. It makes the reader aware of the thousands of former psychiatric patients buried in anonymous, numbered graves in the State of New York and across the United States of America. The history of the treatment of the insane belongs to us all.

The creation of Willard and all state insane asylums was an enormous financial and administrative undertaking for the state; it was also a new concept. For the first time in American history, state asylums for the insane were the first attempts at government intervention where the state assumed the role of parent or guardian for these dependant people, providing for their medical care, food, clothing, and shelter. The charitable poor house system of punishing and isolating the insane began in 1824. Over the course of sixty-nine years, this system transitioned from filthy cells and sheds; to an attempt at humanity with separate buildings, rooms, and pitiable medical care provided by county-run insane asylums; to the ultimate in medical treatment with state insane asylums, and later, state-run hospitals. The miserable poor house system of caring for the insane ended in 1893 when the State Care Act of 1890 took effect.

It is my hope that revealing the inmates' names offers people a sign that the Inmates of Willard State Hospital are not forgotten; they were human beings deserving dignity even in death. According to Darby Penney and Peter Stastny, authors of the book *The Lives They Left Behind*, the remains of 5,776 people are buried at Willard State Hospital Cemetery. Ms. Penney is a national leader in the human rights movement for people with psychiatric disabilities. In an email I asked her, "When did the state hospitals go bad?" Her reply was, "It never went bad. Western society's methods of dealing with people in mental and emotional distress have always been based on punishment and segregation. Anyone who is locked up against their will and kept in isolation is being treated poorly, to my mind."

Willard inmates were not asked if they wanted a headstone inscribed with their name atop their final resting place; they were buried anonymously with numbered metal markers. The exceptions were veterans who have headstones provided by the U.S. government, inscribed clearly with the deceased's name. At some point during the 1980s or 1990s, most of the upright metal markers were replaced with flat aluminum markers or disks that were sunk in concrete poured into PVC pipe to make it easier to mow the vast cemetery lawn. The New York State Office of Mental Health has classified the burial ledger of the Willard State Hospital as a medical record thus denying access to the people of the state. Many of these former patients died over one hundred years ago; they are not under the care of the OMH. The names of the Inmates of Willard can be found on the Internet from such sources as the U.S. Federal Census, genealogy websites, historical documents, and books; everywhere except where they should be; on headstones in former New York State Hospital cemeteries. Unless a descendant approves of the release of their ancestor's name, an engraved headstone cannot be provided either by fund raising efforts or by the state. This rationalization makes me wonder if the people responsible for making these decisions have ever stopped to consider that many of the former inmates may no longer have living descendants. Many patients were dumped at these institutions because their families did not want to be associated with them in the first place. We, the people of the state and the country, have a right to know where our ancestors are buried; and the inmates should have the right to be remembered with dignity. Anonymous burials are common for state mental institutions across New York State and the country. Not only is this unacceptable, it is dehumanizing, insulting and disgraceful. The time has come to accept the mistakes of the past and turn a wrong into a right by releasing the names of the people buried at the Willard State Hospital Cemetery and people buried anonymously in state mental institution cemeteries across America.

As already stated, my great-great-grandmother was labeled a pauper and an inmate of the Yates County Poor House; my great-grandmother was labeled as an insane inmate of the Willard State Hospital. I am not ashamed of them and I do not judge them. I embrace them as family members unfortunately and unnecessarily labeled. Both are buried in unmarked graves not because they were not loved, but because their families did not have the money to purchase headstones. One day I hope to mark their graves with inscribed headstones. The words insane, idiot, imbecile, cripple, deaf and dumb, pauper, and inmate are demeaning and harsh, but these are the words used to identify this dependant class during the nineteenth and early twentieth centuries. Regrettable is the stigma perpetuated about these people who lived at these long-closed asylums and county poor houses. They were human beings, poor, unwanted, separated from society, not physically or mentally well, and they needed medical attention, understanding, and sympathetic care above all else.

The Willard Asylum for the Insane was built specifically for the pauper chronic insane of the state; these people were not only labeled as insane, they were destitute. The majority of paupers were working class people who suffered some type of loss that led to destitution. To be labeled a pauper or lunatic was shameful; it was humiliating for family members to be related to these people because it reflected that their family had not come from good stock. Many inmates were recent immigrants who had no family or friends in the new world. Once incarcerated at the institution, many were destined to remain until death relieved them of their tormented lives. The remote location of Willard and the modes of travel during the 1800s made visitation by family members difficult. Some family members preferred never to see or hear from their insane family members.

In the early twenty-first century, Willard Cemetery remains an anonymous potter's field even though the New York State Office of Mental Health has in its possession the names of the 5,776 people buried there. For two years, I tried to gain access to the burial ledger and the map of the coordinating location of the graves and the burial procedures of Willard to publish my findings and reveal the names in this book. I was denied every step of the way because of HIPAA and NYS Mental Health Laws required to protect the identity of the inmates because they were mental patients. It is hard to believe that I was denied the burial procedures of Willard. To my knowledge, these documents are not protected by law.

I include here my story that you may understand where I am coming from. Besides writing a letter to the former and present Governor, both U.S. Senators, State Senator, Congressman, The Department of Correctional Services, The Commission on Quality of Care and Advocacy for Persons with Disabilities, The Office of Mental Health Counsel, and the State of New York Department of State Committee on Open Government (FOIL), I also wrote a letter to the doctor in charge of the Office of Mental Health Institutional Review Board asking permission to view, record, and publish this information located and stored at the NYS Archives. After waiting seven months for a response, I was told in an official letter, that my proposed study was not approved due to concerns about violating patient confidentiality.

Willard is unique in that patient medical records and photographs dating back to 1869 were never destroyed; only a select few are allowed to see, study, or learn from them because of the HIPAA and the NYS Mental Health Laws. Even though my great-grandmother has been dead for eighty-three years, her medical records are protected under the confidentiality clause of these laws. What the architects of the HIPAA and the NYS Mental Health Law failed to recognize is that U.S. Federal Censuses are released to the public every seventy-two years. Anyone incarcerated in any mental institution present on the day of the census taking shows up on the census as an inmate. If no one is allowed access to their ancestor's medical records, photographs, or burial locations and if no doctors, students, or researchers are allowed to study and learn from them unless approved by the Office of Mental Health, then the question is, "why are they saving them?" I am not suggesting the release of medical records of the living, nor am I in favor of putting medical records of the living on a secure website to share one's medical information with other doctors. What I am in favor of is releasing these unique records to descendants who have gone through the process of filling out and mailing in the paper work. The information should also be made available to serious researchers interested in this field.

From all the information I gathered, I am under the impression that contemporary medical records are usually destroyed within five years of a patient's death, if not sooner. HIPAA should be more concerned with the private, confidential medical records of the living than with the long dead. Who knows how secure our medical records are? They could be at this moment on a doctor's flash drive, lying on a desk in an office or on the doctor's kitchen table. In a recent case in Rochester, a doctor lost a flash drive containing confidential patient information that he intended to take home; it remains unrecovered.

One voice rarely moves the politics of our country. U.S. Senators should be made aware that these laws are prejudicial to deceased people who had psychiatric disabilities and were incarcerated in state mental institutions and asylums. The law denies them the privilege of a headstone as if these people are not worthy of remembrance. A simple modification in the way the laws are written would give former Willard inmates the same privileges as any other human being, U.S. citizen or not. They did exist, they had names, and the silence that has lasted for one hundred forty-two years is deafening.

I went through proper channels to obtain Maggie's medical records and photo. I filled out the paperwork, had my doctor and a witness sign the paperwork, and my doctor sent it in. I waited four months for a response and finally my doctor received a letter. I asked for the medical records and any photos of "Margaret Orr-Putnam." When I received the response from the Greater Binghamton Health Center in August 2008, it stated the staff was unable to locate the requested file on "Margarett Putman." I believe they have her records but will not release them. This doesn't mean that you shouldn't try to obtain your ancestor's medical records and photos. Indeed, you should; my hope is that you succeed. Had I received my great-grandmother's medical records, I would have been satisfied and I never would have conducted this fact finding investigation. Besides being genuinely interested in learning more about Willard, I created this book for family genealogists like me, frustrated trying to find out if and when their ancestor was a Willard inmate, receiving the runaround obtaining their ancestor's medical records and photos, and determining whether their ancestor is buried in the Willard Cemetery.

The final answer came from the Commissioner of the NYS Office of Mental Health in responding to my inquiry by e-mail on October 25, 2010, which basically stated that publicly identifying former patients may be offensive to some families because of the stigma and repercussions that may follow, for example, in some small towns.

We believe that we have come far in eradicating discriminatory behaviors and mindsets; we pat ourselves on the back for our open-mindedness and political correctness. We can see clearly that we have not moved any further in our tolerance or understanding of people with psychiatric disabilities and of people who live in small towns; we are no better than our ancestors who came before us. Willard's inmates who in life were incarcerated, forgotten, warehoused, and controlled by the state are once again controlled and intentionally forgotten in death by the NYS Office of Mental Health. If nothing else, these people had names. Protection provided by these laws is not for long dead souls since U.S. Federal Censuses already reveal many of their names; it is for the protection of the descendants of the insane.

The Inmates of Willard, as well as all former inmates of New York State Hospitals, deserve a clearly marked cemetery that is well maintained and treated with respect like any other cemetery as a place where descendants and friends gather to pay respects, lay flowers, or meditate in silence. California, Georgia, Maine, Massachusetts, Minnesota, Nevada, Oregon, Texas, Washington, and Wisconsin have released the names of former patients buried in anonymous graves at these long closed, state owned mental institutions, and they have allowed engraved headstones to be placed on the graves. In some cases, these states have provided funding for the headstones. It is my hope that the names of the patients buried in anonymous graves in cemeteries owned by the State of New York will be made available to the public in a unified, digital, database. If you share a desire to end the stigma of mental illness by forcing HIPAA and the NYS Office of Mental Health to modify the laws and release the names of these people, along with releasing medical records to descendants and researchers, it is important that you sign the letter located at inmatesofwillard.com and mail it to your two representatives in the U.S. Senate. If these laws are not modified, these graves forever remain forgotten and anonymous.

On May 9, 1992, the Town of Danvers, Massachusetts, acknowledged and took responsibility for the mistakes of their ancestors by presenting a beautiful granite memorial to the people of the state and the country in honor of the twenty villagers unjustly executed at The Salem Witch Trials between February 1692 and May 1693. "The Memorial serves as a reminder that each generation must confront intolerance and 'witch hunts' with integrity, clear vision and courage." Forty-five years earlier between 1647 and 1663, the settlement at Hartford, Connecticut also held witch trials that resulted in the hangings of at least ten innocent villagers, one of whom was my eighth great-grandmother, Rebecca Greensmith née Unknown. The State of Connecticut does not acknowledge, pardon, or accept the mistakes of its ancestors. Will New York State lead by example and end the disgrace of anonymous burials or will it remain as blind and indifferent as the state of Connecticut? The Salem and Hartford executions are grim reminders of the fear, ignorance, and intolerance that permeated America's past, not dissimilar from what happened at Willard. Innocent people were unjustly singled out in shame because they were feared for being different. In both cases, these people were ultimately removed from society and erased from history.

1

THE COUNTY POOR HOUSE

On November 27, 1824, the New York State Legislature passed a law *To Provide For The Establishment Of County Poorhouses.* (Law A) The poor house was the last resort for paupers consisting of a communal life in which inmates were required to work on the farm and in the house in order to eat, have a place to sleep, and to stay alive. This law was harsh and it gave the Superintendents of the Poor and the Keepers of the poor houses unlimited, unregulated power. Many of them were cruel, inhumane and abusive to the people under their charge. If you were a disorderly person, whether sane or insane, it was, "lawful for the keeper of the same house, to place and keep each and every such person in solitary confinement in some part of the same house, and feed him, her or them, with bread and water only, until he or she shall submit to perform the same labor, work and service, and obey, conform and observe the rules, regulations and by-laws." (49)

I first found my great-great-grandmother, Charity, listed as an inmate of the Yates County Poor House in the 1865 Census of the Town of Jerusalem, Yates County, New York. She was 39; daughter, Mary, 18; son, Edward, 8; and daughter, Sarah, age 12, was not listed with them. Perhaps Sarah was fortunate enough to be taken in by a relative or perhaps she was simply overlooked by the enumerator. Charity would not have arrived at the poor house until after the Civil War had begun when her husband, my great-great-grandfather, Aaron H. Griswold; and her eldest son, my great-grandfather, Sylvester Thomas Griswold, went off to war. I am certain that the circumstances must have been hopelessly bleak for Charity knowing that she and her children had nowhere else to go but the county poor house about the year 1862.

The following reports discuss the investigations conducted by the state legislature in 1857 of all county poor houses, work houses, and jails in the State of New York. These reports were important because they exposed the corruption and appalling living conditions that existed in the poor houses, and they conveyed the urgency for special care and provisions for the insane.

"Report Of Select Committee appointed to visit Charitable Institutions supported by the State, and all city and county poor and work houses and jails.

Mr. Spencer from the select committee appointed by the Senate, under a resolution passed February 7, 1856, 'to visit, after the adjournment of the Legislature, all charitable institutions supported or assisted by the State, and all city and county poor and work houses and jails,' and 'to examine into the condition of the said establishments, their receipts and expenditures, their methods of instruction, and the government, treatment, and management of the inmates, the conduct of the trustees, directors, and other officers of the same, and all other matters whatever pertaining to their usefulness and good government,' Reports: Since the adjournment of the Legislature, they have, for five months, with some intermissions, been engaged in the investigations required by the resolution of the Senate. They have diligently examined into the existing condition of the poor houses, work houses, hospitals, jails, orphan and lunatic asylums, and other charitable and reformatory institutions, supported or assisted by the State; and have committed to writing the evidence taken in the course of their investigations, an abstract of which is appended to this report."

"I. Poor Houses, Alms Houses, and Kindred Charities

Exclusive of the alms houses and poor houses in New-York and Kings counties, (which are particularly referred to in the appendix,) there are fifty-five poor houses in the State; the average number of inmates for the year, according to the testimony taken by the committee, being 6,420. The actual number of inmates at the time when the committee was engaged in its examinations, was 4,936, of which 2,670 were foreign born, and 1,307 were children. During the past year, the number of deaths in these fifty-five poor houses was 770. Such a great mortality as this number indicates, should arrest the public attention.

The number of lunatics found confined in the poor houses (excepting those in New-York and Kings counties) was 837, (329 males and 508 females) of which number 301 were received during the last year. Of the whole number, 130 were reported as being in *cells* and *chains*. During the year, 59 improved and 26 recovered. All were *paupers* except 27. Why these twenty-seven should be confined in a *poor house* can only be accounted for by the inadequate provision now made by the State for accommodating the poor insane. This circumstance impressed the committee with the urgent necessity of providing additional establishments similar to the State Asylum at Utica. At least two such are required for present emergencies. A bill was reported to the Legislature at its last session, by a select committee of the Senate, providing for this necessity, which in its principal features, at least, and probably in its details, deserves the favorable consideration of the Senate, and, in the judgment of the committee, ought to become a law. Sufficient reasons for such an opinion may be found in the report of the select committee who introduced the bill, and they are fortified by the facts attested to by the various witnesses whose testimony is appended to this report."

"There was found in these poor houses 273 idiots, 25 deaf mutes, and 71 blind persons. Of those numbered as idiots, many are simply demented and are suitable subjects for lunatic asylums. The average weekly support of the inmates is eighty-three cents. The poor houses throughout the State may be generally described as badly constructed, ill-arranged, ill-warmed, and ill-ventilated. The rooms are crowded with inmates; and the air, particularly in the sleeping apartments, is very noxious, and to casual visitors, almost insufferable. In some cases, as many as forty-five inmates occupy a single dormitory, with low ceilings, and sleeping boxes arranged in three tiers one above another. Good health is incompatible with such arrangements. They make it an impossibility.

The want of suitable hospital accommodations is severely felt in most of the poor houses. The sick, considering their physical condition, are even worse cared for than the healthy. The arrangements for medical attendance are quite inadequate to secure that which is suitable; the physician is poorly paid, and consequently gives only such general attention as his remuneration seems to require. In some cases, the inmates sicken and die without any medical attendance whatever. In one county alms-house, averaging 137 inmates, there were 36 deaths during the past year, and yet none of them from epidemic or contagious disease. Such a proportion of mortality indicates most inexcusable negligence.

A proper classification of the inmates is almost wholly neglected. It is either impossible, or when possible, it is disregarded. Many of the births occurring during the year are doubtless, the offspring of illicit connections. During the last year, the whole number of births was 292. The indiscriminate association of the sexes generally allowed strongly favors this assumption. By day, their intercourse is common and unrestricted; and there is often no sufficient safe-guard against a promiscuous intercourse by night. In one case, the only pretence of a separation of the sexes consisted in the circumstance of separate stairs being provided at each end of a common dormitory; and a police regulation, requiring one sex to reach it by one flight, and the other sex by another, appeared to be deemed a sufficient preventive of all subsequent intercourse.

In two counties, the committee found that the poor houses were supplied by contract, the contractor being allowed to profit by all the labor which he could extort from the paupers. In *both* counties, the contractor was a *superintendent of the poor*; and in *one*, he was *also keeper of the poor house*. In one, the keeper received his compensation from the contractor; and in this case, the food supplied was not only insufficient in quantity, but consisted partly of tainted meat and fish. The inmates were consequently almost starved. They were also deprived of a sufficiency of fuel and bedding, and suffered severely from cold. So gross and inhuman was the conduct of the contractor for this poor house, that two female inmates (lunatics,) were frozen in their cells (or rather sheds,) during the last winter, and are now cripples for life.

The treatment of lunatics and idiots in these houses is frequently abusive. The cells and sheds where they are confined are wretched abodes, often wholly unprovided with bedding. In most cases, female lunatics had none but male attendants. Instances were testified to of the *whipping* of male and female idiots and lunatics, and of confining the latter in loathsome cells, and binding them with chains. In one county, where eleven lunatics were confined, six were in chains, some of whom were females. In several of these cases, the patients were not violent; but it may be proper to say that the severity and inhumanity of their treatment were probably owing to the apprehensions and ignorance of the keepers, rather than to any intentional harshness or any unkindness of disposition.

In some poor houses, the committee found lunatics, both male and female, in cells, in a state of nudity. The cells were intolerably offensive, littered with the long accumulated filth of the occupants, and with straw reduced to chaff by long use as bedding, portions of which, mingled with the filth, adhered to the persons of the inmates and formed the only covering they had."

"Before passing from the subject of poor houses, the committee may be allowed to say that it is much to be regretted that our citizens generally manifest so little interest in the condition even of those in their immediate neighborhood. Individuals who take great interest in human suffering whenever it is brought to their notice, never visit them, and are entirely uninformed, that in a county house almost at their own doors, may be found the lunatic suffering for years in a dark and suffocating cell, in summer, and almost freezing in the winter, - where a score of children are poorly fed, poorly clothed, and quite untaught, - where the poor idiot is half starved and beaten with rods because he is too dull to do his master's bidding, - where the aged mother is lying in perhaps her last sickness, unattended by a physician, and with no one to minister to her wants, - where the lunatic, and that lunatic too, *a woman*, is made to feel the lash in the hands of a brutal under-keeper - yet these are all to be found - *they all exist in our State*. And the committee are quite convinced that to this apparent indifference on the part of the citizens, may be attributed in a great degree, the miserable state to which these houses have fallen; and they would urge upon the benevolent in all parts of the State to look into their condition, and thus assist to make them comfortable abodes for the indigent and the unfortunate."

"III. Lunatic Asylums

For statistical and other details respecting the lunatic asylums endowed or assisted by the State, the committee refer to the appendix to this report. They are as well and efficiently managed as is possible with the means and conveniences at the command of the superintendents and managers, and in conformity to the existing provisions of law. A particular examination of these, has forced the committee to a conclusion which seems to have been generally adopted by the superintendents and managers of such asylums, both in this country and abroad; that the common practice of transferring insane *convicts*, or convicts assumed to be so, from the prisons to the lunatic asylums is impolitic, injurious and unjust. Lunacy has no necessary association with crime; nor should lunatics be enforced to an association with criminals. It is an association every way detrimental to the lunatic, and no way beneficial to the criminal. While lunacy may be wisely deemed a sufficient cause for absolving a convict from punishment, it is not a sufficient one for letting him loose on the community at large, and much less upon that afflicted portion of it, for whose protection and care asylums are founded and maintained. A decent respect for their infirmity demands that they should not be legally associated with those outcasts of society, who, in the possession of their faculties, have degraded themselves by crime."

"A prison is a place of strict confinement and enforced labor, by way of *punishment*; an asylum is simply a place of confinement, by way of isolation, and for the benevolent purpose of protection and *cure*. To make the two places common, is to confound two different intents of the law and of humanity, and to defeat both."

"The Yates County Poor House is located in the town of Jerusalem. It is a stone structure, and including the basement, is three stories high, fifty by 100 feet on the ground - built some twenty years ago, with very low ceilings and without ventilation, and with no provisions for bathing. It is heated by stoves and fire-places, or rather attempted to be. The keeper stated that some of the rooms could not be kept warm in some weather, and that several cases had occurred in the house in which the paupers had been frost bitten, and that one of those was a *lunatic*. Connected with the house is a farm of 123 acres, yielding an annual revenue of $1,000. Fifteen rooms are appropriated to the use of the poor, and as many as eighteen are sometimes placed in a single room. The basement is occupied for dining halls and cooking. Sixty inmates were found in the house - thirty male and thirty female, fifteen foreign and forty-five native born, including twelve children. The sexes are kept separate at night, but not during the day. The house is in charge of one keeper and his wife, who have the management of both house and farm, assisted by the paupers. The superintendent of the poor purchases the needful supplies for the house, provides and imposes rules regulating the diet, and binds out the children when places can be procured, and discharges lunatics when cured. The average number supported is eighty-six, at a weekly cost of $1.40 each. The house is supplied with Bibles, and preaching is enjoyed once in four weeks. The children have been taught eight months in the house, and were at the time attending the district school.

The supervisors have visited the house twice during the last year. A physician is employed to visit the house twice a week. There has been one birth and four deaths during the year. Five of the inmates are *lunatics* - two male and three female, none of whom have ever been sent to the State Lunatic Asylum. They have no special attendants, nor do they receive any special medical attention, and none have been cured or improved. One is kept constantly in a cell. The modes of restraining are by the 'use of irons' and locking in cells, *where one lunatic was frozen*. It is stated as a common occurrence that water is frozen all night in the lodging rooms in the main building. The number of idiots is seven - three males and four females, and four who are blind. During the winter usually about twenty emigrants are provided for here, and two-thirds of the whole number who receive aid here are forced to seek and receive it consequent upon habits of inebriation. The poor house building is quite unsuited and insufficient, *humanely* to meet the wants of the poor." (4)

"Excerpt from Welfare Edition Recalls Evolution of Yates County's Home – Esperanza

Records show that in 1873 the Yates county almshouse was located on East hill in Jerusalem. The 'Poor House farm' consisted of 185 acres and its estimated value was $8,000. In his report to the board of supervisors that year Charles J. Townsend, supervisor of the poor, stated that there were 33 inmates; 19 males and 14 females. Besides these, there were 21 other inmates that spent part of the year at the farm making a total of 54 in 1873. The cost of maintaining the total for the year was $3,284.56. Mr. Townsend described the condition of the home as follows: 'It is the worst, meanest old hovel that ever bore the name of almshouse - not as good as Captain Jack's home in the lava beds, according to the best information I have of them. It is a standing disgrace to Yates County, and there should be a new one built, or abandon the poor house system and let each town take care of its own poor, or turn them out to grass as was Nebuchadnezzar of old. The inmates and keeper have to move their beds when it storms; the rats and other vermin have pretty near a warrantee deed of the old trap and it is dangerous and filthy in the extreme. The farm produces fairly; the barn is good; but deliver me from the house!' " (5)

"Yates County Poor-House

1868. - An old, dilapidated, two-story and basement stone structure, located in the town of Jerusalem, about five miles from Penn Yan. Among the inmates were twenty-four children, two idiots, and seven insane. The insane were in an old building in the rear, with no attendants except paupers. Three were confined in their cells, and nearly all were excited and violent. The children attend school in a building situated upon the poor-house grounds, but when out of school they mingle with the other inmates. No classification is possible in the institution; the sexes are separated at night, but during the day the association is unrestricted. The labor of the paupers, as far as practicable, is utilized upon the farm.

1878. - Near the close of 1868 this county transferred the dependent children then in the poor-house to the Ontario Orphan Asylum, at Canandaigua, and since then it has provided for this class mainly in that institution. The chronic insane, in 1869, were sent to the Willard Asylum, and none of this class are now held under county care. During the past year a new poor-house was erected upon the site of the old structure. This is a substantial, two-story and basement stone building, planned so as to separate the sexes and secure a partial classification. It is heated by steam, has good conveniences for bathing, and is adequate to the present requirements.

1888. - This house is kept in good repair, and affords a comfortable home for its inmates, the accommodations being greatly in excess of the demands. The county sends all of its insane requiring special supervision to the State asylums for this class. The children of the county are temporarily provided for at the Ontario Orphan Asylum at Canandaigua, and thence placed in families." (6)

2

The Creation Of The Willard Asylum For The Pauper Chronic Insane

In 1821, the Bloomingdale Lunatic Asylum opened as a branch of the New York Hospital in New York City. Even though it received quarterly appropriations from the state, it was not state-run. There was no organized medical treatment, provisions, or care for the insane provided by the State of New York until the opening of The State Lunatic Asylum at Utica in 1843. Previous to that time, the insane were subjected to extreme cruelty, neglect, punishment, and starvation in the county poor houses and jails, and many were treated similarly in the homes of family members.

Insanity was thought to be a disease of the brain that could be cured if treated in its early or acute stage. Moral Treatment was the belief that patients should be treated with kindness and sympathetic care. It called for the patient to be removed from family and society in order to relieve the stresses of everyday life. The Willard Asylum was unique because it was created to end the poor house system of caring for the insane. It provided a permanent home for the pauper chronic insane or "incurables" of the state with a higher standard of care than what was given in the county poor houses; which was no care at all. The term *chronic* refers to an individual who suffered from insanity for more than one year. The goal of the asylum was to offer individualized care by *segregating* the insane into two classes: (likely) curable and incurable; rather than treating them all the same by *congregating* them in one massive building. Critics of the Willard bill thought that the words, "All hope abandon, ye who enter here," should be placed above the entrance of the new asylum. Supporters of the bill wanted to remove all insane inmates from the county poor houses in order to provide them with medical treatment and care; and to eliminate the power and vested interests of the county superintendents of the poor. Willard offered kindly care for the insane with a safe, orderly, clean, controlled environment that created stability; work that provided self-discipline; exercise to keep the body and mind fit; a balanced diet; mechanical restraints; and medical treatment provided by physicians. Employing kindly, sympathetic attendants (most of whom had no prior experience in this field and no formal education or training), who were willing to live day in and day out among the insane, in an insane asylum, with little pay, was a difficult task.

The Law of 1836 created The State Lunatic Asylum at Utica. The first New York State mental institution opened its doors to the "curable lunatic pauper" population on January 16, 1843. Within ten and a half months 276 patients had been received into the asylum: fifty-three were discharged recovered, fourteen improved, and six unimproved; seven had died and one hundred and ninety-six were remaining as of November 30, 1843. By February, 1844, the Managers of the State Lunatic Asylum were asking for more money to expand Utica and they had expressed the need for another lunatic asylum to be built, preferably in the western part of the state.

"New York State Lunatic Asylum at Utica. This institution was organized by an act of the Legislature, passed April 7th, 1842, and opened for patients in 1843. It is located about one mile west from the central part of the city of Utica, upon an elevated plateau of ground, commanding an extended view of the city and surrounding country. The building is a spacious edifice, built of stone and brick, presenting a front of over five hundred, and a depth of two hundred and fifty feet, besides cross-wings, extensions and out-buildings, the entire structure furnishing accommodations for five hundred and fifty patients, and apartments for the officers and necessary attendants. The grounds surrounding the asylum are neatly laid out, and planted with shade trees and shrubbery; and the farm comprises two hundred and fifty acres, about one-fourth of which is in meadow lands and the residue under cultivation. The title to the property is in the State, and the institution is controlled by a Board of Managers appointed by the Governor, by and with the advice and consent of the Senate.

The act organizing the asylum provides for the admission of three classes of patients, viz.: pauper, indigent, and paying patients. The first are received upon the application of superintendents or overseers of the poor; the second on the order of a county judge, upon a certificate of indigency; and the third in the discretion of the superintendent, under rules established by the Board of Managers. The present charges for pauper and indigent insane are four dollars, and for paying patients, from four to six dollars per week; but in cases requiring special care and attention, the latter are charged additional.

The asylum was established as a hospital or curative institution, and the act organizing it made no extended provision for the chronic insane. The demands upon it for recent cases have at all times been nearly equal to its accommodations; and the Managers have, therefore, been compelled, from time to time, under the law, to return to their friends or the county poor houses, a large proportion of the chronic cases not violent and deemed incurable. The act organizing the Willard Asylum at Ovid, requires that the pauper chronic insane shall be transferred hereafter to that institution, and prohibits their return to the county receptacles, thus relieving the local authorities of their charge." (7)

In 1865, *The Willard Act* (Law B) authorized the creation of The Willard Asylum for the Insane. This law enacted sweeping changes in the way in which the pauper insane population would be treated. It would also introduce a new policy that "was to relieve the county of their care and devolve it upon the State through the 'Willard,' and the State Lunatic Asylum at Utica." (50)

This partial state care meant that these people were now the wards of the state in a shared kind of way. Although the state was funding the actual cost and upkeep of the land, buildings, equipment, supplies, and payroll of physicians and employees; the counties were still absorbing the cost of the patients' maintenance that was fixed by the Trustees of the Willard Asylum from $2.00 to $3.00 per week. In addition, the counties were required to pay for their clothing which cost approximately $15.00 per year; making the yearly total roughly $170.00 per patient, per year. Prior to the opening of Willard, patients were only allowed to stay at Utica for two years and if deemed incurable or chronically insane, they would be sent back to their home; with relatives or friends; or to the county poor house to be abused all over again. The Willard Asylum for the Chronic Insane opened its doors on October 13, 1869. The following excerpts and documents explain how it came into existence.

The Name Change 1865

"A bill was reported by the committee, of which Dr. W.H. Richardson was chairman, creating a second State lunatic asylum, to be known as the *Beck Asylum for the Insane.* Dr. Willard died April 2, 1865. In a biographical notice published in the transactions of the State Medical Society for 1866, Dr. Franklin B. Hough pays a deserved tribute to the work of Dr. Willard in investigating the condition of the insane poor, his energy in collecting information, and his zeal in promoting the establishment of a new asylum for their care. His biographer remarks: 'His death made a marked impression upon the public mind, and his prominent position (Surgeon-General of the State of New York) suggested a further mark of honor.' The bill then in the Senate was amended, and became a law with the name changed to *The Willard Asylum for the Insane.*" (8)

The Commissioners 1866

"The Commissioners appointed under the organic act to locate and build the Asylum were Drs. John P. Gray, of Utica, Julian P. Williams, of Dunkirk, and John B. Chapin, of Canandaigua. Dr. Gray resigned in May 1866, and Dr. Lyman Congdon, of Jacksonville, was appointed in his stead. The Commissioners were directed first to 'seek for and select any property owned by the State or upon which it has a lien.' This was understood to refer to the grounds and buildings of the State Agricultural College, which was declining and whose actual operation had ceased. The title was acquired, and the Asylum located in December 1865. The erection of the main Asylum building was commenced in July, 1866, and proceeded with till May, 1869, when the Legislature abolished the Building Commissioners and conferred their powers and duties upon a Board of Trustees, viz., John E. Seely, Genet Conger, Sterling G. Hadley, Francis O. Mason, Samuel B. Welles, George J. Magee, Darius A. Ogden and William A. Swaby. This board was created to organize the Asylum and administer its affairs. Their services are gratuitous. Their term is eight years, and their successors are appointed by the Governor and Senate." (9)

The Architects

John Bassett Chapin, M.D., the first Physician Superintendent of the Willard Asylum for the Insane, was undoubtedly the grand architect and driving force behind this new economical plan of state insane asylums that included "cottage style" buildings and the unpaid labor of patients.

"Up to twenty years ago there was little diversity in the plans of asylums throughout the country. They were all constructed upon the compact linear design, introduced by the late Dr. Kirkbride, with which all are familiar, from its frequent reproduction. The first essential departure from this plan was made at the Willard Asylum in New York, where a system of separate structures was designed by the superintendent, Dr. Chapin. These were located in different parts of the large farm, in such relation to the central asylum buildings as to be within easy control of the administrative authority." (10)

According to *The National Cyclopedia of American Biography*, Mr. John R. Thomas, born at Rochester, New York, June 18, 1848, was the architect of the Willard Asylum for the Insane. "Mr. Thomas was architect for the Willard Asylum at Seneca lake, one of the largest in the country (1872)." He was also responsible for the designs of the State Reformatory at Elmira, Sibley Hall of Rochester University, Rochester Theological Seminary and the Natural History Building of the University of Virginia. The Surrogate's Courthouse (Hall of Records) in New York City is one of his most famous architectural designs. (11)

The Trustees of the Willard Asylum for the Insane 1867

"State of New York, No. 12, In Senate, January 17, 1867. First Annual Report of the Trustees of the Willard Asylum for the Insane. *To the Legislature Of the State of New York:* The undersigned, Trustees of the Willard Asylum for the Insane, located near Ovid, Seneca county, beg leave to REPORT: That immediately after their appointment, they took the oath of office and entered upon the discharge of their duties. A meeting of the board was duly called at the dwelling-house on the farm belonging to the asylum on the 15th day of May, 1866, and James Ferguson, Sterling G. Hadley, Genet Conger, and John E. Seeley, being present, the board was duly organized by the election of John E. Seeley as President of the Board of Trustees, and James Ferguson Secretary. No part of the buildings of the asylum have yet been completed or made ready for the reception of patients, consequently the trustees have had little, if anything to do. The farm has hitherto been under the control and supervision of the commissioners - they deeming it necessary it should be so in order to facilitate the completion of the buildings designed for said asylum. John E. Seeley, *President*. Jas. Ferguson, *Secretary*." (12)

The State Board of Charities 1867

"The State Board of Charities was created in 1867, and became a constitutional body January 1, 1895, under the provisions of article VIII of the Constitution of the State of New York, which was adopted in 1894. This article of the Constitution provides that the State Board of Charities shall visit and inspect all institutions, whether State, county, municipal, incorporated or unincorporated, which are of a charitable, eleemosynary, correctional or reformatory character, including institutions for epileptics and idiots, and all reformatories (save those in which adult males convicted of felony shall be confined), and excepting institutions for the care and treatment of the insane, and for the detention of sane adults charged with or convicted of crime, or detained as witnesses or debtors." (13)

The Willard Asylum for the Insane 1869

"This institution located at Ovid in the state of New York is now nearly ready for occupancy. The Trustees have chosen Dr. John B. Chapin, late of Brigham Hall a private institution in Canandaigua, as the superintendent. Dr. Chapin's qualifications for the position are first class and the appointment is an excellent one. The institution is located on a bluff overlooking the Seneca Lake and during the summer months the scenery is delightful. In 1865 the legislature of New York authorized the building of an asylum for the chronic insane poor - a class of persons that are now, and who have been for years confined in the several County houses of the State. The name given to the institution was that of the 'Willard Asylum,' in compliment to the late Dr. Sylvester D. Willard, of Albany, through whose instrumentality mainly it was finally established." (14)

The State Charities Aid Association 1872

"The Legislature of the State of New York, on the 6th day of May, 1893, amended the law under which the State Charities Aid Association has conducted its work for the past twelve years, by extending the visitorial powers of the association, heretofore limited to town, city and county almshouses and poor-houses, to all public charitable institutions owned by the State, including State hospitals for the insane. Another amendment requires the association to make an annual report to the State Commission in Lunacy in addition to that made to the State Board of Charities...Founded in 1872, the object of the State Charities Aid Association was, and is to bring about reforms in our public institutions of charity, through the formation of an intelligent, and educated and organized public opinion. An organization, composed of volunteers, with membership framed upon the broadest lines, could alone hope to accomplish such a purpose, could fairly claim to represent the people. In the ranks of the association, therefore, are to be found men and women, young and old, rich and poor, ministers of all denominations, the farmer, the merchant, the medical and legal professions, representatives of all political parties, the Protestant, Catholic, Hebrew." (15)

The association was able to gain permission to enter and inspect all charitable state institutions with The Right of Entrance Law, Chapter 323, Laws of 1881, which required them to submit their findings in a report to The State Board of Charities. This law was repealed and replaced with Chapter 635, Laws of 1893, which gave the Association more powers, duties, and responsibilities, and required them to report to the State Commission in Lunacy.

The Experiment

Willard was an experiment that lasted 126 years. From the beginning ignorance, politics, money, and power struggles plagued the asylum. In every report to the Legislature, the Trustees of the Willard Asylum along with Dr. Chapin, were constantly asking for more money because the appropriations were never enough, and they were given out in small amounts rather than giving enough money needed to cover the expenses of building the structures properly to completion. From 1866 to 1881, the Willard property was constantly under construction. When it opened in 1869, it consisted of the main building (later renamed Chapin House in 1904), with two wings to accommodate 250 patients; 125 male and 125 female. In 1871, The Branch (Grand View), which was already sitting on the property as the State Agricultural College Building, opened and was fitted up to hold 225 female patients. In 1872, the north wing extension of the main building was completed housing an additional 100 male patients; and most of the first group of five detached or cottage style buildings were completed (Detached Block 1, Detached Buildings 1, or Cottage 1, later renamed The Maples). DB 2 or C 2 (The Pines) was completed in 1876; DB 3 or C 3 (The Sunnycroft) in 1877; DB 4 or C 4 (The Edgemere) in 1880. By 1881, all four groups of cottages were completed. Each block consisted of four buildings used as sleeping quarters for patients (50 patients per building or 200 per group), with one refectory building that housed two large dining rooms, kitchen, supervisor's office and apartments, and a small boiler house and heating equipment located in the rear of each building. Willard now had the capacity to hold 1,375 of New York State's pauper chronic insane.

The first part of this experiment was the law creating The Willard Act which mandated that all the pauper insane were to be removed from the county poor houses and sent to the two state asylums: Utica for the acute insane; and Willard for the chronic insane, thus making the state the guardians and protectors of these people who were being supported by the taxpayers of New York State. The second part of the experiment was making the Willard Asylum an institution for the chronic insane only. The third was relying on patient labor to defray costs; the fourth was the segregation of patients with the introduction and use of cottage style or detached, smaller, inexpensive buildings that would be a departure from the grand scale of the Gothic Revival style asylums of the past. Dr. Chapin best describes the cottages in his report to the State Board of Charities for the year 1873:

"The four dormitory buildings face the Seneca lake and are placed two on each side of the central, or refectory building, arranged *en echelon*. Each building is separated from the adjacent one a distance of twelve feet. The dimensions of each dormitory building are one hundred and twenty-five feet by forty-eight feet. The arrangement of all the halls or floors is similar. Each floor has a day-room forty-eight by twenty-four feet, six single rooms nine by eleven feet, four associated dormitories, two rooms for attendants, and a bath-room and water-closet. There is a hall nine feet wide. Water is distributed through the buildings from the reservoir, and heat is generated from direct and indirect radiators supplied with steam. Gas is used throughout, supplied from the main works. Each floor has accommodations for twenty-five patients. A single building is designed to receive fifty patients comfortably, and by crowding, it will be possible to add to this number. Four attendants reside in each building, one of whom is selected with reference to his experience and trustworthiness, and designated a supervisor. The whole group is under the immediate supervision of a gentleman and his wife, of mature years and discretion. The medical service is rendered by one of the physicians, who visits every hall daily." (16)

First Annual Report of the Trustees of the Willard Asylum for the Insane, for the year 1869, Transmitted to the Legislature, January 12, 1870, Albany, New York.

"To the Legislature of the State of New York: The undersigned trustees of 'The Willard Asylum for the Insane,' have the honor to submit to your honorable body the following report:

Appointed by the last Legislature near the close of its session, we organized as a Board on the 15th day of May last. By the terms of our appointment we succeeded to the powers and duties of the commissioners for building the asylum, as well as those of the former board of trustees of the asylum. Our first duties were those of the building commissioners, for at the time of our organization the buildings were incomplete, and not habitable. They had been inclosed and roofed during the two previous years, some of the inside work had been done, and at the time of our assuming control, a large force of mechanics were engaged on the work with a view to the early completion and occupancy of the buildings. Very soon after coming in contact with the work, and after making a personal examination of its extent and condition, it became apparent to us that the appropriation was insufficient to complete the building, supply the furniture, the steam power and apparatus for heating, the works and fixtures for lighting, and to put the asylum in a condition for habitation for the uses intended.

The question was thus presented to us practically whether we should simply exhaust the appropriation, and then stop and postpone the opening of the institution with all its humane and benevolent results another year, or whether we should concentrate the whole force and work on what was absolutely necessary to put the buildings in condition to receive patients and make them comfortable, and secure and leave incomplete such portions as could be dispensed with. After full consideration it was concluded that it was for the interest of the State, for the well being of the pauper insane, and hence our duty to place the asylum in a condition for occupancy as soon as possible, even if we should be compelled to incur to some extent necessary liabilities to accomplish the desired and important object. The result of the efforts thus made under the direction of this Board, and the supervision of one of our own number, has been the completion of the two wings with their six wards for the accommodation of patients, and of placing the center building in a condition to accommodate the staff of officers now employed and the family of the superintendent. In short the whole institution has been put in complete running order, has now been opened a little over two months, and has securely domiciled in its various wards over one hundred and forty pauper chronic insane gathered from all parts of the State, and is in condition to receive yet others as they may arrive. The center building is in almost every part as yet incomplete, for when the work absolutely necessary for the comfort, security, and proper care of the insane was accomplished, we stopped, not deeming it becoming or proper to go beyond the real necessities of the case in expenditures.

A short description of the buildings of the asylum will not be inappropriate in this our first annual report. The buildings are located on the east bank of Seneca Lake, in the town of Ovid, Seneca County, on the farm known as the farm of the 'State Agricultural College,' consisting of about four hundred and seventy-five acres, lying about half a mile on the lake running back from it one to one and a half miles. Thus located the asylum is easy of access, two steamers passing in each way daily, and landing within fifty rods of the asylum, connecting at Geneva with the New York Central, and at Watkins, with the New York & Erie railroads.

The buildings consist of a main center building seventy by eighty-four feet, on the ground, in height three stories surmounted by a tower. This building is designed and arranged for officers, and for the accommodation of officers of the institution and the family of the superintendent. It occupies a position, as its name indicates, in the center and a little in advance of the wings and is connected with them by circular corridors one story high and fifty feet in length. The wings, or the sections now completed, one on the north and one on the south of main building, are each 171 feet long and forty feet wide on the ground, they are three stories high with basement. Each story above the basement has a hall twelve feet wide running the entire length north and south, with rooms on each side nine by eleven, with a large alcove in the center on the west with bay window which serves as a day or sitting room for the patients occupying the hall, and has a fine and commanding view of the lake and country beyond. The third story of both wings and center building is formed by the Mansard or French roof. These buildings with their connecting corridors extend along the bank of the lake some 600 feet, and present a very fine appearance architecturally. In the rear of the center building, and between and connected with the wings, by a covered passage way (through which food is conveyed to the dumbwaiter which supplies the halls) and with the center building by a straight corridor, is the kitchen, the bakery, the washing and drying house, the engine and boiler, and coal houses, and tool and work rooms, altogether forming a rear wing of 311 feet, a portion of which, viz., the kitchen and wash houses, are two stories high and the others one story. The upper part of the kitchen is designed, and will be finished and used for a chapel. The gas house is located two hundred and nine feet from the rear wing.

All the buildings are of brick with slated roof, the smoke-stack rises from the center of the kitchen, and is connected with the boilers by a wrought-iron pipe five feet in diameter and one hundred and eighty-eight feet in length. This plan of conducting the smoke from the boiler furnaces is in our judgment defective, because it conveys it to the chimney on a slight descent, thereby lessening the draft. This fault of the architect may necessitate the erection of a smoke-stack directly in the rear and contiguous to the boilers. But one boiler has thus far been used, and it is possible that when both are fired up, and in use, the draft will be improved.

The north and south wings are designed for the insane and their attendants only, and are fitted, arranged, and furnished for that purpose, and will accommodate, if crowded to their full capacity, two hundred and fifty persons, or one hundred and twenty five each. All the six halls - three for males and three for females - would be occupied with one bed in every single room, and with from three to eight in the larger rooms and associated dormitories. The heating power and apparatus, the water supply and the gas manufactory, are all on a scale large enough to provide heat, water and light, for the center building and for the sections of the now finished wings, and for other wings still more extensive, if added, than the present ones. The center building is provided with a kitchen in its basement, and the kitchen for the wings is of a capacity sufficient to furnish cooked food, including bread, for both wings and for two others still more extensive. It will therefore be seen, that, in extending the wings so as to double the capacity of the asylum, no expense for heating, for supply of water, or for gas, will be required, except the extension of pipes; and for supplying food, no additional kitchen capacity will be required. Water is supplied from two reservoirs, the first located about half a mile east from, and about one hundred feet above, the ground level of the Asylum buildings. This reservoir covers about one acre of ground, is about seven feet deep, and is supported by walls of earth of strength sufficient for the purpose. Not being subject to floods by surface drainage, or by streams, no danger is apprehended to this reservoir, and it is of ample capacity to furnish a full supply of water to the Asylum, and to every extension required, to provide for all the pauper insane of the State. The other reservoir is about one and a half miles east of this, and is formed by running a dam across a ravine through which a perpetual stream runs, hence has walls of solid, natural earth on three sides. This is the receiving reservoir, and supplies the other, and is itself supplied from living springs and streams which are believed to be perpetual and abundant. The supply of good, pure, fresh water, one of the most important wants of such an asylum, is thus assured and provided for. In case of lack in supply, there are large living springs near the upper reservoir which have been secured and can be made available at small expense.

A very extensive and perfect system of drainage and sewerage has been perfected and carried all about the grounds and buildings, and yards adjacent thereto. The heating of the buildings, both the wings and the centre, is by steam through cast iron radiators placed in the basement, the heated air being conveyed to the halls and rooms through flues in the walls. The apparatus works admirably, and thus far one boiler alone has supplied all the steam for heating, and for driving the engine for washing, etc. The whole cost of the buildings, heating apparatus including engine and boilers, water works, water pipes, drainage and sewerage, gas works, pipes and fixtures, will not vary much from three hundred and fifty thousand dollars, the whole cost including the cost of the land being about four hundred thousand dollars.

In view of what has been done, of the four hundred and seventy-five acres of land purchased, of the capacity provided to take care of 250 insane persons, and in view of the fact that it has all been done, and accomplished when prices ruled high for labor and material, it will, we think, be apparent that it has as a whole been economically done.

Soon after taking charge of the work of preparing the asylum for practical use, our attention was called to the question of heating. It was a vital question indispensable to the working of the asylum, and could not be avoided or dispensed with. The plan for heating by steam through cast iron radiators placed in the basement had been adopted, and the buildings had all been constructed in accordance with that mode of heating. In this connection we also found that our predecessors, the building commissioners, under the law of April 8th, 1865, had contracted in writing with Messrs. Clark & Allen of Dunkirk, for three large boilers, an engine, and other work in connection therewith; that the engine and two of the boilers, together with a large quantity of steam and smoke pipe, had been completed, but had not been delivered or accepted, owing to a misunderstanding between the commissioners, or a majority of them, and Clark & Allen, as to the terms of the contract, and what was covered by it. We learned further that twenty-three thousand dollars had been paid to Clark & Allen on the contract, and that a large sum was still claimed by them for the material and work done as their due. In view of the importance of the subject, the amount involved, and of the indispensable necessity of having boilers to generate steam and pipe to convey it so as to warm the buildings, of an engine to perform work which could not be done by hand, we deemed it our duty to endeavor to settle and adjust the matter on a basis of equity and justice. To this end a committee of this Board visited Dunkirk, examined the work, and conferred with Clark & Allen, and afterward visited Buffalo, and there finally concluded after mature deliberation an agreement and settlement on terms by us deemed advantageous to the State, and which, on report, met the unanimous approval of this board. By this settlement the good faith of the State was maintained, its interest fully guarded, large claims for damage foreclosed; by it the State was released from taking one boiler covered by the contract, but which we regarded as unnecessary, as well as from claims for extra work equivalent in all, including the boiler, to fifteen thousand dollars, at the same time the asylum obtained all that was required to furnish heat and power for all time to come, and, as the event has proved, the boilers, engine and pipe, and material, are of the very best quality and workmanship. We have been more specific and minute in reference to the settlement, because it involves a large sum which we have certified to be due Clark & Allen on their contract, and which had not been estimated for by the commissioners last year, and which was not covered by the appropriation then made, but this balance we believe to be fairly due for material and work actually furnished and performed, and we ask an appropriation to meet and pay it.

The movement of the boilers, each weighing over twenty tons, the large engine, pipes, castings and materials, requiring thirteen large cars from Dunkirk to Ovid Landing, was a work of great difficulty, expense and care, having to take the risk of moving by the terms of the original contract, we kept control of it and it was accomplished by the way of the New York and Erie Railroad, Watkins and Seneca Lake, without accident or mishap, and at a less cost than any responsible party would contract to do it for. All are now in their place, all in prime working order, and all are performing admirably, with the single exception of draft of smoke-pipe of which the location and not the pipe must be held responsible.

An apportionment under the ninth section of the law passed April 8, 1865, fixing the number of patients to be received from each county that had applied, was made July 31, 1869, and received the approval of Governor Hoffman, September 15, 1869, and the Asylum was opened, after due notice given by circulars to such counties as were designated on the 12th day of October; and there has been received up to the date hereof, and are now safely and comfortably domiciled in the different wards, one hundred and forty-one persons from twenty-one different poor-houses in the State. Many of these, the most dependent, helpless, unfortunate and neglected class of our people, have been taken from cells, dens, cages, outhouses, cribs and dungeons, in some instances from chains and worse than prison confinement, from filth, squalor and wretchedness; and are now in neat, clean, warm, well ventilated and comfortable quarters, in a home befitting the great State of New York to furnish for those of her people who have neither home or friends, and who are without the means financially or capacity intellectually to provide for themselves, with intellect shattered, minds darkened, living amid delusions a constant prey to unrest, haunted by unreal fancies and wild imaginings, they now have in their sore misfortune a safe refuge, kindly care, constant watching, and are made as comfortable as their circumstances will allow. This is a result over which every humane and Christian citizen of the State will rejoice.

As a Board, intrusted with the care and management of this great charity, we should be derelict in duty, and fail to meet the requirements which the law of the State imposes upon us, did we not press upon the attention of the Legislature the character, nature and importance of the questions involved in the creation and purpose of the 'Willard Asylum for the Insane.' That purpose involves, as a necessity to its accomplishment, the extension of the Asylum buildings, and of an enlargement of its capacity very materially and very speedily in order to meet the demands which the law imposes upon it as well as to meet the necessities of the pauper chronic insane still remaining in the poor-houses. The law of 1865, which created the 'Willard Asylum for the Insane,' very clearly inaugurated a new policy in regard to the care of the pauper insane, both chronic and recent, of the State. That policy was to relieve the county of their care and devolve it upon the State through the 'Willard,' and the State Lunatic Asylum at Utica. It will be seen that it is a radical change, and it was adopted upon a full knowledge of the facts in the case, and of the actual condition of the insane in the poor-houses, founded upon data which could not be questioned, and which most clearly indicated the necessity of the change proposed.

The condition of the pauper insane has been frequently the subject of official inquiry. As early as 1806 (see chap. 56 of Laws of 1806), a law was passed making an appropriation of twelve thousand five hundred dollars ($12,500), to be paid quarterly, in each and every year until 1857, to 'the New York Hospital,' and, as the preamble to the act declares, for the purpose of providing 'suitable apartments for the maniacs, adapted to the various forms and degrees of insanity.' It is understood, that, in pursuance of this act, the New York Hospital was extended, and the superintendents of the poor, under a law subsequently passed, did, to a limited extent, send pauper insane from some of the counties to be cared for by this noble institution. In 1829, Governor Throop visited this hospital and found only sixty or seventy insane persons confined there, and all well cared for, yet, by the census of 1825, it was ascertained that there were at that time eight hundred and nineteen (819) insane persons in the State, of these three hundred and sixty-three were of sufficient ability to pay for their own support, two hundred and eight were in jail or supported by charity, leaving three hundred and forty-eight insane paupers at large. It is thus quite clear that the New York Hospital afforded but limited relief, although it did what it could to mitigate the sufferings of the unfortunate lunatics.

In 1830, Governor Throop, in his annual message to the Legislature, called special attention to the condition of the insane poor, and recommended the establishment of an asylum for the gratuitous care of that most destitute class of the human family. As a result of this recommendation, a special committee was appointed to investigate this subject. In the succeeding year they reported, and a commission was appointed to locate an asylum for the insane. In 1836, a law was passed authorizing the State Lunatic Asylum at Utica; its history is well known, it has relieved and ministered to thousands of the insane, and is now full to repletion; and yet the poor-houses of the State, in 1868, had confined in them over fifteen hundred insane paupers, a considerable number of whom have graduated into chronic cases at Utica. See report of Commissioners of Public Charities, made to the Legislature of 1869.

In 1843, Miss Dix visited the poor-houses of the State, and made to the Legislature of 1844 one of the most eloquent and pathetic appeals ever made for the suffering pauper insane; she suggested a plan of relief, but no action was had.

In 1855, the county superintendents of the poor from the different counties of the State met in convention and appealed to the Legislature of 1856, asking relief for the suffering and neglected pauper insane. As a result of this earnest appeal, a legislative committee was raised, a full investigation entered upon, a report made to the Legislature of 1857; and yet the poor-houses continued to overrun with insane paupers; indeed, the Legislature of the State, in its progress on the subject, made them the only places where the pauper chronic insane could go, for county judges were prohibited from sending to the 'State Lunatic Asylum' cases of more than one year's standing, and the managers of the State Lunatic Asylum were directed by law to send back to the county poor-houses all who had been there two years. (See Laws, chapter 282, passed April 10, 1850; also see act amendatory of the act to organize the State Lunatic Asylum, passed July 9, 1851, giving county judges discretionary power to send indigent persons either to the county poor-houses or State Lunatic Asylum.) It will be seen that the operation of these laws of necessity filled the county poor-houses with the pauper insane, and made them the only places where the chronic pauper insane could find refuge, from 1850 to 1865; the legislation of the State then made the county poor-houses the only home for the chronic pauper insane.

We now come to the establishment of the 'Willard Asylum for the Insane,' and to the law creating it, by which the policy of the State was fixed, and by which its former policy and legal status on the subject was changed. A brief allusion to the facts and circumstances which led to the law of 1865, before the examination and analysis of the law itself, will not be out of place.

The Legislature of 1864, by act passed April 30, 1864, authorized Doctor Sylvester D. Willard, secretary of the New York State Medical Society, 'to investigate the condition of the insane poor in the various poor-houses, alms-houses, and insane asylums and other institutions where the insane are kept.' This investigation was not made by Doctor Willard in person, but by a series of questions addressed to an intelligent physician residing in the county where the poor-houses were located, and in reply he received answers from all but two or three counties. The facts were gathered from intelligent and honorable men of the localities, not likely to overdraw the picture or misrepresent, and they disclosed a terrible condition of neglect, abuse and suffering. In fifty-five counties not including, New York and Kings, thirteen hundred and forty-five lunatics were found, nearly all of whom were chronic cases, and whose condition, in the language of Governor Fenton, was 'deplorable.' This report, backed by the recommendation of Governor Fenton, was the origin and base of the Willard Asylum for the Insane, taking its name from the author of the report, and aiming by the strong power of the law to change the policy of the State in regard to the case of the pauper insane by removing all such from the county poor-houses and with them to remove the reproach of barbarism which their treatment there involved. From the origin and history we proceed to the examination of the law itself.

It was passed April 8, 1865, and its title declares it to be 'an act to authorize the establishment of a State Asylum for the chronic insane, and for the better care of the insane poor, to be known as 'The Willard Asylum for the Insane.'

After authorizing the Governor to appoint commissioners to select a site and to erect the buildings, and as the buildings progressed to designate counties from which the pauper chronic insane should be received (see the law from 1st to 9th section) we come to the final and sweeping mandate and provision which, in the end, were to remove every insane pauper from every county poor-house in the State and place them either in the 'Willard Asylum for the Insane,' or in the 'State Lunatic Asylum.' The 10th and 11th sections of the law read thus:

10. The chronic pauper insane from the poor-houses of the counties that shall be designated as provided in section nine hereof shall be sent to the said asylum by the county superintendents of the poor, and all chronic insane pauper patients who may be discharged not recovered from the State Lunatic Asylum and who continue a public charge shall be sent to the asylum for the insane hereby created, and all such patients shall be a charge upon the respective counties from which they are sent.

11. The county judges and superintendents of the poor in every county of the State except those counties having asylums for the insane to which they are now authorized to send such insane

patients by special legislative enactments, are hereby required to send all indigent or pauper insane coming under their jurisdiction, who shall have been insane less than one year, to the State Lunatic Asylum.

In these two sections the intent is unmistakable, the language is imperative, limited only to the capacity of the Willard Asylum as it progresses to accommodate, and when it reaches the full capacity and can provide for all the chronic insane in the county houses, then all must be sent there; meantime none of the recent cases can be sent to the poor-houses, all must go to Utica, and if not cured must go from there, not to the poor-houses, but to the 'Willard Asylum for the Insane.' In this latter provision there is a complete reversal of the laws of 1850 and 1851. By this legislation and the establishment of this Asylum the State assumes the guardianship of the insane paupers of the State; it makes provision for all not heretofore provided for. The chronic cases it sends to its State institution known as the 'Willard Asylum for the Insane,' and the recent cases it sends to its other State institution 'The State Lunatic Asylum.' This was the beginning of a new era in the care of the insane poor. It was doing what has never before been done, making distinct provision for the chronic pauper insane, and on a scale sufficiently comprehensive to embrace them all. In order to give the policy practical effect, the commissioners appointed under the law, two of whom, viz., Dr. Gray, of the State Lunatic Asylum, and Dr. Chapin of 'Brigham Hall,' Canandaigua, gentlemen of very large experience in the care of the insane, at an early period adopted certain principles and plans for buildings on a very extensive scale consisting of a main hospital building and of detached groups of less expensive cottage buildings. The first or main asylum building was projected on a very extensive plan, and was designed for at least five hundred persons, while the others were less expensive, and could be extended so as to embrace all the pauper insane from all the poor-houses of the State. Appropriations were made, a large farm was purchased as the base of these extensive operations, and the main asylum buildings were commenced, and are now so far completed as we have stated elsewhere in this report. The accommodations thus far provided are but the beginning, and should they stop where they now are, the result would be a total failure of the policy as foreshadowed by the law. The poor-houses of the State would of necessity still continue to swarm with pauper insane, would continue to be in the future as in the past, entirely inadequate and unfit for their care and treatment. The law of 1865 would have to be changed or disregarded, some good would have been effected, a new and splendid asylum would have been created for a few paupers; but the great mass of the pauper chronic insane would still remain the suffering inmates of the miserably provided; ill-ventilated poor-houses.

In view of this state of facts and sincerely impressed with the wisdom and humanity of the policy inaugurated by the law of 1865, we have caused plans to be made for extending the wings of the present asylum buildings, and for one group of a cheaper class of cottage buildings detached from the main buildings, and have caused estimates to be made covering the expense of their erection and for which we ask an appropriation.

These plans cover as a whole one wing extension, and a group of four two-story plain substantial buildings, and a refectory to be used in common by the four, and they would provide accommodation for three hundred or more insane persons, viz.: one hundred in the wing extension, and two hundred in the four cottages, and would cost, according to our estimates, one hundred and forty thousand dollars. When completed, these additions would provide, with what is now furnished by the main hospital buildings, for five hundred and fifty persons in all. Another year, another wing and cottage group could be erected, adding capacity for three hundred more, and thus in three or four years the grand design would be reached, and all the chronic pauper insane of the State find comfortable homes, kindly care, due restraint and skillful medical treatment in the Willard Asylum for the Insane, at a cost in the aggregate and per capita much less than any similar institution of like extent in this country, and so fully and perfectly adapted to its purpose, has ever been constructed, furnished and put in operation. In this home thus provided for the chronic pauper insane of the State it is essential to its full and complete success in our opinion, that all be gathered together with one controlling head. To take a portion and leave the balance, does not cure the evil, it would mitigate and improve the condition of a select number, but would leave the rest in their present condition. The policy of the law, and the demands of humanity, required that every county poor-house be emptied of the insane, that they be transferred to the better home provided for them by the State, where they can be properly sheltered, cared for, restrained and provided for. A careful examination of the subject will satisfy you, we think, that this concentration of all the chronic pauper insane is really necessary if not indispensable to the perfect and most successful working of the policy foreshadowed by the law of 1865. However many other asylums there may be for the insane, or wherever in the State located, necessary and useful as all these may be, there should, nevertheless, be but one for the chronic pauper insane. In this institution there is land enough, and sufficient room for extension, and with all here concentrated under a single head and control, a better classification can be made, better care provided, and with less cost per patient, their labor can be made more available, their out door exercise better arranged, less restraint imposed, and sanitary measures provided, more perfect and efficient than it is possible to have, or provide, in smaller asylums, where a smaller number are supervised and provided for.

Here, collected from the wretched poor-houses, they become the wards of the State; their home is public property and open to constant visitation and inspection. The superintendent, officers and attendants are under direct State supervision and amenable to State authority; liability to abuse without notice is removed; constant and skilled medical attendance is assured; the sexes are separated; cruelty or neglect cannot be practiced without exposure and correction. In carrying out this policy, so broad and comprehensive, and yet so wise and humane, it will not require palatial edifices nor large expenditures for simple show and display. The most costly buildings, including water and gas works, engine, boilers and heating apparatus, for the full development of this grand system are already erected, and will not have to be duplicated in order to enlarge the Willard Asylum for the Insane so as to provide for every chronic pauper insane person in the State outside of the large cities. A careful examination of this whole subject in all its bearings has satisfied us that on the asylum farm at Ovid there is room enough for all, that the organization is broad enough, and that sound policy, wisdom and true humanity alike demand that all should be gathered here as soon as suitable accommodations can be provided. The very full and able report made to the Legislature by the commissioners of the board of public charities leaves no doubt as to the necessity of removing from the poor-houses, as soon as may be, the insane confined therein. In the very nature of the case these houses cannot be made fit and proper places for the care and treatment of this class of persons. In view, then, of this question in all its relations, we earnestly call your attention to it and ask for an appropriation to carry into effect the just and humane policy of the State. In connection with this subject, and particularly in regard to the plan character of buildings hereafter required, we refer you to the accompanying report of Dr. Chapin. We cannot doubt that his views in regard to the less expensive yet comfortable and substantial class detached cottage buildings will meet your approval as it has ours.

From inquiry, and the best information we can obtain, as well as from our personal observation of the patients now in this asylum, we think that at least two-thirds of the chronic insane have become so fixed in their habits and are so easily managed as to require, first, a directing will, and secondly, kindly and considerate treatment, to be properly controlled. From this it will appear that after properly restraining and taking care of one-third of the more violent and dangerous, there is but little practical difficulty, with intelligent direction, in managing and controlling the remaining two-thirds. With twelve hundred patients gathered here, four hundred of the most restless and troublesome could be restrained and provided for in the insane hospital or asylum buildings, where all the appliances and facilities for control and management have been provided, while the remaining eight hundred of fixed habits and of feeble intellect, could be divided into male and female, then properly classified so as to occupy in comfort and entire safety the cheaper cottage buildings, where, surrounded by gardens, orchards, and cultivated fields, they could labor and exercise in the open air. It will be easily seen how much this system of treatment would conduce to the comfort, the health and good government of the chronic insane, and how much the cost of their support would be reduced thereby.

Twelve hundred is about the number of chronic pauper insane which would be congregated here at any one time if the policy of removing all from the county poor-houses were fully carried out, excluding a few large counties when suitable provisions have been made in connection with their large cities for their insane, we estimate the number remaining to come here from the county poor-houses, provided all were sent, would be about twelve hundred, a number which, in our judgment, could be better classified, more economically provided for, and better maintained than a less number, and to these might be added with comparatively small expense, the three hundred idiotic paupers now confined in the poor-houses of the State.

In our estimates and plans for extension and furnishing increased accommodation for the insane poor, we have omitted the improvement and remodeling the large and elegant college building located on the farm about three-fourths of a mile east from the present asylum buildings, not because we do not think this extensive and expensive building could not be used in connection with the Willard Asylum for the Insane, but because it has been suggested by good and wise men who have given the subject much thought, that it can be better used by the State for a kindred class of unfortunates, who now, like the pauper insane, have no other home than the poor-houses - the pauper idiots of the State. This class, like the chronic pauper insane, are friendless, hopeless, and helpless, but as a general thing they are harmless, like children, and still more than children dependent, requiring constant care, attention, and direction.

The college building, a noble brick structure, five stories including the basement, and fitted and furnished with rooms designed for students, can, with slight alterations, be made to accommodate in comfort and safety, it is believed, three hundred idiots. In the poor-houses these demented ones do not and cannot have proper care and training, and hence the suggestion to devote this great edifice to the humane purpose of furnishing them with a proper and comfortable home, where they could be cared for and protected. The alterations required for its occupancy by this class could be easily made, and at comparatively small expense. As it now is the building is not only useless but going to decay. It is too good and costly a structure to remain useless.

According to the last report of the Board of State Charities it appears that there is outside of New York and Kings counties, three hundred and fourteen idiots in the different poor-houses in the state. It will therefore be seen that this college building on the asylum farm at Ovid can be made to accommodate nearly if not all the pauper idiots of the State. The estimated expense in fitting up this building for the use of the idiots is $15,000 to $20,000, and we do not think it will exceed the first named sum. No one will question the great good to result to the counties, to the idiots and to humanity from such a result. By some it is proposed to put the idiots thus gathered together under the same board of trustees and general supervision that now manage and care for the Willard Asylum. If this is done it will necessitate the appointment of but a few new officers; an assistant superintendent and matron and a few attendants would be all that would be required, with perhaps an assistant physician to carry into full effect this plan which would provide for all the pauper idiots from all the county poor-houses of this State. It would certainly present an interesting fact if all the county poor-houses of the State could be relieved of both the insane and idiotic persons now confined in them. It would be an important era in the history of our public charities as well as in the history and management of the poor-houses of the State, if these two classes were removed from them. Many of these miserably provided institutions might possibly be dispensed with altogether.

If in the wisdom of the Legislature it is thought best not to place the pauper idiots under the care of the Willard Asylum management in the college building, then we ask an appropriation of $20,000 in addition to what we have estimated, for extensions of one wing and one group of cottage buildings, to enable us to remodel the college building for the occupancy of a class of mild female insane patients. In our judgment it can be fitted for that purpose for the sum named, and that when all the pauper insane are concentrated here two hundred of the class named can be selected, who in safety and comfort can occupy this building. This would supply the place of a detached group of cottage buildings, and would save the State at least $50,000 - the cottage group costing at least as much as that more than it would to fit up the college building. We have thus presented our views covering this entire subject, and submit them to the superior wisdom of the Legislature, asking for them a careful and thoughtful consideration.

If our views are correct, and the law making power second them by necessary legal provisions, it will not be long before the improper, and in some instances disgraceful, treatment of the unfortunate insane paupers of the State will be changed, and the reproach which it has cast upon the counties of the State entirely removed. It is worth consideration whether it will not be more in accord with the now settled policy of the State, to make the support and maintenance of the pauper insane entirely a charge upon the State, to be raised by general tax, and not through the poor authorities of the counties. The counties would be thus entirely relieved of all care, except in the simple act of sending all the pauper insane to this and the State Lunatic Asylum, and the tax for support would probably be very equitably distributed, but this is a question for your body, and not for us to settle.

In this connection we may say, that the price now fixed, viz.: two dollars per week to be paid to this asylum for the board of patients by the counties, is less than the actual cost per person. The expenditures thus far are however no fair criterion of what they will be hereafter, when the asylum is full, and all things are reduced to system and order, but under the most favorable circumstances for a time, at least, we do not think the cost of boarding will come down to two dollars per week, although in time it may do so. The cost of support will depend a good deal upon the amount of labor which patients can perform and the productions of the farm. Commencing as this institution did late in the fall, with every thing new and incomplete, we can hardly form an intelligent opinion as to the value of the labor of patients or of the cost of their support, but from the results thus far, it is fair to presume that, in any event, and particularly if all are sent here from all the counties of the State, the value of the labor of patients will be very considerable, and reduce a good deal the cost of maintenance. We do not ask that the price of board be raised at present, but thought it proper to state the fact as it is, as the State must make up the deficit. When the cost is settled by actual results, if the system of county support is continued it will be right and proper to fix the amount in accordance with the actual cost, and make the counties pay the full amount for maintaining their insane poor. It is worthy of consideration whether it may not be well for a still more stringent provision of law compelling the county authorities to send their pauper insane to this asylum, where the State has made such careful and expensive provision for their support and care; and the removal of all the insane from the poor-houses being so clearly in accord with a sound and humane policy, we are satisfied that the poor authorities in many of the counties of the State either do not understand or do not heed the law of 1865. All ambiguity should be removed from the subject, and as fast as the work of extension proceeds, so fast the counties should send away their insane paupers to the home thus provided for them.

It affords us great pleasure to express our satisfaction and approval of the conduct of the general and medical superintendent, Dr. John B. Chapin. He has fully met our expectations in the discharge of his very responsible duties, and shown capacity, discretion and adaptation. The assistant physician, Dr. Charles L. Welles, the steward, Abram C. Slaght, and the matron, Mrs. Sarah H. Bell, have performed the respective duties of their offices since July last with untiring devotion to the interests of the asylum.

The opening and working of the institution has been easy and smooth, hurried as were many of the preparations and rapid as was the filling up; yet no accident or serious disturbance has occurred, notwithstanding some of the worst and most violent cases from the different poor-houses have been sent here. Under the kind, considerate treatment adopted, all has proceeded orderly and with comparative quiet. The patients have been comfortable, their general health improved, and, although all who have been received are chronic cases and of long standing, yet we are not without hope that some, under the change of treatment and care here, will be restored to their right mind. This number, of course, will not be large, but of all it may, with entire safety, be said that their condition has been greatly improved and that they are made as comfortable as their situation will allow. It should be remembered that this is an asylum for the chronic pauper insane, and for no other class; that as such it is unique in character and differing from all other insane asylums in this country, and we believe it supplies a want long felt and presents in its character and operations one of the best and most unmixed charities in the land.

We herewith transmit the report of the treasurer of the asylum, showing in detail the expenditures made under our direction and the present condition of the funds subject to draft. We submit, also, plans and estimates for the extension of asylum buildings and furnishing them for use, alluded to in the body of this report; also estimates for completing the present building, together with deficits, including amount certified to be due on boilers, engine and pipe, under contract of the building commissioners. We also add the estimated cost of a slip and dock for the accommodation of boats bringing coal and other supplies to the asylum. At present the harbor is insecure, and at times dangerous for boats.

We ask the appropriation with the discretion to expend it for a new dock and slip on the asylum property, or for the purchase and repair of the storehouse, dock, and hotel property of fourteen acres, now used as a steamboat landing, hotel, etc., and which adjoin the asylum property. This storehouse, dock, hotel and land, is a productive property, and can be made to yield a good revenue; it would be a desirable addition to the asylum property, and should be subject to the control of this board, for the use and convenience of the asylum.

John E. Seeley, William A. Swaby, Sterling G. Hadley, Genet Conger, Francis O. Mason, George J. Magee, Samuel R. Welles, D. A. Ogden. Willard Asylum for the Insane, Ovid, January 1, 1870."
(17)

Admission 1869

"Form of an order for the admission of a patient at county expense.

To the Superintendent of the Willard Asylum for the Insane:

You are hereby authorized and requested to receive into the Willard Asylum for the Insane, _____ an insane pauper, provide _____ as may be necessary, and charge the expense of _____ maintenance to _____ county. Dated _____, Signed _____, *Superintendent of the Poor.*

Bills are made out and transmitted quarterly to the county treasurers, on the first of December, March, June, and September, by the treasurer of the asylum. Patients should be brought to the asylum in a cleanly condition, and free from vermin. All patients require two suits of clothing adapted to the season, and should be brought by some person competent to furnish a history of the case. Applications for the admission of patients should be made before they are brought to the asylum. All correspondence concerning patients and the business of the asylum should be addressed to Dr. John B. Chapin, Superintendent, Ovid, N.Y." (17)

3

INSPECTION OF THE WILLARD ASYLUM FOR THE INSANE

The following partial report is one of several surprise inspections of the Willard Asylum for the Insane conducted by the Commissioners of the State Board of Charities in 1884. This report stated that of 1,823 patients, 118 or 6.47 percent were sleeping on the floor because of lack of accommodations. The mechanical restraints mentioned in the report were: the camisole (canvas straitjacket); leather belt (strapped around chest or waist to restrain in a chair); wristlets (leather wristbands to restrain in a chair); and muff (hands on top of each other inside a heavy canvas or leather muff, secured on both ends with leather straps). It does not appear that the institution owned or used the Utica Crib but it did have at least one padded room. As time went on Willard and all other state insane asylums strived to abandon all forms of mechanical restraint. All assaults and deaths of patients, whether they were patient on patient; patient on attendant or doctor; or attendant or doctor on patient, had to be reported and swift action was required to be taken by the medical superintendent.

"Our inspections were without notice, and generally made in the following order, viz.: First, examinations of the wards, including the attendants, the patients, sleeping-rooms, bedsteads, beds and bedding, bath-rooms, water-closets, day-rooms and the dining-rooms; second, the kitchen, bake-rooms, laundries, furnaces with heating and ventilating apparatus, out-buildings and other property; and third, the books of the medical department, including those of the superintendent, and the books of accounts, including those of the steward."

"...The general 'condition of the buildings, grounds and other property' of the several State institutions appears to be good... Another exception is 'The Branch,' formerly called the Agricultural College, now used as one of the buildings for patients in the Willard Asylum. This structure is not properly adapted to the care of insane people, but is peculiarly adapted to furnish a holocaust of victims in case of fire."

"SCHEDULE 'F.' Willard Asylum for the Insane. Visited by Commissioners Craig and Milhau of the Committee on Insane, September 5 and 6, 1884.

Dr. John B. Chapin having resigned September 1, the position of superintendent is now filled by the former first assistant, Dr. P.M. Wise, who escorted us through the south wing of the main building. On the day of visitation there were 850 male and 973 female patients in the asylum, making in all 1,823. The asylum is beautifully situated on the eastern bank of Seneca lake, and the farm contains about 1,000 acres, almost all of which were under cultivation. There are six groups of buildings, the groups being at some distance from each other. A physician resides in each group with the exception of one, where Dr. Hopkins, resident physician of the 'Branch' has charge. A railroad runs to all the groups, by which means connections are made with the main building. Three large reservoirs store the water taken from a branch fed by springs. Water is also pumped from the lake. Besides this, each group of buildings has a well which supplies water for drinking purposes. On the grounds are also paint, carpenter, tailor, shoe and plumbing shops, in each of which a number of patients are employed.

The wards in all the buildings are numbered from the north, beginning with No. 1 on the ground floor and numbering up, then again starting on the ground floor and running up, and so on until the south end is reached. An amusement building has lately been built, the upper floor of which is utilized as sleeping apartments for some of the help.

MAIN BUILDING. The main building is divided into three parts: the center, north and south wings. In the center are the offices, apothecary shop, officers' rooms, telegraph office, etc. In the telegraph office is a telephone which connects with all the groups. There is also another telephone which runs along the line of railroad to Ovid, about two miles distant and Hayt's corners, about five miles distant.

SOUTH WING (FEMALES). On each floor of the wings are three wards, called a department. Each department is in charge of a supervisor who accompanied us.

Hall 1. This is for a quiet class, and contained forty-one patients in charge of four attendants. Some of the patients were filthy in their habits, and two slept on the floor. The superintendent stated that the patients are classified with regard to the benefit that would accrue to them, and not with regard to their violence or filthiness. If a patient is apprehensive that he or she will be injured, such a one would not be placed where there were noisy or violent patients. The walls in this and in all the buildings are covered with a silicate enamel, which can be washed with soap and water. There are three dormitories in this ward, each seventeen feet long, twelve feet wide, and eleven high, and seven beds were in a room; all the rest are single rooms. Wooden bedsteads are used throughout the institution. The woven wire spring mattress is used on this hall; besides which each bed is supplied with a thin hair mattress, two sheets, white spread, and a feather pillow. The beds for filthy patients were supplied with rubber sheets.

The windows were curtained, pictures were on the walls, and some of the rooms were carpeted. The settees were cushioned, making it very comfortable for the patients. The clothes room was in neat order and well ventilated, and there was a separate box in this room for the clothing of each patient. The clothes are all marked with the name of the patient, so that they never become mixed in the wash or otherwise. The sheets are also marked with the number of the ward and letters of the building. This is the rule throughout the institution. The wash-room contains one iron sink with running water. The floor is tiled and every thing was in neat order. There are two hoppers in the water-closet, and the water is kept running at all times, except when the patients are out on the grounds. The plumbing was in good order, and no bad odor was perceptible. The flooring is of tile and was clean. The bath-room contains two iron tubs which were clean and in good order. Here also is a tiled floor. This room does service for two wards. The patients are bathed once a week, and only one in the same water.

The beds and bedding were clean, and the general appearance of the ward was very good. One patient was sick in bed; all the rest looked well and were neatly dressed. None were in restraint, and no restraint is used except on the written order of the physician in charge. The medicine is received by the supervisors of all the departments, and by them distributed through the wards. Each cup bears the name of the patient and contains one dose. The dining room was neat, and knives, forks and crockery are used. The day-room is small, but was in good order. The seating capacity of the ward was ample.

Hall 7. On this hall there were twenty-two patients, mostly epileptics, and two attendants. Many were filthy in their habits. Nine slept on the floor. Single rooms are on one side of the hall, and windows looking out on the grounds on the other. A cross-hall is used as a dormitory. Straw mattresses are here used and when soiled, clean ticks and fresh straw are supplied. The ticks are all sewed up, and when necessary to change the straw, the seams are opened. Many of the patients were feeble, and some slept on the floor to prevent their being injured by falling out of bed. The strap iron springs are here used. It is necessary to change some sheets every day. The seating capacity is sufficient, but no cushions were on the settees. Pictures were on the walls, and as in all the halls, near the ceiling was a stencil border. A number of rocking chairs were in use. The clothes-room was in good order and well ventilated. The dining-room is small. The bath-room, the floor of which is tiled, contains one tub and was in good order. The water-closet is arranged as those in the halls already described, has tile flooring, and was in good order. General appearance of hall good. No one in restraint. The dead-room, a room in the cross hall, is fitted up with two marble slabs and an iron sink, for making autopsies. An iron staircase leads to the upper stories, one being at the junction of every two sections.

Hall 2. This hall is for the violent class, and contained forty-eight patients, many of whom were of filthy habits, and five attendants. Five patients slept on the floor, as there were no accommodations for them. No restraint is used on this hall. The superintendent stated that one congenital idiot on this hall is maintained at a cost of about $500 a year; she is deaf and dumb, almost blind, and destructive. On the first hall of each department is a speaking-tube connecting with the main office; also an electric bell to signal the attendants. A night-watch goes on duty at ten o' clock, whose duty it is to go through all the halls (nine) in this building. There is also a night-watch for the north wing and one for each of the groups of buildings. Each night-watchman carries a watchmen's clock, keys to which are on the different halls; this tells at what time he or she visited the halls. The superintendent said he would prefer the electric register in the office, to record these visits, if $2,000 were appropriated, for which sum an offer to furnish the register had been received. The rooms, bedding, etc., were in good order. Some of the patients had to be bathed five or six times daily, and many beds were soiled every night, but all were found clean at the time of inspection. The seating accommodations were adequate.

Hall 9. On this hall there were twenty-five idiotic, demented and filthy patients, in charge of three attendants. Three patients slept on the floor for lack of accommodations. Rooms are arranged on one side of the hall, and on the opposite side are windows; two of the rooms are single, the others are dormitories. One patient was sick in bed. The clothes-room, dining-room, etc., were in good order, the patients were well dressed, and the hall throughout was well kept. Pictures hung on the walls of all the halls of the institution, and in this wing and the north wing stained glass windows with curtains gave a pleasant appearance to the halls. The floors in the building are in good repair. The superintendent said: 'Some patients are sent to us who are not insane; they are idiots; and the asylum was not created for that class of persons. On this hall is a congenital idiot who is really not a fit subject for the asylum, and we always protest against receiving such patients. They may have a convulsion and they object at the Idiot Asylum to have patients of that class there. They may occasionally be a little irritable and have delusions, as idiots often have. This patient is quiet and harmless. I do not object to them where they are manifestly insane, but where they require no medical care, what is the use of paying medical officers to care for them?' In the wings is an arrangement for letting steam in the attic, and there are also plugs for hose in the buildings in case of fire. The line of hose is kept in the halls of the main or center building, as are also fire extinguishers. There is also a steam fire engine on the grounds. The female patients of the institution make all their own clothing besides making much for the men.

NORTH WING (MALES). The north wing is a duplicate of the south. Dr. A. Nellis, Jr., escorted us through this wing. Most of the patients in this wing, as in the south wing, were of the most violent class in the institution.

Hall 1. This hall is for a demented class and contained forty-five patients and four attendants. Five slept on the floor, and one was filthy day and night. One patient was sick in bed. This hall, like all the halls in this building, is neatly decorated and pictures are hung on the walls. The seating capacity is sufficient, and the settees are cushioned. There are three dormitories and each contained eight beds, two more than intended. The rooms were in neat order, and the patients were well dressed.

Hall 4. On this hall was a mixed class of thirty-eight patients in charge of four attendants. Fourteen slept on the floor for lack of accommodations. One bed was found dirty, and the attendant stated that the patient had made it up himself. The ward generally was in good order. A muff, wristlets and belt were placed on one patient at night by the physician's orders, as he tried to strangle himself.

Hall 7. This hall is for the demented and epileptics, and contained twenty-three patients in charge of three attendants. Some of the patients were filthy in habits and seven slept on the floor. Besides the settees a number of rocking chairs were in use. A camisole was occasionally placed on one patient to prevent his interfering with a sore on his face. There is a dissecting room on this hall similar to the one in the south wing. A clothes chute is in the public hall of each wing, down which all the soiled clothing and linen is thrown.

Hall 8. This hall is for the most violent class in the institution, and contained twenty patients in charge of three attendants. A number were filthy at night, and six slept on the floor. Rooms are on one side of the hall only, and windows on the other. By the order of the physician, a muff, belt and wristlets were placed on a destructive patient. A slight odor was noticed in the water-closet, which was caused from lack of running water. The rooms generally were in good order. One sheet and a mattress were found soiled, but otherwise the bedding was clean. The seating accommodations were sufficient.

Mr. Borst, who appeared before a committee of the Legislature some time ago, was found locked in a cross hall of this ward. He was almost nude and very violent. The physician stated that Mr. Borst was very destructive, and in one quarter had destroyed $250 worth of property. At such times he is restrained with a muff and belt about a week night and day, after which time he will generally promise to behave himself. The last time he was so restrained was about six weeks previous to the day of visitation, at which time he broke his bedstead at night, knocked off the window screen, broke the guard and threw the furniture out of the window. His bed is now made on the floor. The attendants are frequently assaulted by him, and Dr. Nellis stated that only that morning Borst tried to strike him and spat in his face. The other patients were well clothed and looked comfortable.

Hall 2. This hall is for a violent class, and contained sixty-one patients and five attendants. The hall was overcrowded, eighteen patients being obliged to sleep on the floor for want of accommodations. The rooms and bedding were clean, and the patients comfortably clothed. The patients were seen at dinner, which consisted of salt mackerel, potatoes, tomatoes, bread and pudding. Knives, forks and crockery are used. No restraint is here used.

Hall 5. An excitable and violent class was on this hall. Four attendants were in charge of the forty patients, seventeen of whom slept on the floor. No restraint is here used. One sheet and a mattress were found soiled, but the bedding generally was clean. The walls were decorated and the rooms in good order. A number of patients complained of ill-treatment, which, on inquiry, was found untrue. No restraint is used on this hall.

Hall 3. This is for a mixed class; many of the patients were of filthy habits. There were fifty-four patients on the hall in charge of four attendants. Six patients slept on the floor from lack of accom-modations. Five feeble patients were in bed. The attendant stated that most of these were filthy, and had to be bathed every twenty minutes. On one side of the hall the partitions have been taken out between the rooms, making a long dormitory, in which were nineteen beds. Rubber sheets were on most of the beds. The hall was in good order and the bedding clean. A night watch or attendant is on this ward at night to attend to the wants of the patients and keep them clean. The patients were seen at dinner, which, for the feeble, consisted of corn starch, milk and beef tea. Some were not able to swallow meat or coarse food. No restraint is used. The attendant stated that one patient had had his pantaloons and shirt changed as often as fourteen times in one day, on account of his filthiness.

Hall 6. This hall is for the demented and feeble class, and contained twenty-eight patients and four attendants. Two slept in beds in the hall. Three dormitories are on this hall, and no single rooms. The rooms and bedding were clean, and the patients well clothed. Quilted sheets are used on the beds of a number of destructive patients. The seating capacity is sufficient. The patients were seen at dinner; two were eating in the hall, an idiot boy and an old man, the latter taking care of the former under the belief that he was his son.

Hall 9. This hall is for idiots and epileptics, and contained twenty-one patients and three attendants. Many were filthy in their habits, and two slept on the floor for want of accommodations. Dormitories are on one side of the hall and windows looking out on the grounds on the other. On one bed there was no mattress, but a number of heavy blankets instead, and a canvas pillow, which could not be destroyed by the patient. One patient was sick in bed and had to be fed with a spoon. The patients were seen at dinner; they were well clothed and looked comfortable. Every thing on the hall was neat and clean. The superintendent stated that about five-sixths of all the patients in the asylum were sent out on the grounds every pleasant day. The doors to the rooms in each wing were raised about four inches from the floor, with an open fan-light above, thus making good ventilation throughout. The buildings are in good repair, and the patients appeared well cared for.

In a long two-story brick building connected with the main building by a corridor, are the kitchen, milk cellar, laundry, etc. The kitchen is in the basement or lower part; the floor is of tile, and was in good order; here all the cooking is done for the two wings. A track runs to the elevators in the basement of each wing. All modern improvements are in the kitchen, and the cooking is done by steam. Besides the ordinary list, an extra diet list, with the names of the sick, is kept here. A number of patients were seen at work preparing the meals. Everything was in neat order. In the milk cellar, cans holding 280 quarts are kept in an ice-box used for that purpose. Milk is only given to special diet patients. In the boiler-house are three large boilers for heating the main building, and supplying the steam to run a large engine, which furnishes the power for running the machinery in the laundry. In this building is also a large fan-wheel, which forces a current of air through the main building and wings.

LAUNDRY. Here the washing is done for the whole institution. On the ground floor are fifteen washing-machines and two wringers run by steam. On this floor the drying is also done by steam. Most of the patients here employed were men. The ironing is done on the upper floor, where a number of female patients were employed. One steam mangle is in use, all other ironing being done by hand. In one room a number of patients were engaged in sorting out the clothing for the different groups and wards, all of which is marked. The building is well ventilated by means of air being forced through it. An amusement hall has lately been built a short distance from the main building. The intention of the building was to furnish sleeping accommodations for some of the help. It was not quite finished at the time of this visit, but when completed, the lower floor will be used for giving private theatricals, concerts, lectures, etc., and the upper for rooms for the help. It is a neat structure, and well adapted for the purpose intended, and will be heated by steam from the basement.

D.B. (DETACHED BLOCK) No. 2 (FEMALES). This is the first group south of the ravine. Dr. Bristol resides in the center building, attached to which on each side is a wing for the patients. The ground floor of the center building is divided into an apothecary shop, two dining-rooms, one for each wing, and a kitchen. In the rear of the group is a boiler-house which supplies hot water and steam for heating purposes. The buildings are two stories and attic, and the wards are numbered as in the main building, commencing from the north. There are three groups the exact duplicate of this, so that the description of the one will answer for the others. The most violent cases are in the main building, although many of the patients in the detached groups are somewhat disturbed and violent. Dr. Bristol escorted us through the buildings. On this occasion there were 242 patients in this group, most all of a quiet class. All, with the exception of the sick, go out walking every pleasant day.

The dining-rooms are large, and were furnished with long tables and chairs. Knives, forks and crockery are used by all the patients. The rooms were in good order, and every thing clean. The kitchen contains all modern improvements, and was in very neat order. The dining-room for the help opens into the kitchen. A matron is in charge of each group for females and looks after the housekeeping. The supplies are kept in the main building, and only issued to the detached groups on a written requisition signed by the matron in the female department, and by the steward in the male department. The requisition book was examined. There is a duplicate list of articles on each page, one of them (on the stub) being kept in the book, and the other signed by the matron, which is then sent to the main building, to be signed by the superintendent, and when the goods are received the matron signs the stub in the book.

Hall 3. This hall is for a quiet class, and contained thirty patients some of whom were of filthy habits, and two attendants. None slept on the floor and no restraint was used. The dormitories are of two sizes - nineteen by fifteen, height eleven feet; twenty-five by twelve, height eleven feet. In each dormitory there were six bedsteads. All the dormitories in the buildings are of these dimensions. On this hall there were seventeen patients at work in the day room, (which is also used as a sewing room), making clothing for the male patients. The goods are cut in the tailor shop and finished by patients on different halls. One sewing machine is used by the woman in charge only. The work turned out the month previous was 154 pairs of pantaloons, six coats and one vest. The rooms and bedding were clean, and the patients well dressed. The female patients make the clothing for their separate wards. The woven wire spring mattress is used on all the beds but three, which were occupied by patients of filthy habits. The seating capacity is sufficient, and the settees are cushioned. The clothes-room was in good order and well ventilated. In the bath-room are two iron tubs in good order. The water-closet was in good condition, a continuous stream of water being kept running in the hoppers, except when the patients were out on the grounds. The floors of both rooms are of wood, but in good condition.

D.B. No. 4 (FEMALES). On the day of visitation this block contained 244 patients. Dr. Sylvester, the resident physician, being absent on his vacation, we were escorted through the buildings by Dr. Bristol who had charge during his absence. This block is a duplicate of the one already described.

Hall 3. This hall is for the quiet class, and contained thirty patients and three attendants. Five were filthy in their habits, none slept on the floor. A set of muffs was shown, but the supervisor stated that they had not been in use for six months. The seating accommodations are sufficient, and most of the settees were cushioned. Many of the patients do fancy work. The rooms were in good order, and the bedding was clean. No bad odor was noticed in the water-closet or bath-room. The patients had all been bathed by half-past eleven on this morning. The walls were decorated, and the general appearance was neat. The patients were neatly clothed and looked well.

THE BRANCH (FORMERLY THE AGRICULTURAL COLLEGE). This building is a four-story brick structure, and contained on the day of visitation 190 female patients. It is not adapted for use as an asylum; the halls are not well lighted and look cheerless; and the main stairway is also dark. Dr. Hopkins, the physician in charge, escorted us through the building. Besides the main stair-case, the building is supplied with one iron and one wooden stairway. The kitchen, store-room and bed-rooms for the help are in the basement, which is damp and unfit for such use. The doctor stated that the help often complained of being sick from sleeping there, but it was the only available place. A line of hose is in the cellar, which is the only means of protection in case of fire. One hall is on each floor.

Hall 1. This hall is for the quiet class, and contained fifty-two patients and four attendants. None slept on the floor in this building. About twenty shirts are made by the patients each month. The halls are decorated and pictures are on the walls. The seating capacity is sufficient, and the settees are cushioned. A supervisor has charge of the building. Many rat-holes were noticed in the floors, and the physician stated that two attendants killed seventy-two rats in one night.

There are no single rooms in the building, and the dormitories accommodate from three to ten patients each. The wire spring mattress is used on all the beds but one in each dormitory, but on this, the iron strap mattress is used. The following are the sizes of the dormitories: 21 by 9, 11 feet high, each contains three beds; 21 by 27, nine and ten beds; 21 by 13, each contains five beds; 21 by 15, seven beds. The rooms were in good order, and the bedding was clean. The patients were well clothed. All who are well enough are taken out to walk every pleasant day. The hall is used as a day room. The seating accommodations were adequate, and some of the settees were cushioned. The clothes room was in neat order. Each patient has her own box. The bath-room contains two iron tubs and was in good condition. The floor is of wood. The water-closet, also with wooden floor, was also in good order. The patients were all bathed on the day of visitation. The dining-room was neatly arranged. Knives, forks and crockery are used throughout this building. The halls were decorated, and pictures were on the walls.

Hall 3. This hall is for a disturbed class, and contained fifty-four patients and five attendants. Ten were of filthy habits. The patients make about fifty shirts a month. A pair of wristlets were on the hall but not in use. The rooms were in neat order, and the bedding was clean. The seating accommodations were sufficient, and most of the settees were cushioned. The water-closet and bath-room were not in good order, and a bad odor was noticed. Two patients are bathed in one water contrary to the directions of the physician. The clothes and dining-rooms are arranged as in the other wards, and were in neat order. The patients were well clothed and in good condition.

D.B. No. 3 (MALES). This block is a duplicate of those already described with the exception that the wings are detached and connected by a corridor. Dr. Myron D. Blaine is here in charge and escorted us through the buildings. In the rear of the block is a large yard inclosed only on three sides. In this inclosure are two neat summer houses or sheds for the patients, many of whom were seated in them while others were amusing themselves on the grounds. They were neatly clothed and appeared contented. In this block on the day of visitation there were 265 patients, about 150 of whom work. They are not classified but are mixed throughout the wards. Filthy patients were on every hall. Most all were out on the grounds at this time.

Hall 8. On this hall there were thirty-four patients in charge of three attendants. Straw and hair mattresses are here used, and iron straps are on the bedsteads. A few soiled sheets were noticed on the beds. The doctor explained that this was the day on which the sheets were to be changed, but at that time the change had not been made. No restraint is used in the building with the exception of a guard room which is simply a regular room with an iron screen on the window. This was not in use on this occasion. The clothes-room was neat and well ventilated. All the male patients are supplied with slippers which are worn in the buildings, but shoes are put on when they go out. The day-room was in good order. The seating accommodations were sufficient, and the hall generally had a pleasant appearance. The water-closet and bath-room were in good order, but the floors are of wood. The plumbing was good and no odor was noticed.

D.B. No. 1 (MALES). This group is arranged as the others, with the exception of two detached buildings connected with the center by corridors, which are on each side of the main building. Dr. Hopkins, who has charge at the Branch, has also charge of this block, and, with the supervisor, escorted us through the buildings. This group accommodated 257 patients, all of whom were out on the grounds, with the exception of those sick. The patients were seen in the yard, which is a duplicate of that previously described. Many of them were working. They were neatly clothed and looked well. Water-closets are in the yards for the use of the patients when on the grounds. The patients are not classified. The dining-rooms, kitchen, etc., were in neat order.

Hall 6. Here were thirty-two patients and two attendants. A camisole was worn by a patient at night to prevent his committing suicide; no other restraint is used. The rooms and bedding were clean, the seating accommodations adequate, and the general appearance of the hall was good. In the water-closet and bath-room there were wooden floors in good repair.

Hall 3. This hall accommodated thirty-two patients in charge of three attendants. This is for the most filthy patients in the building. An occasional bed was found soiled, but the excuse was that the bedding was to be changed throughout the building that day. The general appearance was neat. The floors of the water-closet and bath-room are tiled, and the plumbing was in good repair. No restraint was used. The seating capacity was adequate.

GROUNDS. In company with the steward we were driven over the grounds, which were almost all under cultivation. Springs supply water for the cattle while in the pastures. The asylum owns twenty horses, five colts, eighty cows, twenty head of young cattle and 430 pigs. The cows give about 150 gallons of milk a day, which supplies the needs of the institution. The garden consisted of about thirty acres of land. The hog-yards are paved with brick, which was found to make the feet of the hogs tender, and it was suggested that the brick be covered with a layer of earth which could occasionally be cleaned out. The cow-stables were neat, but it was evident that the cows were tied too closely together and there was not enough air space for the number. The cows were all out on the pastures. The culvert, for which an appropriation was received last year, was almost completed.

The sewage of the 'Branch' and of D.B. 3, empties into the creek which runs through the ravine, and finally enters the lake not far from the main building.

BOOKS OF THE ASYLUM. A large number of books are kept in the asylum, which were examined. The case book has printed forms. It is written up from time to time, and all changes in the condition of patients are entered at the time they occur, and as a matter of routine entries are made in every case once a year. Under title 3, section 10, general laws. Record of superintendent's doings each day is kept in the following books: Each head attendant on every ward makes out a daily report, which is presented to the attending physician in the morning at the time of his visit. That report gives the number of patients on the hall, number sick, number taking medicine, number wet and dirty night and day, number admitted and discharged, number in restraint, and the kind of restraint used and for what purpose, the number employed and how, number sleeping on halls, and every thing special that occurs during the day. These reports are summarized into departments, and the supervisor of each department presents it to the physician. These are then collected by the apothecary, and a general summary made in a book entitled 'day reports.' The summary for September 4 is as follows: 1,823 patients; forty-one in bed; 241 taking medicine; 125 wet and dirty during the day; 264 wet and dirty during the night; two admitted; one restrained in belt during the day for destructiveness and violence; one restrained at night in a camisole to prevent suicide; one restrained in a muff during the night to prevent suicide; one restrained in camisole during night and day for surgical reasons; one restrained at night in camisole for surgical reasons; forty-five engaged in employment on the farm; nineteen in the garden; nineteen at the barns; thirty-three in the laundry; seventy-seven in the kitchens; eight in the centers; one in the bakery; one in the matron's office; 140 at needle work; three assisting engineers; three in tailoring department; thirty in tailoress' department; three assisting the carpenter; three painting; three shoe making; 112 at work on the grounds; 218 employed at various occupations on the halls; 1,120 out to walk. The book is kept and the papers from which it is compiled are all on file. At any time during the day, when his action is required, the physician makes a special report; and at the end of the month these are made into a book and placed on file in the superintendent's office. A report is made by the chief cook of the diet for the day. Such reports are made in all the buildings and filed in the office. The assistant physicians all keep a clinical record book. Census book, which gives the census of the various buildings daily. Record of night watch. Each night watch makes a written report in the morning of every thing that happens during the night.

The rate for the coming year was fixed $2.55 a week *per capita*. The actual cost for the year ending August 30, 1884, was $2.63. There was a rebate for the last quarter of twenty cents a week, on account of surplus from former maintenance fund. The superintendent also called our attention to a 'register of patients' which contains a catalogued alphabetical list of all persons admitted since the opening of the asylum, with name, age, date of admission, county, number of admission, and the result of treatment. Register of interments of patients buried in the asylum cemetery, with name, age at death, nativity, date of death, date of burial, number of the grave, number of the form, and the number of the lot, the signature of the witness of the burial. Books required by the board of health. Medical record of each group of buildings, which gives record of diseases, name, location, diagnosis, commencement of disease, result and remarks."

"Employees – Pay Scale (Per Month)

MALES:	FEMALES:
TOTAL NUMBER OF SUPERVISORS 7	TOTAL NUMBER OF SUPERVISORS 8
HIGHEST WAGES $35	HIGHEST WAGES $22
LOWEST WAGES $20	LOWEST WAGES $16
TOTAL NUMBER OF ATTENDANTS 69	TOTAL NUMBER OF ATTENDANTS 79
HIGHEST WAGES $27	HIGHEST WAGES $18
LOWEST WAGES $16	LOWEST WAGES $9"

(18)

4

DEFINITIONS OF INSANITY

According to the Merriam-Webster Dictionary, the definition of insanity is: "1: a deranged state of the mind usually occurring as a specific disorder (as schizophrenia). 2: such unsoundness of mind or lack of understanding as prevents one from having the mental capacity required by law to enter into a particular relationship, status, or transaction or as removes one from criminal or civil responsibility. 3 a: extreme folly or unreasonableness b: something utterly foolish or unreasonable." (19)

Contrary to current pop culture belief, the definition of insanity is not, "doing the same thing over and over and expecting different results." No one is quite sure who coined that phrase but it is incorrect. This should be a great learning experience for us all. Don't believe everything you watch on television and read on the internet because it may not be true. Always dig deeper and check your sources especially when trying to uncover the facts. This also proves a wonderful point that people, educated or not, from any era, will believe almost anything if it has been repeated over and over again, and especially if it comes from a person or persons who are in a trusted position of power and authority.

In order to understand the maladies that afflicted our ancestors in the 1800s, it is best to describe them using the definitions of that time period. Many of us know someone who suffers from a psychiatric disability and most of us have been made aware of these illnesses by reading magazines and watching television commercials put out by the drug companies. People of the 1800s did not have the option of taking prescription drugs to control their moods and behaviors. I am not advocating prescription drugs; I'm making an observation. If you exhibited the symptoms of prolonged, debilitating depression or melancholia, it was considered a form of insanity worthy of admission into an insane asylum.

What you will see in Chapter 9 is the 1880 U.S. Federal Census – Schedule of Defective, Dependent, and Delinquent Classes – that defines insanity into six general categories: Mania, Melancholia, Paresis (General Paralysis), Dementia, Epilepsy, and Dipsomania. You may also see the terms: Paroxysmal, Chronic, Periodic, Subacute and Acute next to the term Mania which describes the type or duration of Mania. There is one additional term included in the Mania category: Puerperal Mania, which was not included with these six but is listed for one woman in 1880 under the heading "Form of Disease." There are two more terms that you may see listed next to your ancestor's name, they are: Idiocy (Idiot) and Imbecility (Imbecile). In the twenty-first century, these terms are known as mental retardation or intellectual disabilities. These two labels are not included in the definition of insanity but the patients who were labeled as such were marked on the Willard census as insane.

In 1898, Dr. John Bassett Chapin, first Physician Superintendent of The Willard Asylum for the Insane, wrote a book entitled *A Compendium of Insanity*. This book is complete with all the definitions used in the 1880 census. It is disturbing to note that his book contains photographs of patients who had each particular illness described. These patients were used as examples of what each outward appearance of a particular psychiatric disorder should look like. Apparently physicians and alienists (physicians who devoted their specialty to insanity) of this time period could look at someone's facial features and deduce that a person was insane. Two scientific theories that were quite influential in the nineteenth century were Phrenology and Physiognomy. The first is the study of the shape of the skull based on the belief that it is indicative of mental faculties and character. The latter is the belief that the facial features expressed the qualities of the mind and character of the person by their configuration or expression. (19) The shape of the head and features such as a low sloping forehead, high cheekbones, and shifty eyes could be measured with special tools called craniometers and calipers, and the measurements could then be analyzed.

With the great influx of insane immigrants into the United States along with the fear that insanity was escalating, these two schools of thought would give rise to another frightening science called *eugenics* that used forced sterilization from the 1910s through the 1930s on patients incarcerated in mental institutions. This new science was utilized in order to prevent undesirable people from having children and spreading the defective genetic trait or germ plasm of insanity onto future generations causing the offspring to become continual, dependant, wards of the state. From all the information I have read, I found no evidence that Willard used forced sterilization at any time.

Two men who were very influential in the scientific community of the time period were Charles Darwin who in 1859 wrote *On The Origin of Species*, and Sir Francis Galton who invented the term eugenics in his book published in 1883, *Inquiries Into Human Faculty and Its Development*. In 1869, Galton coined the phrase, "nature versus nurture," in *Hereditary Genius*, which by the way uses genealogy to trace genius in families.

Dr. Chapin's definitions are obsolete as they are over one hundred years old. It is important not to judge your insane ancestor especially considering that psychiatry and neurology (two competing professions in the 1800s), were in their infancy. The purpose of this book is not to be judge and jury of the insane or of the people who put them away, but to be understanding and knowledgeable of the circumstances that changed our ancestors' lives and the era in which they lived. Antibiotics, such as Penicillin, would not be discovered until 1928 which would have potentially saved the lives of patients suffering from Paresis (Syphilis).

Excerpts from Dr. John Bassett Chapin's A Compendium of Insanity

"IDIOCY; IMBECILITY: A person born without mental faculties or capacity is an idiot. Idiocy is a congenital condition due to arrested or abnormal development, prenatal conditions, disease, or accident. It is accompanied by physical defects, as short stature, deformity, irregular gait, or defective articulation. Many idiots show evidences of cerebral meningitis in infancy. An idiot does not become insane, though he may have psychical explosions, because the mental faculties are not sufficiently developed to pass into a state of disorder or disease. He is one who requires the consideration of, and who is both by legal fiction and in fact, an infant throughout the whole life-period. The terms idiocy and imbecility are frequently used as synonyms, but by general agreement it is an aid to regard both as meaning a congenital defect, differing rather in degree, as might be expressed by the words partial and complete. The term *imbecility* has been applied with great convenience to partial or arrested development which begins to show itself early in life and before the age of puberty. The child may be well formed and the mental faculties seem to be developing in a normal direction, but when he reaches a period when new and enlarged relations are usually established, and an advance might be expected, he shows an incapacity to receive instruction, falls behind his fellows, has an ungovernable temper, is not amenable to discipline, is cruel to dumb and helpless animals, is devoid of affection, has no capacity for any business, and may have even criminal instincts from an apparent lack of all normal faculties. Though he may reach an adult age, yet it comes to appear that he has not advanced beyond the capacity of a child of six or eight years. Idiocy and imbecility, which imply deficiency of mind, are regarded as instances of congenital defect. They are not, however, to be confounded with or brought within the category of insanity, which is rather recognized as a disease or disorder of the mind. An imbecile may have an attack of insanity, depending on the degree of mental development. The several classes are treated and cared for in institutions that are quite unlike, although in a legal sense the insane, idiots, and imbeciles are regarded as persons of unsound mind.

A child may grow to manhood and then show an irregular development, as a strong will and vacillating judgment; a vigorous understanding and be destitute of affection, have peculiarities of dress and manner, a disposition to walk in certain fixed directions, to touch persons and places in passing, to talk aloud when alone and gesticulate in periods of abstraction, or to assume unusual modes of dress and living. Channels of thought are formed which become habits from frequent repetition. None of these peculiarities amount to insanity, but may be strictly in the line of a normal growth and development. They are the characteristics that normally belong to some individuals, and are regarded as *eccentricities*, but do not in themselves amount to a state of insanity, and need not have consideration here further than to place them properly as indicating a degree of degeneration inherited or acquired."

"INSANITY DEFINED. An attempt to formulate a definition of insanity may seem as futile as an effort to define a sane mind; yet writers have made the endeavor, in order to limit the range of the subject, to facilitate discussion by agreement about terms that have an understood meaning, and to aid medico-legal proceedings. Many refrain from giving any definition, but announce a classification of forms of insanity, and furnish extended descriptions of each.

Esquirol has defined insanity to be *'a cerebral affection, ordinarily chronic, without fever, characterized by disorders of the sensibility, of the intelligence, and of the will.'* Maudsley declares *'insanity to consist in a morbid derangement, generally chronic, of the supreme cerebral centers-the gray matter of the cerebral convolutions-giving rise to perverted feeling, defective or erroneous ideation, and discordant conduct, conjointly or separately, and more or less incapacitating the individual, for his due social relations.'*

According to Conolly, *'insanity is the impairment of any one or more of the faculties of the mind, accompanied with, or inducing, a defect in the comparing faculty.'* Regis (1891) without pretending to give an accurate definition of insanity, observes that *'it is a special disease, is a form of alienation characterized by the accidental, unconscious, and more or less permanent disturbance of the reason.'*

Bucknill regards insanity as *'a condition of the mind in which a false action of conception or judgment, a defective power of the will, or an uncontrollable violence of the emotions and will, have separately and conjointly been produced by disease.'* The courts are not disposed to accept professional definitions of insanity, but prefer to furnish an interpretation of the legal relations of the insane. Blackstone has said that *'a lunatic, non compos mentis, is one who hath had understanding, but by disease, grief, or other accident hath lost the use of his reason.'*

Insanity may also be defined to be *'that mental condition characterized by a prolonged change in the usual manner of thinking, acting, and feeling-the result of disease or mental degeneration.'* The last definition is to be commended, as it is in accordance with medical requirements in the sense that it presupposes the existence of disease, and is readily comprehended by a court and jury.

To establish the existence of insanity it is essential to determine that there has been a departure from the ordinary and usual way of thinking and acting - that it is a prolonged change, and that it is the result or accompaniment of disease or mental degeneration. This definition, with its limitations, excludes from the category of insanity cases of sudden unconsciousness, as from injuries or shocks, delirium of fever, abuse of alcohol and drugs. Cases of this character are not to be certified for admission to the hospitals for the insane, for detention and treatment. The delirium of bodily disease is purposely excluded from the definition. While an insane person may have delirium from toxic agencies, as a temporary accompaniment of some physical disease - as, for instance, a fever - consisting mainly of hallucinations of the senses, of brief duration, the definition is intended to place the latter mental symptoms rather among the complications of bodily disease. So also must be excluded those so-called popular delusions - as spiritualism and the belief in false religions - which are not due to the existence of disease. Persons addicted to the habitual use of alcoholic liquors or drugs are not included as coming within the scope the definitions applicable to insanity and the insane. Such use is rather a habit than a disease, and, though seclusion may prove beneficial, and prolonged indulgence may even result in insanity, cases of the opium-habit or alcohol-habit cannot be certified to be insane, nor legally detained in a hospital, as our lunacy laws are usually construed.

It is a frequently recurring question that the judges are called upon to meet, in the discharge of their duties, how far the term insanity shall be used to exonerate and excuse the acts of persons who habitually allow their passions to have unbridled sway, or those who indulge in theoretic vagaries until their conduct is a constant menace to human life and even the fabric of society. The definitions of insanity that have been furnished are not intended to include nor wholly to relieve from responsibility those who commit acts that accompany sudden explosions of anger, or those instances of social and fanatical speculation that render their promoters incompatible with the safety of society and with public order."

"DELUSIONS. The insane, as a rule, act from motives very much the same as those that govern and influence the sane. They may show anger, resentment, and pleasure, but they are influenced and impelled to action by erroneous beliefs and ideas. The incorrect judgments of the insane are called delusions. *A delusion is a false, perverted, and, in a medical sense, an abnormal belief.* As an illustration a person may believe that he is full, or that his digestive functions will not act again, and persistently refuse to take food; that his head is enveloped in a shield, and to get rid of the encumbrance may beat his head against a wall; that he is the Almighty; that he is the oldest person in the world, having been well acquainted with Adam and Eve; that he has great wealth, although surrounded by the appearances of wretched poverty. Erroneous opinions of the sane are not to be confounded with delusions of the insane, as they are constantly and easily corrected by ordinary experience and knowledge. No argument or persuasion can, as a rule, correct the false beliefs of the insane. Delusions are almost universally present in acute forms of insanity, and are easily recognized. When the disease develops slowly it is difficult to detect their nature, and they become apparent only by long and careful observation of the patient in all his varied relations to his occupation, to the community in which he lives, and to his family. Delusions of the insane are both objective and subjective. They are evolved from the external and internal sources of consciousness, as well as from an incongruous association of stored ideas. They are evolved from, and are symptoms of, disorder of the intellectual and moral faculties. The existence of a single delusion that in itself may be harmless, if that delusion comprises the whole case, and does not materially change the relations of the person to his various interests, is not a sufficient warrant for legal lunacy-proceedings or for advising admission to a hospital. If, however, there exists evidence of physical disease, together with delusions, or a delusion that dominates or controls the patient, then he is insane. If he commits a criminal act as the direct consequence of a delusion, in that case he is irresponsible in a legal sense. Out of this an attempt has been made by the legal profession to recognize a distinction between what is called 'medical' and 'legal' insanity, which physicians are not disposed to accept, while admitting that there may be a modified degree of mental capacity and responsibility."

"HALLUCINATIONS are false perceptions. Ordinarily, if an object is actually present, or any one of the special senses is excited, an afferent sensation is conveyed to the sensorium. If the mind takes cognizance of the sensation, the result is a perception. If there is an act of perception when no object is near, it is without foundation and is unreal or false. Hallucinations are sensory symptoms of insanity as well as of delirium. The patient seems to hear voices of persons and see objects that are not present. Everything may be tinged a crimson color. Every pane of glass in a window may have a face in it, and the faces and forms of relatives long deceased may seem to appear. A person with hallucinations is noticed standing in one position in an abstracted manner, as one absorbed in deep contemplation, or gesticulating and conducting in an audible tone a conversation which to a spectator may seem somewhat one-sided. Another manifestation of sense-disturbance is the statement occasionally made by patients that someone is reading their thoughts, and the patient claims that what he reads or what is passing through his mind is being repeated in an audible voice.

So annoying is this persecution through days and nights that sleep and repose are destroyed. The patient may attempt again and again to read, and is observed to lay aside the book and walk away. Men and women complain that wicked, obscene, and profane expressions are constantly addressed to them, and they are persecuted - tormented to do terrible things by some unseen agency. It is common with the insane suffering from hallucinations of hearing to assert that they have communication with spirits, that they are in connection with all parts of the world by telegraphic wires, and that they receive messages by telephone to which they make replies.

The senses of taste, smell, and feeling are all liable to perversion, but hallucinations of these senses are not as frequent as those of hearing and sight. The natural taste is changed so that food may seem to be compounded of disgusting substances, putrid or poisoned, and is persistently refused. One patient insisted that the room was filled with smoke and bad odors; another held a handkerchief to her face or waved it to dispel the imaginary vapor of chloroform which she said enveloped her.

Individuals suffering from hallucinations of hearing may have a feeling that they are literally pursued. Their peace of mind is destroyed, their judgment and self-control are gradually undermined, and delusions of persecutions come to be formed. Criminal acts are performed under the influence of hallucinations of hearing and sight; suicides and homicides have been committed under the influence of commands from a higher power; and assaults occur, in and out of hospitals, incited by imaginary and invisible agencies. The sense of feeling is disordered, producing itching or uncomfortable sensations of heat and cold; clothing is burdensome, explaining the tendency to remove it and to denude the person. All of the senses may be involved in the same case. Individuals laboring under hallucinations by the influence of association often fix upon persons who are nearest to them as the authors of their persecution. Mysterious assaults and even homicides are explainable sometimes on the hypothesis that they are committed under these circumstances. The experienced observer comes to recognize a characteristic physiognomy of these cases - an appearance of abstraction and fixed attention-which affords a clue to the nature of the mental disorder. Visual and auditory hallucinations are uniformly present in delirium accompanying extreme physical exhaustion, disease, and toxic conditions of the blood. The wandering, furtive movements of the eye, the seeming incoherent conversation - quite like that which may be heard at one end of a telephone line - are indications of hallucinations of both sight and hearing.

The question will arise as to what extent auditory and visual hallucinations may exist before a physician is warranted in making a certificate of insanity. It is true that many suffer through the greater part of their lives from some disturbances of this nature which prove to be harmless. They seem to hear the sound of bells, hear reports, and see familiar faces. These are not the actions of a normal brain, yet they do not interfere with the usual business or other relations of a patient who recognizes the sensory disturbance and whose better judgment and self-control do not permit it to influence him. But if hallucinations exist to a degree to induce beliefs that have no better foundation, and which influence the actions of the individual, then he is insane, although the mental disorder may be partial or general.

Any explanation of hallucinations must be regarded as largely speculative. Why extreme nervous prostration, the exhaustion that follows alcoholic excess, indulgence in the opium-habit, or the presence in the circulation of toxic agencies should produce not only hallucinations but such hallucinations as are characteristic of the various causes that produce them, is beyond explanation. It may be said of all acute insanities, and of delirium attended with hallucinations, that there is a defective state of nutrition of the brain due to the quantity or quality of the blood circulating within it, or to some degree of cell destruction. The phenomena of hallucinations are subjective: there is no object present to excite them. They are not instances of mistaken identity, as they have an internal origin. It has been said that, like dreams, they are but reproductions of former actual sensations which memory recalls incongruous, disorderly association, as it is known that the blind and deaf are subject to them. They may occur only to those who have at one time possessed their senses, and subsequently lost the use of one or another; but the fact may have a bearing on the hypothesis that memory performs an unconscious function in the reproduction of former sensations or images.

Observers agree that hallucinations of hearing are more frequent than visual disturbances, although some have stated that in acute insanity the reverse is true. Hallucinations of hearing appearing early in the attack of insanity and persisting until the chronic stage, or appearing in a case that begins insidiously, are looked upon as a prognostic sign of unfavorable import. New habits of thought are formed in consequence, which become gradually changed into permanent channels that cannot be easily broken up."

"ILLUSIONS. Another symptom of insanity is the occasional presence of a class of false beliefs closely allied to disordered sensations, and to which the term illusions has been applied. Illusions are the distortions of actual objects by the senses. The identity of persons and things is mistaken. A stranger may be addressed by the name of a familiar friend or as some distinguished character, and things stationary and moving are converted in the mind of the person into unreal objects. Hallucinations of the senses are subjective, while illusions have an objective origin."

"MELANCHOLIA. (a) Simple Melancholia Without Delusions. Melancholia is a form of insanity characterized by prolonged and profound mental depression. Many persons are at times conscious of some depression of spirits, which may be a reaction after a period of excitement and exhaustion, which passes away after a temporary duration. Such instances are examples of psychic disturbances that arise from unexplainable functional states of the brain, or they may be dependent upon toxic or other agencies in the circulation that affect the nutrition of the nervous centers or pervert mental functions. As they are corrected, the gloom and weight of depression are lifted and disappear.

It is proper to make a distinction, and in many cases to draw a line of demarcation, between melancholia and hypochondria. The melancholiac and the hypochondriac experience depression and are sad and gloomy; but one may be insane and the other does not come within the category. The depression of the melancholiac is mainly mental, and relates to subjects having a relation to the mind of the patient, while that of hypochondria relates mainly to supposed bodily conditions. The hypochondriac may be worried about his head - he may say it is 'numb;' that he is destitute of feeling; he looks at his face, his tongue, and his body, and seems to see evidences of disease; and, while in fact his general health is below its normal standard, he exaggerates every abnormal sensation. He carefully watches his excretions. Every strange feeling, as palpitation of the heart, indigestion, is a symptom of disease of the heart and stomach. Every organ may thus have its turn. Actual symptoms of functional disorder indicate to the sufferer organic changes. The physician is constantly changed, and the patient is a victim of quacks who impose upon him by a promise of relief by nostrums and excessive medication. The willpower is weakened, and the patient is listless, vacillating, and passive, until he is disposed to surrender to the dominating influence of a stronger character than his own. So long as the hypochondriac is not seriously affected in his relation to his business or his family affairs, and is not influenced and changed by actual delusions, he cannot be considered insane. Hypochondria may, however, progress to melancholia. Sensory disturbances, hallucinations, and delusions may develop and change and influence the ordinary actions of the patient. At this stage the patient may be pronounced insane, and in some of the nomenclatures the term *hypochondriacal melancholia* has been used to designate this class of cases.

Depression, sadness, or gloom may be an early stage of an attack of mania or other form of mental disorder, or may follow an acute mania, or attend the pre-natal and puerperal state, the physical debility of fever, influenza, or other physical ailment that affects the nervous system. It is a stage too often overlooked in the study of a case. Profound depression may be a premonitory symptom of some form of mental disease, in the same sense that a chill, languor, and debility are often the precursory symptoms of physical disease. Cases that throughout present a history of prolonged depression may be classified under the term *simple melancholia without delusion*. It is rather an exception to the rule of experience that a case of insanity is fully developed without a preceding stage of depression. It may be of brief or prolonged duration - of a few days or several months.

When a case is presented for examination or treatment, it is usual to find that the friends of the patient date the beginning of the attack to some outbreak or unusual acts of the patient. As a rule which is established by uniform experience in the largest proportion of cases, insanity is not a disease of sudden development, but has an incipient, formative, and prodromal stage... It will appear that the patient has perhaps a neurotic heredity, and unstable mental and physical organization, either acquired or inherited; that there have been worries attending the household, business affairs, or school studies; bodily sickness or frequent child bearing may have occurred.

From some one of these experiences of human existence, singly or together, there has been produced a great tension or strain. These are only relative terms, so that what one person may seem to bear without appreciable injury will be followed in another by ill-health, insomnia, loss of appetite, derangement of digestion, and disturbance of all the bodily functions. The blood on which the nutrition of the nervous mass depends is generally impoverished, and the circulation is imperfectly performed from a lack of nervous stimulus. While the bodily condition gradually approaches a state of invalidism, some marked mental changes are noticeable. The patient may become irritable, easily annoyed by trifling circumstances, forsake his accustomed haunts and friends; the usual occupation is burdensome; he complains of a weary, tired feeling, and, as a matter of fact, is tired and exhausted with slight mental or physical exertion. The gait is slow, the manner is languid, and the patient has a worn, exhausted appearance. He may complain of headache, a sense of pressure located at some definite portion of the head, indigestion, vomiting, or mental confusion.

Without rational or positive evidence of any organic disease, a stage of invalidism exists which may have been developing for months or years, consisting wholly of functional disorders. A clergyman who had suffered from many of the symptoms named above during the incipiency of his disease aptly likened his condition to that of an engine in perfect order, but in which the means to generate the force to move it were lacking. The term *neurasthenia* has been given to those conditions of 'nervous weakness often accompanied by perverted nervous disorders' (Billings). Its meaning is synonymous with the terms 'nervous prostration' and 'nervous exhaustion,' in more common use. In 1868, Van Deusen published an essay on 'A Form of Nervous Prostration (Neurasthenia) Culminating in Insanity.' Beard in 1869, and Cowles in 1889, in his admirable memoir on 'The Mechanism of Insanity,' and others, have discussed the relation of neurasthenia to nervous diseases and the production of insanity. The views announced by these writers have been confirmed by extended observations of other observers. Nerve-strain may thus come from the whole range of those causes that operate upon either the mental or the physical system in such a manner as to exhaust strength, or vital force, more rapidly than recuperation takes place, so that the term nervous exhaustion is also properly used.

Various disorders of the nervous system are among the manifestations of neurasthenia, as neuralgia affecting several parts of the nervous system; headache; vertigo; chorea; disorders of the circulation; palpitation of the heart; heart weakness; angina; disorders of the digestive system, as dyspepsia; prolonged vomiting simulating gastric irritation; functional disorders of the liver and kidneys, from which may come failure to eliminate excrementitious matter; or a change in the chemistry of digestion. The relation of neurasthenia to many bodily diseases may yet be found to be more intimate than is now recognized. As a factor in the production of insanity, neurasthenia must be considered the most important. The largest proportion of hospital admissions received in an acute stage have a history of neurasthenia. It is fitly called the 'soil' out of which insanity develops. It is too often the formative stage, or incipiency, of insanity. If with the prominent symptoms of nervous exhaustion there is depression of spirits together with a decided loss of weight, if there is emotional disturbance, it may be considered that the patient has received a serious warning."

"MANIA. Under the term mania may be grouped a large number of mental manifestations quite the opposite of those described as belonging to melancholia. Mania is a condition characterized by an abnormal exaltation and activity of the mental functions - the intellectual faculties, the emotions, and the will - and may show itself by irrational talking and acting, by delusions, illusions, and hallucinations, and by unusual muscular activity or movements. Here again a comparison of the condition of the individual in the disordered state in which he is found with what it was prior to the attack is necessary. It is important to learn the history of the patient in respect to his intelligence, his everyday life in relation to his accustomed occupations and to his family, his normal and usual manner of acting, and to learn whether any heredity or eccentricity-history exists. As it is difficult to find two persons who think and act exactly alike, so it is equally difficult to find two cases of the same form of insanity that are precisely similar. There are complex combinations of ideas, and complications of mental faculties and psychic forces to deal with in every case.

While it is an easy matter, and quite the rule, to find one case of uncomplicated fever or pneumonia very much like every other case, in dealing with the form of disease now under consideration it would be most difficult to find one case in all respects the counterpart of another. Yet, without regard to the dissimilarity that exists in normal mental development, the activity of the emotions or the imagination, the brightness or the stupidity of different individuals, there is a sufficient similarity in the symptoms that are observed to make a subdivision of all cases of so-called mania into subacute mania, acute mania, chronic mania, and recurrent mania. These terms have reference mainly to degree, intensity, duration, and frequency. The number of so-called 'manias' that have been actually described and named - usually from some prominent characteristic or persistent delusion - exceeds sixty. To present the refinements of nomenclature adopted by various writers upon insanity, no one of which is universally accepted, would consume more space than has been allotted to this subject, would not be helpful, and would only result in confusion. The given classification will sufficiently aid an intelligent comprehension and study of any case that may ordinarily occur, and will answer the present purpose.

In subacute and acute mania there is usually a history of physical or mental overwork and protracted mental application without repose, resulting in strain; also, reverses or successes in business, profound moral shock, resulting from loss of property or kindred, and from disappointments, the exhaustion attending the puerperal condition, and alcoholic or sexual excess - all of which operate directly or indirectly to impair the normal standard of health, to cause loss of sleep, and to produce a functional irritability of the brain.

It is so unusual to meet with a case of mania in the acute stage that is not preceded by some symptoms of depression that the rule may be stated that this form of mental disease does not occur instantaneously as a transition from a normal state of physical health. As was stated of melancholia, there is here also a prodromal stage. A careful inquiry will reveal some disturbance of the physical health, or that a moral shock has been received, producing a profound depression upon a person possessed of a neurotic temperament or heredity. The patient may show a disposition to devote his whole thought to some matter that concerns his personality or welfare, to seclude himself, and to dwell upon religious subjects, perhaps studying the Bible more than usual. Business matters may not be wholly laid aside, but as other subjects engross a great deal of attention the usual occupations are neglected, or are a constant source of perplexity. In the case of a woman, her personality or concerns engross her thoughts, and she may give herself up to emotional disturbance, as fits of weeping, laughing, and demonstrations of extravagant conduct of an hysterical character.

It will be noticed that there is a loss of appetite, that food is taken irregularly, and that the body-weight is diminished. Complaint may be made of insomnia, and that the small amount of sleep is disturbed and broken by dreadful dreams. There is an ill-defined sense of apprehension that something is to happen. There may be functional disturbance of the circulation, pain or discomfort in the head, flushing of the face, or vertigo. There may be unusual demonstrations of irritability or anger, outrageous conduct of some kind, or manifestations of erotic propensities. In women the function of menstruation is usually suspended. While the physical and psychical symptoms of an incipient stage of mania may furnish a warning to an experienced observer, they are usually regarded as insignificant in proportion to the conditions they foreshadow, so that they may wholly escape serious attention.

The symptoms which have been named form the history of the incipient stage of a large proportion of cases of subacute and acute mania. The patient who may be suffering from them is seriously threatened with an attack of insanity, although if he will co-operate with the measures the physician may propose, a further development of the disease may be arrested. The question will arise whether the patient should at once be sent away from his home for treatment. The decision should depend upon a willingness to submit absolutely to such rational treatment and advice as the physician may direct, until sufficient time has elapsed to determine whether improvement is to take place, or whether other more serious symptoms are to appear. If the threatening symptoms abate, it would then be advisable that some change of environment and absolute rest from business should be enjoined, and that all such measures as will promote sleep and the complete restoration of physical health should be systematically followed. A companion possessed of common-sense, firmness, and mildness, with a course of tonics and generous living, may often be most helpful at this stage.

After a period of incubation, which may last from one to three months, marked changes may appear, and in the progress of the case the patient enters upon an advanced stage of the disease, during which the symptoms of maniacal disturbance are pronounced, or prove to be of the most aggravated character. Singly or together the emotions, the intellectual faculties, and the will are exalted beyond the normal activity. On an analysis of the mental symptoms, they may not be found to be due to delusions and hallucinations, but rather are limited to an exaggeration of the emotional and intellectual faculties. The disordered manifestations result from morbid functional activity, all of which may subside gradually, followed by partial hebetude and recovery.

If the case advances to an acute stage, accompanied with delusions and hallucinations, emotional disturbances, consisting of immoderate laughing mingled with tears, exhilaration, anger, affection, lewdness, frenzy, and revenge, will in turn appear. The patient becomes garrulous in the extreme. Ideas originate with such rapidity that the conversation appears to be a disconnected confusion of words, which are uttered so rapidly and with such effort that they come forth as if propelled by some inward force. If the attention can be attracted, the answers to questions are often non-responsive; not for the reason that they are not wholly comprehended by the patient, but because, with the rapid discharge of ideas, he attaches but little weight to what he deems an intrusion in comparison with the importance of his own incessant, disconnected, rambling jargon. The conversation of both men and women may be carried on with a voice pitched to a high key, and with dramatic enunciation. Such is the conceit and egotism, that this may be one form the patient takes to attract attention by the noise he can make, or as a manifestation of his self-importance. The nature of the conversation is often obscene, profane, or trifling, directed promiscuously toward those who are near, or carried on when entirely alone. The feelings of modesty and decency which belong to men and women seem to be impaired, and self-respect is gone. The conduct of many patients of this class is exceedingly trying and vexatious to those about them and to the nurse in charge.

They cause a variety of mischief, provoke assaults, and make attacks upon others; they rend their garments and destroy furniture with apparent joy. Their habits are often dirty; they even smear their persons and the walls of their rooms at night with dirt, urine, and excrement. There is a propensity to make a noise, as by the destruction of glass or whatever can be damaged or moved about - sometimes to demonstrate their strength or to attract attention. They resist efforts made to control them, and become exceedingly violent. As the majority have a confused recollection of what has occurred, they are too likely to misconstrue the efforts of friends and attendants to control them into acts of actual abuse, which come to form the groundwork of nearly all of the complaints of ill-treatment.

There is always much motor disturbance in acute mania. All the muscles appear to be in a state of activity. The patient may even dance or leap; or he may try his strength, which is usually much overestimated by others, in various ways. The patient is disposed to add force and emphasis to his harangues by demonstrative gestures with the hands, feet, and body, keeping time continuously to rhythmic sentences. While these muscular demonstrations and the loud tones of the patient seem quite formidable, and offer a strong temptation to attendants to overcome them by force and the use of mechanical restraint, yet it is possible to avoid much or all of this by judicious care, tact, and as little interference as may be consistent with safety in respect to non-essential things. If the physical condition is good, there is no objection to the noise or the muscular activity of the patient, and, if he really enjoys it, even to taking him out in a carriage or for a prolonged walk, in order that he may expend in a harmless way some of the superabundant force."

"The egotism and vanity of these persons stand out prominently. The patient is loquacious, perhaps talks about everyday matters; but running through the thoughts and conduct are an egotistical exaltation and exaggeration of manner, and a self-assurance and aggressiveness that are wholly unnatural."

"PUERPERAL INSANITY. The insanity of pregnant and parturient women should be noticed in this connection. Women become insane both before and after confinement, and the term 'puerperal insanity' has been applied to this class of cases, because the disease has a relation to the puerperal state. The disease may appear in a few days or several weeks after confinement, or during lactation. The form, for convenience, may be called puerperal melancholia, puerperal mania, mania with delusions, simple depression or excitement, according to the degree or prominence of symptoms. The insanity of gestation, or prenatal insanity, usually takes the form of depression. It is due to the worry, strain, and physical exhaustion that in some cases accompany gestation.

Post-partum insanity is usually maniacal in form and complicated with delirium. It is more frequently due specially to sepsis. The observations at the Pennsylvania Hospital for the Insane, if they are confirmed by general experience, would go far to strengthen this opinion. Since the introduction of stricter antiseptic measures in obstetrical practice the number of cases of puerperal insanity has decidedly decreased. For a period of ten years preceding the year 1897, twenty cases of acute puerperal insanity were admitted. For a corresponding period preceding 1877, ninety-nine cases were received. The opinion is entertained that if in every obstetric case a rigid exclusion of every source of septic infection should be observed there would be a further reduction of the number of cases of puerperal insanity. If practicable to obtain, the temperature and pulse changes will greatly assist the formation of a correct diagnosis in all these cases, and will prove most suggestive as to the proper treatment if septic conditions are thus shown.

The mental symptoms that characterize melancholia or mania as they have been described, are not essentially different in these cases, except that the onset is rapid and may be either mild or severe. The rapidity with which some symptoms appear may be partly owing to the sudden change that takes place in the patient's condition at the delivery of the child. Slight emotional disturbances, as weeping or laughing, sometimes called hysterical manifestations, petulance, irritability, worry about the newborn child, are not infrequent immediately after confinement; but these conditions soon pass away with rest, returning sleep, food, and quiet, and may be managed at home. If these manifestations are prolonged, characteristic symptoms, such as have been described as belonging to the acute stage of mania, will appear. They are usually of the most aggravated character. The language and actions are inconsistent and at variance with the established character of the patient. The words may be profane, obscene, and uttered in a loud voice. The suspicions relating to persons and food are intense, and necessitate tact and patience in the management, and frequent changes of attendants. The agitation, jactitation, and general motor disturbance are very marked, and contribute to the exhaustion of strength and vital force. If the temperature and pulse do not rise, if there is no complication, if the delusions and hallucinations are associated with the persons and things actually surrounding the patient, and if she will take food and procures sleep, then the prognosis is favorable, and no unreasonable anxiety need be felt about the result.

On the other hand, if there is a temperature ranging from 100 to 104, and the pulse over 100, with a rising and variable tendency, there is sufficient reason to suspect sepsis. To the maniacal condition there may be superadded a mental condition in the nature of delirium, confusion, and symptoms of meningitis. The attention of the patient cannot be aroused, the sensory disturbance is active, distressing, and exhausting. The tissue-waste is so rapid that emaciation goes on faster than the loss can be made good by liberal administration of nutritious food. The tongue may be coated and inclined to dry. While the threatening symptoms last the patient's condition is to be considered critical in the extreme.

If it is decided that the patient has passed the incipient stages and that she is likely to continue insane for several weeks, if the strength is good and the home cannot conveniently or for any reason be converted into a hospital, removal to a hospital should be effected without delay. It is a common hospital experience to receive acute puerperal cases which have been transported long distances in a feeble condition at great risk to life. There should be no haste to undertake a journey if the patient is exhausted, as it is far better to convert the house into a hospital for two or three weeks, when a critical stage may have passed. The attending physician and the nurses must meet the emergencies until the strength of the patient will permit removal. As a rule, removal to and treatment in a hospital furnish the best guarantee against suicide, accidents, or any other calamity, as well as the best assurance of recovery. The probabilities are that the largest proportion will recover in from three to five months. If sepsis exists, it is a serious complication while it lasts.

The tendency to suicide, to the infliction of self-injuries and mutilation, or to some act of violence to the newborn child, are all indications of extreme perversions of natural instincts in these cases, and should be borne in mind and guarded against. The precautionary measures should comprise constant observation, the removal from the room of all instruments that can be used as weapons, the security of the windows so that they cannot be opened beyond a few inches and the care of keys and the bathrooms. It is the wisest course to make the patient absolutely safe at all times.

The recognition of melancholy or other alterations of the usual manner that attend the prenatal stage, and the diagnosis of puerperal mania and the insanity that accompanies the period of lactation, as well as the septic conditions that so often complicate this form of disease, are important to the proper treatment and care of the patient. The melancholy of prenatal insanity, and the subacute mania which may follow, as well as the acute maniacal stage which succeeds to delivery and lactation, may be mainly due to exhaustion of nervous force. They may also be incident to gestation, to the delivery of the child with accompanying hemorrhage, to the additional drain from lactation, or to septic causes which supervene."

"CHRONIC MANIA; PAROXYSMAL MANIA; RECURRENT MANIA. The active symptoms of acute mania may subside and leave the mental faculties permanently damaged. The disease then assumes a chronic form. In all cases complicated with meningitis some organic change may have occurred, involving the capillary circulation, and affecting the nutrition and blood-supply of the brain. The term 'chronic' has reference to time, and in hospital-reports is understood to imply a duration of insanity beyond one year. Chronic insanity is not necessarily incurable. After the acute constitutional and mental symptoms subside, if recovery does not take place, the patient may yet resume to a degree an orderly habit of living, but does not return to his usual, or to any useful, occupation. The patient may show peculiarities and some mental weakness. He may laugh or talk aloud have no capacity or desire for self-support, be irritable, impatient, or fault-finding, and self from the society of his family and friends. It cannot be said of these patients that lucid intervals, but the remission of the active symptoms is so marked that they may on.. .ischarged from a hospital when the habits of orderly living have been established. The periods of remission can hardly be called lucid intervals, for delusive ideas and decided instability and vacillation remain. Many such cases in and out of hospitals may, in the further course of their lives, have paroxysms with a recurrence of all the active symptoms of their disease, such as require hospital care, so that at no period can they be pronounced mentally well. The term *paroxysmal mania* has been applied to designate appropriately this form of mental disease.

The tendency of chronic mania is toward continued deterioration and mental degeneration. A case of chronic mania presents during the life of the patient varying degrees of mental impairment, so that in every hospital will be found a number who have passed through the acute stage and are hopelessly wrecked and damaged as to their mental organization. They are often continuously noisy, turbulent, destructive of clothing and property, dirty and filthy in their habits, discharging their excrement in their clothes or in their beds. All traces of decent and orderly behavior, and the facial expression which may have characterized the patient in his normal condition, seem to be obliterated. They need the care of attendants to bathe and dress them in the morning, to place food before them during the day, to control their outbreaks of violence and their dangerous propensities, and to undress and place them in bed at night, where they pass so many sleepless nights that the night attendants can never report them as asleep. The care of these cases is incessant, and may extend through months and years.

In all of these cases the hallucinations and illusions, which are prominent and dominating, have become fixed, and out of them have grown an infinite variety of delusive ideas and confused beliefs. The natural emotions and feelings are blunted or obliterated. They have as a class, however, a certain resemblance in respect to their disordered judgments, their manner and habits, their disconnected, incoherent conversations, their changed and perverted feelings, and the tendency to gradual mental failure and enfeeblement, sufficient to classify them under one general head. The Germans have used the term *Secundare Verrucktheit* to indicate chronic mania with mental confusion, and for the disconnected ideas and delusions following an acute attack."

"TREATMENT OF MANIA. The general therapeutic principles that are laid down for the guidance of the physician in the treatment of functional disorders and recognized pathologic conditions in general practice, so far as they have an application to mental cases, are of equal force here. The treatment of mania is both moral and therapeutic. The moral treatment embraces all that concerns the environment, the personal attendants, the room or ward, the discipline - for the insane are amenable to discipline, which does not of course imply punishment. The quarters of the patient should be prepared by removal of all furniture not absolutely required; all articles that might be used as weapons should be secured, and an attendant procured, if the patient is in private care."

"The patient needs plenty of food, which may be given freely at the usual time for daily meals and at other times. It is hardly probable that he will get too much. He needs sleep, fresh air, and, if there is no fever and the strength permits, plenty of exercise out of doors. It is a good rule to allow the patient to move about under reasonable restrictions, to avoid unnecessary, irritating interference, or non-essential antagonisms of any kind, and, so far as practicable, to insist that he conform to his usual habits as to rising, dressing, taking of food, bathing, walking out of doors, exercise, and removal of clothing at night.

If the habits of the patient are destructive, the bedstead and all movable furniture may be removed, as the broken pieces may be used to destroy property or as weapons. The mattress may be protected by a covering of strong, painted canvas, and laid upon the floor. If clothing is persistently destroyed and the patient denudes himself, a suit of canvas or twilled moleskin cloth may be prepared for men. For women a combination or union suit of twilled goods, composed of waist and pantaloons, buttoned or laced behind, over which a skirt may be worn, will be found useful in an extreme case. If force is to be used at any time, it is the more prudent course to employ plenty of assistance, so that a serious struggle be avoided. If it appears that a struggle is likely to occur in placing a patient in a bath-tub, it is the better course to substitute a sponge bath. Much of the nervous irritability noticed in all of these cases, it should be remembered is due to an altered or defective state of the nutrition, and tonics and iron should be administered for a long period. If the state of the circulation or of the heart is such as to require support, stimulants, digitalis, and strychnine should be given."

"The insomnious condition of all maniacal patients is one of the most embarrassing symptoms to overcome. It is persistent for weeks and months, but need not in itself create alarm, for the endurance of these persons is astonishing, and, as a matter of actual experience death does not often take place from this cause, even in acute mania…Sleep is, therefore, promoted by medicines as well as other measures that tend to reduce the functional activity of the brain and excessive motor disturbance. Of all the narcotics, opium is the most certain and powerful, but its administration is not, on the whole, satisfactory in mental cases. The constipation that results renders opiates very objectionable; but the greatest objection to their use is the capillary congestion that follows the narcotism, and which is likely to be one of the conditions to be met and counteracted in the critical states of acute cerebral disease. The after-effects of preparations of opium are so unsatisfactory that their use is not to be recommended in the case of acute mania, or in one of insomnia with the delirium of fever, or from the excessive use of alcohol.

Sulfonal alone, or sodium bromide and tincture of hyoscyamus, in combination, will often produce sleep and chloral may be occasionally added. This combination is thought by some to be attended with average good results for a short time; but there is objection to the effects of chloral and the bromides when used continuously for a long period…Hyoscyamin and hyoscin hydrobromate exercise a marked influence in controlling excessive motor activity and in inducing sleep in cases of mania… The effect of hyoscin in controlling excessive motor activity is one of the excellent results obtained from the use of this drug in conserving the strength and reducing tissue-waste. Sulfonal, one of the new hypnotics, will undoubtedly have a place until a better is obtained, as it produces sleep in 80 per cent of administrations without constitutional disturbance or serious after-effects. Sulfonal may be given in doses of from 15 to 20 grains. As it is insoluble, it may be best administered in suspension in a tumbler of warm milk. It is slow in its effects. Trional has produced very satisfactory hypnotic effects in doses of gr. xv. All medicine should, as a rule, be administered to the insane in a liquid form. If given in pills the chances are that the patient will not swallow it. Noisy and sleepless patients are known to sleep better if they have abundance of outdoor exercise and fresh air.

In the general management and treatment of mania in the acute stage, the indications throughout are to sustain the strength of the patient and repair the waste that goes on rapidly, rather than to place the chief reliance upon medication. In this, as well as in all forms of insanity, the greater advantage of hospital treatment lies in the systematic and persistent application of all measures and the administration of all medicines directed by the physicians. In the hospital treatment and care of the chronic insane the regularity of the daily life of the patient tends to establish orderly habits of living, to the development of self-control, and the abatement of paroxysms of excitement. A chronic case of insanity may acquire habits of industry which divert the mind from introspection, from the influence of delusions and hallucinations. New paths of thought become fixed, which in turn supplant suspicious and delusive ideas, the patient gains self-control, and may often be discharged from the hospital to reside among his friends."

"DEMENTIA. It has been stated that the two opposite conditions - mental depression and mental activity with general exaltation, described as melancholia and mania, with its several subdivisions - may have a terminal stage in mental enfeeblement, which is called *dementia*. Dementia is an enfeeblement of the mental faculties. Mental enfeeblement peculiar to childhood, from arrested development, congenital idiocy, or imbecility, is not included under this term. There are varying degrees of the abatement of vigor of the judgment or understanding, impairment of the will-power, and of subsidence of the manifestations of the normal feelings and affections, showing degrees of deterioration, even to complete obliteration of all power to form thought, to act, or to show any feeling. In brief, in complete dementia the mind is damaged or destroyed. Dementia may also occur as the result of organic disease of the brain, of cerebral hemorrhage, of embolism, or of changes in the cerebral circulation, such as may result from endarteritis that may interfere with the nutrition of the brain; it may be due to the presence of tumors, syphilitic gummatous growths and degenerations, or to alcoholic excesses; it may be a sequence of disease, as malarial cachexia and typhoid fever; and it may follow the trophic changes incident to old age. The more frequent form of dementia met with in hospitals is that which follows as a terminal and consequential stage of melancholia and mania. Dementia may be either primary or secondary, partial or complete - terms indicating order of development and the degree of impairment.

Dementia appears sometimes, but rarely, as a *primary* condition. Under such circumstances it may be the result of sudden shock, physical or moral, or of excesses, either sexual or alcoholic. There is no preceding stage of excitement, and, while the symptoms are quite like those of secondary dementia, to make a differential diagnosis for the purpose of treatment it is necessary to study the history of the case carefully, as the one condition offers more hope of recovery than the other. If the patient has passed through an attack of illness, as fever, or has been exhausted by close and long application to business or brain-work of any kind, or has been profoundly impressed by some moral shock, such as may occur from domestic affliction, sudden disappointment, or injury of the head, as from a fall, the mental functions are inactive and feebly performed. The patient undergoes a change, may become apathetic, lack decision, be indifferent to his surroundings, laugh when alone, show little interest in his family, appear to be confused, be unable to collect his thoughts or to write a letter (which may be noticeable by the number of omitted words and sudden breaks in sentences which are left incomplete), and talk slowly, while the memory of recent dates and events is indistinct and evanescent. The mental condition is that of hebetude not due to organic brain changes, but is dependent upon a suspension or abeyance of mental function.

The dement shows rather physical weakness than physical defect. In accordance with the degree of dementia, the mind receives only transitory impressions which may leave no trace. They come and go, so that the memory neither recalls events that are past nor notices present occurrences. The face of a familiar friend may elicit a momentary sign of recognition, but the impression is a fleeting one and is forgotten. Life may seem to be but an animal existence, destitute of emotions, the pleasure of the society of kindred, and all interest in former concerns is ended, the patient standing or sitting in a state of passive indifference to all environments."

"SENILE DEMENTIA. As the mental faculties of infancy are weak from lack of development, so in old age they have failed from prolonged use, from degeneration of the cerebral vessels, and trophic changes in the cerebral mass. Here the enfeeblement - characterized usually by the term senile dementia - seems to be a primary change, although in a small proportion of cases it is ushered in by a state of subacute delirium and insomnia. The patient seems confused, forgets his way, or, thinking he is not in his own home, attempts to wander, and may show resistance if opposition is interposed. Loss of memory is one of the earliest symptoms of dementia of mental failure due to old age. Lack of attention must not be confounded with absent-mindedness and inability to recall names, dates, and events, which is quite common even in middle life by persons much engrossed in business affairs, who pay little heed to matters not exactly in their line. Memory does not alone fail, but there is a general failure of all the mental powers, together with loss of physical vigor, and the state called 'second childhood,' or senility, appears. The vacillation, loss of will-power, and erotic propensities, which senile dements so often exhibit, render them an easy prey to designing persons who bring about marriages, or procure the execution of papers that often give rise to vexatious litigation, or wills are changed and codicils added which are subsequently disputed. Persons who have well-marked symptoms of senile dementia at sixty-five, or subsequently, do not recover their reason, and their friends should be so advised. Senile dementia rarely occurs prior to the age of sixty. If subacute mania or delirium seems to precede the failure, the friends of the patient will often consult the family physician about the necessity of taking the patient to a hospital. While this alternative must sometimes be adopted, this stage will probably be of brief duration, and will be followed by a passive and manageable condition.

The nervous system seems susceptible to the deteriorating influences and changes produced by syphilis, and primary dementia may be one of the sequences of syphilis. According to Savage, idiocy and moral perversion may be due to inherited syphilis. Acute and recurrent insanity, with optic neuritis, impairment of sight, ptosis, and strabismus, may all follow constitutional syphilis. Syphilis may be a cause of melancholia and acute mania; also of epilepsy, locomotor, ataxia, hemiplegia, and amaurosis. It is associated with the history of 80 per cent of cases of paresis. As there are no symptoms, and none of the forms of nervous and mental disease already mentioned that belong exclusively to syphilis, it is important to get as much history and as many clues as possible in any given case that may lead even to an inferential diagnosis of the existence of syphilis, that may be suggestive of a course of treatment.

Primary dementia, or profound hebetude, with a history of syphilis, may simulate paresis. If the history, for any reason, leaves the physician in doubt as to the cause or form, an anti-syphilitic course of treatment is fairly warranted. Recovery sometimes is equally surprising and rapid. A hospital case recovered from a state of apparent complete dementia after fourteen weeks treatment with mercuric chlorid and potassium iodide, taking 70 grains of the latter three times daily.

Primary dementia may follow the exhaustion attending prolonged physical and mental strain, such as may attend military campaigns, homesickness, deprivation of food, and the vicissitudes of war. After the late war thousands who had been prisoners, or who had passed through the terrible experiences of the field, were left as mental wrecks. No one who reviews a procession of the survivors of the war can fail to discern in their fixed and immovable faces, often their prematurely old look and loss of physical vigor, the disastrous effects of the severe ordeal upon their nervous organizations - a disability not perhaps to be exactly estimated, and conclude that it is appreciable and equivalent to the added wear and tear of from ten to fifteen years of life in the case of each one.

Dementia may follow melancholia and the various forms of mania, epilepsy, and, as we shall see, paresis or general paralysis of the insane, as a secondary or terminal stage. It is, as has been observed, 'the goal of all insanities.' After a prolonged period of depression or exaltation there ensues a stage of quiet and repose. The violence and force of the shock of the disease has expended itself, and the brain has been damaged. Nutrition may have recommenced and gone on actively, with increased body-weight, but there is no mental improvement. The patient has lost his vigor, and has settled into a passive, indifferent state.

Memory is weakened, the natural affections are blunted, the powers of attention and concentration are gone. There is an indifference to personal appearance and dress; ideas are evanescent, although some of them - perhaps a remnant of the active stage - remain, and excite but a momentary emotion. There are no fixed and prominent delusions; the face wears a placid, smooth, expressionless look, for the facial muscles have lost their characteristic responsive action. The man is in no respect what he was before his sickness, and is like a ship after a storm, having form and motion, but without a pilot or rudder to guide.

A patient partially demented may remain in a stationary condition during the remainder of his life. He may have some capacity to receive impressions, but he has no capacity to formulate ideas. A near relative, a judicious attendant, or a hospital organization furnishing the will-power that has been lost, may be able to keep the patient up to his highest attainable standard, and this may be all that can be done for him. Yet, despite all that may be attempted, the dement has a tendency to deteriorate physically and mentally, and may sink to the lowest state of animal existence. The functions of animal life are performed, the food is received into the stomach and digested, but the psychic storms are ended, and there is no recognition of days, dates, or kindred. The contents of the bowels and the urine are discharged in the clothing or in the bed, and saliva flows from the mouth. The countenance has lost the natural expression, the extremities are cold, livid, and perhaps edematous from the feeble state of the circulation, and the downward tendency is progressive until death occurs."

"PARESIS. Paresis is a form of insanity in which there is mental disorder of several types, accompanied with progressive muscular paralysis. The terms that have been applied to this disease in medical literature are 'general paralysis of the insane,' 'paretic dementia,' and 'paresis,' all of which are synonymous, or are so intended and understood. The last has equal significance from its derivation, and is short. It is a disease of the brain and spinal cord, characterized usually by maniacal disturbances in the early stage, with enlarged and grand ideas of wealth, power, and greatness, followed by mental failure and dementia, defective articulation, gradual progressive paralysis of the muscular system, with occasional epileptiform convulsive seizures.

For convenience the disease may be divided into three stages:

1. A prodromal stage, or period of incubation.
2. A stage of decided maniacal activity, or dementia, with symptoms of paralysis.
3. A stage of profound mental enfeeblement, with physical helplessness.

Although it has been usual to refer to a prodromal or incipient stage of general paralysis, the symptoms that may be called characteristic, or those that indicate the coming disease, are not definitely determined in the initial stage. It is a stage that precedes the outbreak, or that period in its progress when a convulsive seizure may have occurred, or when the friends of the patient or the public authorities interpose to control or restrain the liberty of the patient, lest he commit some outrageous act. Then, for the first time, probably, the case comes to the knowledge of a physician, and the acquaintances of the patient will recall peculiarities in his conduct covering a considerable period of time. It may appear on inquiry that there has been a period of depression or hypochondria, that the patient has been extravagant beyond his income, that he became intemperate and licentious, unmindful of marital relations, negligent in respect to business, and sleepless; he may have complained of headache, dyspepsia, general loss of vigor, and loss of memory of recent events. The individual has undergone some change, and is an object of solicitude to his friends. He may have been noticed to be abstracted, as if absorbed in deep contemplation, and to be reserved or taciturn. There is no apparent constitutional disturbance, the appetite is ravenous, the sexual propensities are strong, and the patient seems to lead a contented, abstracted life. How long these symptoms may have lasted is usually a matter of uncertainty. They appear in some cases to have existed for several weeks or months. Not one of these symptoms can be regarded as pathognomonic of general paralysis, but taken together, when occurring in an individual of thirty-five or forty-five, who has enjoyed exceptionally good health, who has the reputation of living what is called a 'fast' life, they are threatening and alarming premonitions. The mental symptoms that belong to the initial stage are sufficient to excite an apprehension of some impending and serious disease.

The second stage furnishes unequivocal signs of the existence of this fatal disease. The patient's manner now undergoes a marked change. Whatever may have been the previous mental symptoms, his sleep is short and broken; he rises early; he is restless, moving about from one place to another, but really accomplishing nothing. If he has been depressed or despondent, his manner is changed; he is exhilarated, the voice is elevated and the manner more self-assertive. There is a disposition to make purchases of useless articles and property, without any regard to the extent of the obligations incurred. There are ideas of great wealth, of investments that will return great profits, of enormous business projects, of great physical strength and prowess, and food is taken ravenously and in large quantities. If the physician at this stage inquire of the patient as to the state of his health, he will almost invariably answer 'first-rate' - that he never was better. If close attention is given to the articulation, the existence of some hesitation or peculiarity may be detected. There is a slight thickening of the speech, caused by an inco-ordination or paralysis of the muscles of the tongue and lips. If at this stage of the case, exalted, expansive delusions of wealth, power, or strength are observed, though the patient's condition does not reach a maniacal stage, but is one of general comfort, indifference, and good feeling, the cause of which the observer does not succeed in drawing out, and if, in addition, there is noticed a hesitation of speech, the kind of articulation so much like the thick talk of a person under the influence of alcohol, there need be no doubt as to the diagnosis. The motor disturbance of the tongue may be obscured at first by the activity of the maniacal symptoms;

but the peculiar pronunciation of words containing several syllables with consonants will sooner or later become quite marked. This is the first sign of a beginning of general and progressive paralysis. The patient seems to stumble over words or enunciates them with an omission, perhaps, of one or two syllables. There is a propulsion given to the word with an evident effort of the facial and labial muscles. The tongue appears to be protruded with a similar effort, as if there was a gathering of strength, followed by a sudden movement. Part of the effort is due to a mental incapacity to comprehend the question at first. When the tongue is protruded fibrillar movements will be noticed to be quite active and distinct, giving to it a tremulous appearance. The altered speech seems to be the first indication of approaching paresis, although there is another physical symptom that may also appear quite early, and should be looked for - an inequality of the pupils, or unequal dilation, or the opposite - a contraction to pin-head size.

The experienced observer may discover in the exalted and grandiose delusions the mental symptoms of paresis, yet a conservative judgment and diagnosis will be better fortified by awaiting the manifestations of characteristic physical evidences furnished by the altered articulation and inequalities and changes of the pupils, when it is of great importance that conclusions should be correct.

If the patient is physically broken down at the onset, and of a mild disposition, there may not be any extraordinary maniacal development, and he may pass through this stage quietly, pleased with his good health, his imaginary riches, and his supposed comfortable surroundings. These are, however, the exceptional cases. The general activity and exaltation, the amount of imaginary business to be transacted, and the general exaggeration of the *ego*, the personal individuality of the patient, lead to an enormous amount of letter-writing. In hospitals, in addition to the stationery that may be issued, newspaper margins and book leaves are appropriated to write upon. The handwriting here throws some light upon the diagnosis of the case. The handwriting is altered and bears evidence of inco-ordination in the wavy lines; the spelling of words is incomplete from the omission of letters and syllables, and whole words or sentences are broken, run together, or omitted. The substance of the letters shows the mental condition; they may contain orders, notes of hand, or checks for fabulous amounts. Now and then a person who is actually rich is seized with paretic dementia, and enters upon new and enlarged schemes, which are the actual growth of disease, and may seriously compromise an estate or a trust before the real condition is understood. Men who have been accustomed to manage their own affairs will not brook control and advice, and if opposed are violent and dangerous. As a matter of actual experience, these paretics are so full of business, so good natured with their vast possessions, that they are easily managed or diverted, even in their excitement. They rarely commit violent or criminal acts as a result of their delusions, although, if opposed, as, for instance, in attempting to leave their homes or in attempts to travel about the country, they will persist in their efforts, even to a forcible resistance of all control. Although they may boast of their great strength, that they are trained athletes, and delight in displaying their muscles, their strength is expended in a single effort, which leaves them exhausted."

"Disturbances of the cerebral circulation are frequently observed throughout the disease. The partial paralysis of the vasomotor system results in hyperemia of the brain. The face is flushed and turgid, and convulsive seizures may take place during the second and last stages of the disease. The convulsive seizures are epileptiform and apoplectiform, and characterized by unconsciousness and convulsive muscular movements. The convulsions of general paralysis have some peculiarities to distinguish them. They are oftener confined to the upper extremities, affecting one side of the face or an arm or a leg, and are followed after a return of consciousness by a convulsive twitching of the facial muscles or an arm, which may continue for a period of one or more days; or there may be a succession of these seizures. The convulsive movements may be unilateral, clonic, or tonic. If the convulsion is severe and attended with a rise of temperature, death may take place from cerebral effusion at any stage. The presence of a convulsive seizure during the early stage is a very strong diagnostic symptom in any case that is not otherwise clear.

The maniacal symptoms of the second stage usually soon subside, and the patient may assume a quiet, natural manner, and be regarded by his friends as improved. There may be a remission or complete abatement of the active symptoms, and the patient may even be discharged from a hospital to reside at home. The remission may continue a few weeks or months, to be broken by a convulsive seizure, followed by decided mental failure. If no remission occurs the mental failure and paralysis proceed and constitute the third stage. In the future progress of the disease the characteristics of dementia appear. The comfortable, indifferent appearance and manner are preserved through all stages. Memory fails. Impressions are evanescent; a visit from a relative is forgotten when ended, and all the conditions of mental enfeeblement that have been mentioned as characterizing advancing dementia are present. The paralysis gradually becomes general if life is prolonged. The gait is staggering or ataxic; articulation becomes indistinct; solid food cannot be masticated, and only liquid food should be offered. If the patient does not die during a convulsive seizure, he gradually becomes helpless and bedridden and is a pitiable object. It is not unusual in this stage, after the patient is confined to bed, that extensive bed-sores and sloughs appear, notwithstanding every precaution and care that may be taken. At every stage of paresis the patient may have a convulsive seizure, which may be followed by others in succession. While a convulsion, or a series of attacks of this nature may occur, and the patient returns to his usual condition, yet, for prognostic purposes, the temperature should be frequently taken. If the temperature is noticed to rise to 104, with an upward tendency, the case may then terminate fatally in a very brief period."

"The causes of general paralysis have been the subject of most careful inquiry. The largest proportion of cases occur in the male sex. It was formerly supposed that women were exempt, but this has been shown to be incorrect. The disease is believed to be not inherited, but acquired. The history of the large majority of cases is one of intemperance, licentiousness, sexual excess, syphilis, or some nervous exhaustion incident to excessive application to business, or the great strain attending reverses. Fifty per cent of the males admitted to the Pennsylvania Hospital for the Insane have had a history of syphilis, and, of eight women, six had a history that furnished the strongest presumption of the existence of syphilis. It has been remarked by several careful observers that they have never known a well bred lady to be affected with general paralysis. It is always a delicate question to determine the existence of sexual excess, and it is usually a matter of conjecture. On the other hand, as has been stated, paresis is a disease known to occur most frequently among the people more advanced in civilization. It is most frequent in the Anglo Saxon race. Neither can we accept the allegation that business activity is an important factor, as the Hebrew race, always engrossed in business affairs, shows an exemption from the disease next to the negro. (Savage.) So, of syphilis as an element in the causation, how far its existence is a coincidence, and to what extent it is a cause, is yet to be regarded as unsettled. Of 20,000 cases of syphilis, it is reported (Lewin) that one per cent became insane, but not a single case of general paralysis was observed. Others, however, insist that paresis is but one of the several manifestations of brain-degeneration from syphilis. While, therefore, the cause of general paralysis is still unsettled, the fact remains that the largest proportion of its victims have led a life marked by some kind of excess, and a large percentage are known to have had syphilis, and whose brains on post-mortem examination show the peculiar changes produced by that disease in the nervous tissue and in the vessels.

Of the treatment of a disease that all experience goes to show progresses by gradual but certain steps to a fatal termination, but little can be suggested with a probability of averting the inevitable end. In hospital practice an attempt is made to ameliorate and cut short the paroxysms of maniacal excitement by medicines, one of the best of which is hyoscin. The action of digitalis is sometimes attended with excellent results. Chloral may aid in averting a recurrence of convulsive seizures, and in promoting sleep. If there is reason to suspect a syphilitic complication, mercuric chlorid and potassium iodid will often bring about a subsidence of acute symptoms and establish a remission.

With the loss of muscular power, if life is prolonged, a time arrives when the patient will be confined to bed, and will require attention to the bowels and bladder, and much care to prevent bed sores. With every attention, it frequently happens that gangrenous sloughs form rapidly from pressure as well as from trophic changes. It is important that the patient be kept dry, and the pressure upon sensitive parts be relieved by padding. An application of alcohol, alum, and solution of tannic acid has a tendency to harden the skin. Remembering the gluttonous habits of a paretic, and the general muscular impairment and paralysis that exist in the later stages of the disease, danger of suffocation from the lodgement of solid food may be averted by dividing it into small pieces or administering it in liquid form. The prognosis of paresis is unfavorable for recovery. The delusions, propensities, general disturbance, and disposition to squander money are so pronounced that the wiser course is to place the patient in a hospital rather than to attempt the care at home."

"EPILEPSY. The mental disorders that result from epilepsy deserve a brief notice. An epileptic seizure is characterized by sudden unconsciousness, convulsive muscular movements, a slight cry or moan, pallor of the face at the onset, followed by a flushed, turgid appearance of the countenance, frothing at the mouth, labored respiration, with deep inspirations, and sleep which is more or less prolonged. The seizures return from time to time, but not in accordance with any known rule.

It is usual to describe two forms of epileptic seizures: (1) One showing the graver symptoms described, and called by some *epilepsia gravior*; by the French, *grand mal*. The symptoms above alluded to seem to comprise a complete attack. (2) The seizure may be characterized by temporary, even momentary, unconsciousness, by pallor, and a slight convulsive twitching of the eyes and mouth. This incomplete form has been named *epilepsia mitior*, a milder form of epilepsy; also by the French, *petit mal*. The attack may be so mild that the individual may pause while walking or engaged in conversation, a slight twitching of the muscles of the face and pallor appear, and at once resume where the interruption occurred.

In one view a convulsion is simply a sudden interruption of those normally acting and constantly existing co-ordinating functions of muscles, of those restraining factors that are called inhibitory. The intensity of contractile power that a muscle will show depends upon the degree of force emitted from the nervous centers. If there can be a conception of a high tension of psychic force, with such a sudden discharge or explosion as will disturb or destroy all balances or restraining powers, then there can be some appreciation of those irregular movements of the muscles that make up a convulsion. But the convulsive movements are not the whole of the case. There is, in addition, a state of unconsciousness, resulting in part from a disturbance of the circulation within the cranium. The convulsive seizure may be preceded or followed by mental changes; and these, when present, consist in irritability, hebetude, dullness, or restlessness, unusual mental and motor activity, passionate outbreaks, even to maniacal outbursts of fury. This changed condition of the patient may exist from one to two or three days before, or subsequent to the seizure. The convulsive action of the muscles is only one of the manifestations of epilepsy, as epilepsy may exist without actual muscular convulsion. There may be unconsciousness of a momentary duration, so brief that a person engaged in writing, or in his usual occupation, may suspend and resume it without changing his position. There may also be a brief frenzy, continuing from a few moments to several hours without convulsion, or of such a slight nature that a friend will only notice a change in the countenance and a stare of the eyes. These peculiarities are in the nature of a discharge of a psychic force and temporary suspension of will-power, of which we know nothing except through its manifestations. To this condition, generally recognized, the term 'mental epilepsy' has been applied. An epileptic paroxysm is often preceded by some sensory disturbance or sensation called an 'aura,' and which is uniformly of the same kind.

An epileptic may pass many years without perceptible mental change, but the usual experience is that he is observed to gradually become irritable and passionate, and that the mental vigor abates. Some of the most terrible crimes recorded in the criminal annals of the insane have been perpetrated by epileptics. 'The maniacal fury of these patients is of the wildest and blindest kind, which nothing can tame, the individual acting automatically, as it were, and in a state of unconsciousness.' The mind of the epileptic is left after a fit in a morbidly irritable condition, in which the slightest provocation will derange it entirely. The tendency is toward enfeeblement, and the epileptic may eventually pass into a low, stupid state of dementia. Many of these persons go through life without visible mental impairment. Mental failure seems to depend on the frequency of the attacks and the degree of cerebral congestion that accompanies the seizures.

Epileptics have committed acts of incendiarism, homicides, and petty crimes, of which they retained no exact memory or consciousness. In some of these cases a confused recollection of some terrible struggle or mental oppression remains, in which hallucinations and illusions of sight and hearing have played an important part. In these cases, when criminal acts are committed, the courts usually hold that an epileptic during the interval between the seizures is not necessarily in a disordered mental condition, and the question of legal responsibility for acts committed during this intermission is submitted to a jury. It is, of course, true that during the progress of a case in which the seizures occur at long intervals little or no impairment may be observed; but when it is shown that a criminal has epilepsy, and the well-ascertained deteriorations and changes that attend epilepsy - such as irritability, uncontrollable passion, dementia - are demonstrated to the court by a medical expert, or if the criminal act is committed at about the usual time of the occurrence of a convulsion, too great caution cannot be exercised about pressing a conviction in these cases. In those cases in which an act was perpetrated in close connection with a convulsion, there should be little doubt about the irresponsibility. During and immediately succeeding the fit the epileptic is in an unconscious condition, unable to exercise self-control, having no recollection of what has transpired, and is legally irresponsible.

Epileptics rarely die in a convulsion, and of the two forms, the milder form, or *petit mal*, is believed to exercise a more decidedly deteriorating influence upon the mental faculties than the other form. In a doubtful case, in which the mental conditions and changes peculiar to epilepsy appear from time to time, such as intermittent, periodic manifestations of delirium, maniacal outbreaks of a transitory nature, dullness, stupidity, and hebetude in the morning, reasonable suspicions may be aroused that a convulsion has occurred, but had not been observed. It would be advisable in such a case that the patient be watched at night, as seizures are always more frequent at this time, and sometimes only nocturnal attacks occur. The tongue should be examined to ascertain whether it bears any mark of the teeth, and the bed, to learn whether an involuntary discharge of urine occurs during the night.

The *status epilepticus* is a prolonged unconsciousness and semi-comatose condition accompanying a quick succession of seizures. If there is a marked rise of temperature a fatal termination may be expected from cerebral effusion or from exhaustion of vital force."

"Recovery from epilepsy rarely occurs as a result of medical treatment. The number and frequency of fits may be decidedly reduced by the administration of potassium or sodium bromid alone, or combined with fluid extract of ergot and strychnine. This must be accepted as the best result now attainable from medical measures. The effect of the prolonged use of the bromids is understood, yet the improved condition and comfort of the patient from their use is considered as a sufficient warrant for their indefinite administration. If the seizures recur with frequency, chloral with strychnine may be administered by the mouth, or by enema with good results." (20)

Dr. Chapin did not include the definition of dipsomania in his book, as it is listed under the broader term of monomania. But, Dr. Daniel Hack Tuke, a highly regarded, British contemporary alienist, included a definition in one of his books, *A Dictionary of Psychological Medicine*. This book, written in 1892, also includes photographs of insane patients.

"DIPSOMANIA. 389A. Pure Dipsomania. - *Dipsomania is a morbid condition, characterised by the irresistible obsession and impulse to drink, coming on in attacks, during which the patients are in a condition of impotence of will and manifest great anguish.* According to our general facts, it appears that dipsomania must not be considered as a distinct disease, but as a secondary symptomatical condition, for the same reasons as the other impulses in a mental condition, the nature of which we shall have to determine. Studied by itself, dipsomania may be methodically described, because it always presents identical characters. It generally comes on in attacks presenting the character of intermission; so much so sometimes that certain patients have one attack only during the whole course of their existence. The attack is preceded by a *prodromic stage*, then it enters on its *course*, which is followed by a period of *recovery*.

Prodromic Stage.-This is almost constantly characterised by mental disorder of a depressive nature, which is very vague, consisting in an indefinite sadness and uneasiness; the patients lose energy and courage, have a feeling of inability, and throw up their occupation; they have the presentiment of some approaching event; their affective sentiments are diminished; indolent and apathic, they suffer from a kind of moral anaesthesia, which takes complete possession of them. At the same time anorexia, insomnia, and a sensation of praecordial anxiety may be observed."

"*Course.*-From the time the patient falls he ceases to struggle against his temptation; he has not even time to think about it. He goes from debauchery to debauchery, from degradation to degradation, and finds himself in drunken revelries without the slightest attempt to resist. He has one purpose only; to procure by all possible means the drink so ardently desired, and this imperious desire to satisfy the impulse completely deranges intellect and sentiments. Reason has no longer any regulating control, and the patient has no time to appreciate the import of his actions. The faculties are completely disordered, and the dipsomaniacal impulse causes an actual *delire des actes*, making the patient dangerous to himself and his surroundings. Most reprehensible actions (robbery, prostitution, begging, &c.) are committed without hesitation, supposing that the object be to procure intoxicating drink."

"*Diagnosis*.-Understood as we have described it, dipsomania can be compared only to itself, and it seems superfluous to state the diagnosis. But it is necessary, if only for the purpose of establishing once more an absolute line of demarcation between alcoholism and dipsomania.

(1) An alcoholic patient becomes insane because he drinks; a dipsomaniac is insane before he commences taking to drink. (Magnan.) Dipsomania may be complicated by alcoholic symptoms, but alcoholism never leads to dipsomania. (2) Alcoholism is an intoxication has as its cause-alcohol; dipsomania its cause in a defective mental condition, and alcohol is but a secondary factor, which may be replaced by any poison, leaving to the syndrome all psychological characters. (3) Dipsomania proceeds in paroxysmal attacks, and the appetite for strong drink is absent during the intervals between the attacks. Alcoholism has no definite course; its development depends directly upon the more or less considerable or prolonged consumption of alcohol. (4) A dipsomaniac satisfies a pathological and imperious want; he does not like alcohol, and takes it against his will. He strives energetically without the necessary power of resistance, and suffers greatly through the sense of impotence; an alcoholic individual has no actual want; he only obeys a vice, a proclivity, and an alteration of his moral sense; he does not strive although he has the power, and would suffer if he were prevented from taking drink. (5) A dipsomaniac is conscious of his condition, he is ashamed of his degradation, and hides himself in order to drink. An alcoholic individual is sometimes unaware of, but more often indifferent to, his condition; he does not regret his excesses; but he even boasts of them. (6) Lastly, dipsomania is a syndrome, always identical with itself, whilst alcoholism is an intoxication varying much in its clinical symptoms. The prodromic period of an attack of dipsomania might be mistaken for the commencement of an attack of melancholia, but this period is very short, and the appearance of the impulse makes the diagnosis certain. The knowledge of a previous attack of dipsomania must put the observer on his guard."

"*Treatment*.-The treatment of dipsomania may be clearly seen from our explanation. To deprive the patient of the stimulant by sequestration is the first indication. It has a double purpose: to cure the attack and to protect the patient against himself, by preventing him from committing those actions, of which he often makes himself guilty, in order to procure the desired drink. The second indication is to calm, by all possible means, the erethism of the cerebral cortex, which is the first cause of the attack, lukewarm baths, alkaline bromides - in one word, all sedatives are suitable. It is well, however, to avoid the use of narcotics (morphia, cocaine) which might awaken in the patient an appetite for a new sort of poison. Bitter drinks, given copiously, are a good adjuvant. Lastly, during convalescence, tonics will improve the general condition of the dipsomaniac. At this period moral treatment may often be useful; its purpose is to raise the courage of the patients, to comfort them by rehabilitating them in their own eyes, by showing that their excesses are disease and not a vice, by exhorting them to patience, and indicating to them the cerebral hygiene which they have to adopt. This moral treatment encourages the patients, and makes them have confidence in themselves." (21)

5

1870 UNITED STATES FEDERAL CENSUS - EMPLOYEES & INMATES OF WILLARD

Employees & Family Members

I thought it might be interesting to add the employees and family members of employees who lived on the Willard property and who were included in the first federal census of the Willard Asylum for the Insane, Romulus, Seneca County, New York. There was an additional page for 1870 consisting of farmers and their families but it was not clearly defined by the enumerator if they were employed on the Willard farm or just residents of Romulus, so I did not include the people listed on that page. The employees and family members are listed in the order in which they appeared on the census.

First Inmates

The Willard Asylum for the Insane opened its doors on October 13, 1869. One woman and three men were the first to enter the asylum. According to the 1870 U.S. Federal Census, taken on July 26th, the first four inmates listed were: Mary Rote, Alonzo Hopkins, Abram Lewis and John S. Page. These people would be the first of thousands who would enter this grand, Second Empire structure with a Mansard Roof; many would not exit until they were carried out wrapped in a shroud.

About The United States Federal Census

In the ninth (1870) U.S. Federal Census, one of the questions asked if anyone in the household was: "Deaf and Dumb, Blind, Insane or Idiotic." The tenth (1880) census also asked this particular question with an additional one that asked if anyone in the household was: "Maimed, Crippled, Bedridden or Otherwise Disabled." Most all of the eleventh (1890) completed census forms no longer exist as they were destroyed in a fire. The twelfth (1900) census did not include the above questions but the instructions to the enumerators were greater and more detailed, and the questions asked of the public became more numerous and invasive. The federal census is taken every ten years and is released to the public every seventy-two years. If your ancestor, like my Maggie for example, was an inmate of Willard after 1920 and died before 1930, their name will not appear on the census.

The Enumerators went door to door to collect the census information and spoke personally to who-ever answered the door. In the case of Willard and other large institutions, I am quite sure that the enumerator was furnished the information by an office worker or physician, and did not actually speak to the people who were incarcerated. An interesting fact about the location of Willard is that it sits on two towns: Romulus and Ovid.

All of the Enumerators who completed the Willard censuses wrote in cursive, which at times, was difficult to read. In many cases, I had to make a best guess on the spelling of the name and the age of the inmate due to the enumerator's poor handwriting. The original census page number from where your ancestor was listed is noted on each spreadsheet. These are not scientific statistics.

The Enumerator:

The Enumerator for The Willard Asylum for the Insane in 1870 was, Mr. Burroughs Roberts, Assistant Marshal. On the left hand side of each census page, he wrote, "Willard Asylum for the Insane." The headings "Occupation; Value of Real Estate Owned; If Married Within the Year; Attended School Within the Year; Cannot Read and Cannot Write," were left blank. Under the question, "Whether Deaf and Dumb, Blind, Insane, Idiotic, Pauper or Convict," all inmates of Willard were listed as "Insane." This census was taken on July 26, 1870, and consisted of eight census pages. Mr. Roberts listed males and females together and not in alphabetical order. For ease of finding your ancestor, I have listed them in alphabetical order.

Total Males & Females for 1870: 250

TOTAL MALES: 115	TOTAL FEMALES: 135
WHITE: 115	WHITE: 135
BLACK: 0	BLACK: 0
MULATTO: 0	MULATTO: 0
CHINESE: 0	CHINESE: 0
INDIAN: 0	INDIAN: 0
INSANE: 115	INSANE: 135

The census spreadsheets for The Inmates of Willard are located at inmatesofwillard.com, under the "Names" tab.

6

1870

In 1870, Charity Griswold was 44 and still listed as an inmate of the Yates County Poor House along with two of her children: Sarah, 17; and Edward, 14. Mary, age 21, was not listed with them as she married about the age of nineteen. According to a local census of 1875, Charity and her children were no longer listed as inmates of the poor house. She and her son, Edward, were found living in a home next door to her eldest son, my great-grandfather. Edward married about age twenty-four and had at least one child; his death is unknown to me. Mary, her husband, and four children, were also found living next door to my great-grandfather. Mary died at the age of thirty-five on September 24, 1884; cause of death listed as convulsions. As is the case when tracing women on censuses, I could not find Sarah. When women marry and you don't know their husband's surname, it is difficult to find them again.

When you share your GEDCOM on a genealogy website, you often receive emails from other family researchers, and every once in a while, one of them actually gives you some valuable information. I received such an email from a woman who said that Sarah was her great-great-grandmother. Sarah had married about the age of eighteen, moved from Yates County, had five children, and died at the age of fifty-nine in 1913. This newly found cousin had also found Charity's maiden name which I had been unable to find. It is to your advantage to share your database and your decision to accept emails from strangers, but a word of caution; it is in your best interest to hide all living individuals including yourself and your immediate family in order to protect everyone's privacy. Most genealogy software has the privacy option that you will want to perform before uploading your GEDCOM onto a website.

1869 First Patients

"The first patient admitted was a feeble, demented woman, brought in irons. Dr. Hoyt, Secretary of the Board of State Charities, in noticing this case, states, 'She had been confined over ten years, and for most of the time had been in a nude state. She was found crouched in a corner of a cell, partially covered with blankets, but without any other clothing or even a bed.' Since her admission your attention has been directed to her appearance, and the room occupied by her at night. She has been daily dressed, and at all times presentable. Her general appearance and habits of cleanliness are much improved. On the same day three men were brought in irons. One of these men had been occasionally industrious. All, when excitable, had been confined for long periods in rooms called cells. One man, immediately on his removal from the State Asylum to the county house, was placed in a cell with his hands and legs confined in irons and chains, receiving his food through a hole in the door. In this condition he passed three years. One patient was brought to the asylum who had been an inmate of a county house twenty-two years, spending the greater portion of the time in a room five by six feet in size, without a window. This person from long disuse and debility had quite lost the control of his limbs." (17)

1870 Labor in the Asylum

"The question of labor, as connected with the chronic insane, is an interesting one. It not only bears upon the cost of their support, but also upon their comfort and health. In past years' experience, it has been fully demonstrated that a very considerable amount of labor can be realized from both male and female patients; that such labor is to some extent remunerative, as well as attended with good sanitary effects. Two-thirds of the labor of the farm and garden, the avails of which amount to over $5,000, has been performed by male patients. In addition to this, a large amount of labor connected with the building operations, and with the internal administration, not embraced in the above has been done by them. The female patients have worked in the laundry, and in the kitchen to some extent, and, in addition, have made with the needle a large number of articles of clothing, bedding, etc. In view of these results we feel greatly encouraged and gratified. This work will be still more effective when it can be still further systematized, when the confusion and obstructions incident to extensive building operations are removed. The work is done cheerfully, and the influence upon the patients is salutary. In the future, when the institution is in complete order, the detached groups or branches properly located contiguous to the gardens and orchards, we expect that a large part of the labor for their cultivation and care, as well as the lighter class of farm labor, will be performed by the male patients; and that the females will make most of their own and the male patients' clothing, as well as the beds and bedding to be used in the asylum.

The cost of maintenance has for the year averaged a trifle over three dollars per week per patient. This embraces the period of the opening, when the expenses were necessarily large and the number of patients small. During the last six months the average cost has been less than $2.75, showing a considerable decrease, which we are confident will continue to diminish. It is not yet time to determine with certainty the actual cost per week for the maintenance of the insane at this asylum. The cost will depend upon numbers, upon labor of patients, upon the system adopted and the character of patients. Not until the policy of the law is fully carried out, and all the pauper insane are gathered here, classified, and brought under a clear and well-defined system, can the question as to cost of maintenance be fully settled." –Trustees (22)

1871

For the insane, life at Willard meant the loss of personal freedom, personal property, and privacy. For the most part, inmates were treated as incompetent children. The State of New York had not kept pace with the growing pauper chronic insane population which in turn resulted in an act passed by the state legislature in 1871. Within a year and a half of Willard's opening, *An Act in Relation to the Chronic Pauper Insane* (Law C) was quickly enacted to relieve the counties from sending all their insane to the two state asylums for these reasons: overcrowding in both asylums; and some counties did not want to pay the expense of supporting their pauper chronic insane in state institutions.

This new law was a giant step backward in the care and treatment of the insane. It allowed the county Superintendents of the Poor to keep their insane at the county poor houses, especially the chronic insane who were considered incurable, and only send the most disturbed and violent cases to Willard. It was considered safer and in the best interest of the patient to be sent to Willard which had been built specifically for them with doctors and attendants trained in the care of the physically and mentally ill rather than to remain in the county poor houses where there were no doctors; the attendants were often pauper residents, and in some cases they were insane pauper residents; and there was no specialized care. The indifference and abuse inflicted on the insane population by the County Superintendents of the Poor and the Keepers of the poor houses took place on a daily basis.

"It will be borne in mind that 'The Willard Asylum for the Insane,' to the great mass who go there, is to be a life-long home. In the main they are incurable. As a class, they have no means and few friends. They are the wards of the counties or the State, and so must remain as long as they live. Bearing in mind all these facts, we have devised a system of care and treatment, and adopted a plan of buildings to meet the wants and satisfy the demands of the case." –Trustees (23)

1872

"By the enactment of last year we are required to charge to the counties only the actual cost of maintenance. We are left really without funds for repairs. There are frequent accidents, such as the breaking of the banks of the reservoirs (which has occurred twice during the year); the washing away of culverts and bridges, and many other unforeseen casualties, and to meet which, we have no fund to draw upon. *Since writing the above, the roof of the gas-house has been destroyed by fire, doing some damage to the works, aside from the roof." –Trustees (1)

"On reflection, we think few of the good and thoughtful people of this State, will deny its obligation to look after this class of people. They are bereft alike of reason, friends, the means of support, unfit and unsafe to be at large. Society is endangered by contact with them, and restraint or confinement is a matter of necessity. Is not the conclusion alike logical and irresistible, that the proper and the best custodian of them, is the supreme authority, the aggregate power of all the people, the power and authority which we call the State? Who so able, who so likely in a becoming manner, who will so well and so wisely provide a proper home, with appliances and means for care, restraint, and, if need be, the confinement of this irresponsible, crazed, yet dangerous portion of our people?" –Trustees (1)

"We have again experienced the periodical anxiety attending the organization of a new addition to the Asylum, and the reception of a large number of patients rapidly collected together. It was a legitimate inference from the law creating the asylum, from its antecedents as well as its phraseology, that it contemplated the ultimate removal of all the insane from the county alms-houses, and the gradual substitution of State custodial care for the arrangements provided by the counties. It was a question whether all the insane should be taken from certain counties which the law directed should be designated, or whether all the counties should be designated with the exceptions specified, and the accommodation apportioned among them. Having regard to the humane intent and purpose of the law, the latter course was, in the exercise of your judgment, deemed the proper one, and the additional accommodation which has been added from year to year has been placed at the disposal of the superintendents of the poor as equitably as was practicable. The practical relief which it was contemplated the asylum should afford has thus been brought within the reach of the whole State. In availing themselves of the accommodation, we have observed, from the opening of the asylum, that the principle which has governed all the officers engaged in making a selection of patients for transfer, has been to prefer the helpless and filthy. Under this rule we expect to receive but a limited number of the able-bodied and industrious insane, and are liable to receive, as we have, cases which survive but a brief period, serving to add to our mortality rate fictitiously, while that of other establishments may seem to be declining. It is perhaps as well that the course pursued has been so far carried out. It has had the effect to bring under a central observation the nature of the burden of chronic insanity, which the people of this State have felt disposed to assume here, in a becoming and decent manner. It has led to the improvement of every county-house in the State, as we are warranted in stating, from the report of the secretary of the State Commissioners of Public Charities, and enabled the vexed question of provision for the chronic insane, to be so compassed that a solution may yet be arrived at." –Chapin (1)

"To the 30th of September, 1872, the total amount expended for construction of buildings, site and land, water-works, gas-house, farm, barns, fences, piggery, docks, maintenance and supplies, was $916,534.66. This sum, includes all expenditures, and, of course, those made upon the five 'detached buildings,' erected and nearly ready for occupation. Their capacity will be 200, in addition to our present number. From the data in our possession we estimate there has been paid of this sum for maintenance, fuel and land not embraced in the original purchase, the sum of $115,500." –Chapin (1)

1873

The Long Depression began in October 1873 and ended in March 1879.

"The 'branch,' or college building, is the most exposed to fire. It has lath and plastered walls, and a fire once fairly started would be likely to consume it very rapidly. There are over two hundred female patients in the building, and there are but two stairways, both of wood, as a means of escape in case of fire. We recommend an additional flight of brick and iron stairs, fire-proof, which we estimate would cost $2,500." –Trustees (24)

"We have continued the price for support at $3.00 per week per patient. The cost for clothing has been a trifle over $15.00 per patient for the year. The whole cost to the counties therefore for a single patient for one year is about $170." –Trustees (24)

"During the past year, as in former years, applications have been made for the admission of idiots and imbeciles. These cases are not regarded as coming within the law designating the class to be received here. The condition of these persons is represented to be wretched in the extreme and should receive attention, but it is questionable whether it would be practicable to mingle the insane and idiots under our organization." –Chapin (24)

1874

"Experience has demonstrated, that the present location of the cemetery is a bad one, though the most appropriate one on the asylum farm. It is inconvenient because of its distance, from the nature of the soil, and it also interferes with the enlargement of the upper reservoir, which is indispensably necessary. We therefore desire to change the location. Twenty-five acres of land can be purchased a short distance to the north, and adjoining the lands of the State, for twenty-five hundred dollars, which we regard as very desirable, as a location for the cemetery, and we recommend an appropriation of that amount for that purpose." –Trustees (25)

"We submit that it would be better for all and result in no increase of expense or taxation for the State, in its sovereign capacity, to relieve the towns and counties of the entire care and control of this class, treating all as the wards of the State, but exacting pay from those who have means to support themselves. Under State support with a well-digested system, the counties would be taxed no more, while they would be relieved from a charge and duty which they cannot fulfill as it should be, and, as a final result, all the insane of the State would have the improved care, protection and comfort, which is now afforded to only a portion. We earnestly press this whole subject on your careful attention and bespeak for it thoughtful consideration." –Trustees (25)

"We have now in operation a telegraph between the Asylum and Ovid, a distance of three miles, where we are brought in connection with the Western Union Telegraph. The machines in use at the Asylum branch, and at Ovid, are called the Gray Automatic Printer, and work admirably. They connect the Branch and the main Asylum and both with the treasurer's office at Ovid, and are a very great convenience as well as a saving of labor and time in correspondence. Attached to these telegraph machines are fire gongs or alarms, by which knowledge of fire in any of the buildings at any time of night or day could be speedily communicated to the center and thence to all parts of the institution. This we regard an important matter in case of fire." –Trustees (25)

"It may cause some surprise, that a long period of continued observations, should have added so little to our knowledge of the pathology of insanity, of practical value in the treatment, when the inherent difficulties which surround the subject are not appreciated. Notwithstanding the great additions which have been made to our knowledge of the history, the causes and symptoms of insanity; the improved character of the buildings for the care of the insane; the marked improvement in their management and moral treatment; the new remedies which have been added to the *materia medica*, and the light which the microscope is supposed to shed upon the pathology of the disease, the percentage of recoveries has not increased but seems to be diminishing." –Chapin (25)

1875

"From the opening of this institution there have been more applications for women than for men. This excess has been greater than the relative proportion of insane females over males. We account for this from the fact that the poor authorities of the counties find it more difficult to provide for and protect insane females than insane males. Be the cause what it may, there is greater solicitude to gain admission here for women than men. Knowing as we do that in the alms-houses no proper and adequate provision can be made to separate the sexes, and to guard and protect insane women, we have felt it our duty to provide more room for the latter class. Had we ample room for all, no discrimination would be made, but, restricted as we have been, we have felt that the weaker and more helpless demanded our first consideration." –Trustees (26)

"If an examination were made to determine the antecedent social position of the mass of the insane, it would be found that the middling classes and the laboring class contribute the larger proportion, and not the wealthy or pauper class. It is, also, true that the former furnish the amount of insanity which becomes a public burden. This, perhaps, may be explained on the hypothesis that there are causes operative among the middling classes to the production of insanity which do not exist among the wealthy, and that the latter possess the means to secure appropriate relief promptly which the former do not have. Nevertheless the inquiry is pertinent. In our observation, the insane of the middling classes do not receive the prompt treatment in the early stages of insanity which is rendered the indigent or the independent classes. Hundreds of cases which have come in our line of duty to examine presented a uniform history of neglect of early treatment by reason of pecuniary inability; of detention in close quarters at home until the hope of recovery had passed; of gradual exhaustion of means threatening to involve entire families in pauperism; and of final transition to incurable dementia and life long dependence. We are not in a position to suggest more than a partial remedy for a state of things we are quite sure ought not to exist. It is clear the state, in a matter of such vital interest, should pursue a decided policy. It should, in every way, encourage the prompt transfer of all recent and curable cases to an asylum for treatment, and prevent, as far as practicable, the interposition of obstacles of a pecuniary nature to such a course, so that no person of moderate means be excluded from the public charities of the state from this cause alone." –Chapin (26)

Admission 1875

This admission form appeared in the Sixth Annual Report of The Trustees of The Willard Asylum for the Insane in 1875 that required two physicians to sign commitment papers. Prior to *The Laws of 1874* (Law D), the Superintendent of the Poor, who was not a physician or an alienist, was the only person required to send an individual to the Willard Asylum for the Insane.

"On the admission of a patient there should be presented the certificates of two physicians, sworn to, and approved by a judge in the county in which the patient resides. The following is the form of certificate prescribed by the Commissioner in Lunacy in these cases:

State of New York, County of _____. I, _____, a resident of _____, in the county aforesaid, being a graduate of _____, and having practiced as a physician, hereby certify, under oath that on the _____ day of _____, I personally examined _____ of _____. (Here insert sex, age, married or single and occupation) and that the said _____ is insane, and a proper person for care and treatment, under the provisions of chapter 446 of the Laws of 1874. I further certify that I have formed this opinion upon the following grounds, viz.: (Here insert facts upon which such opinion rests.) And I further declare that my qualifications as a medical examiner in lunacy have been duly attested and certified by (here insert the name of the judge granting such certificate). Sworn to and subscribed before me this _____ day of _____, 187_. State of New York, County of _____. I hereby certify that _____, of _____ is personally known to me as a reputable physician, and is possessed of the qualifications required by Chapter 446 of the Laws of 1874. _____ Judge of _____." (25)

1876

"With the increase of our population it has been found impossible to prepare asylum accommodation on the plans usually proposed, to equal the demand. When a new hospital is projected appropriations for its construction are made in small sums compared with the whole cost and it is found to be a work extending over several years. On completion it is immediately filled and large numbers still remain unprovided for. In 1871, it was ascertained the number of persons taken insane in one year in this State was sixteen hundred and seventy. If accommodations were to be provided for these cases alone, on the plans usually insisted upon, one new asylum would be required to be erected every year." –Chapin (26)

1877

"We have demonstrated here that the chronic insane can be maintained for at least three dollars per week in safety and comfort. Suppose it to cost a dollar less per week in a poor-house, with no comfort, safety or protection, who so mean and contemptible as to withhold the dollar? For the whole State it would be but a paltry sum, increasing no man's tax so that he would feel or know the difference. We protest against using poor-houses for the custody of the insane. If the counties will provide separate hospitals, equip and provide them with proper attendance and medical care, then we have no word to interpose, but few counties can or will afford to do this, and without such, humanity and Christian civilization raise their voices in protestation. We come asking nothing for this asylum." –Trustees (27)

1878

"The front walls of the main asylum buildings, and the wings on either side, have been painted during the year. Built at various periods, and of different colored brick, the appearance was unpleasant. The buildings have now a uniform color of light-grey, and their appearance greatly improved, as well as made more permanent and durable." –Trustees (28)

"The labor of the employes should be paid for when due. To meet all the monthly payments as they become due and payable, the treasurer of the asylum depends upon the county treasurers to remit the quarterly bills rendered to the counties for board of patients, promptly. From various causes delays in making collections frequently occur. For these reasons, it would be the exercise of a wise foresight and preparation to have on hand a moderate sum in reserve to meet the various contingencies, to which we are liable from time to time." –Chapin (28)

1879

"Willard Asylum is now the largest institution of the kind in this country. In all its enlarged proportions it is easily managed, safely conducted, and controlled. Personal restraints are used only as a protection to the insane themselves, and to save life and property." –Trustees (29)

"We ought always to have, to meet contingencies and unforeseen emergencies, at least $10,000 or $15,000 on hand and available. The counties, as a whole, are usually from $10,000 to $15,000 in arrears in their payments." –Trustees (29)

"Attendants and Employes. - The number of attendants assigned to duty in wards is 133. In addition there are 150 employees engaged in various offices about the establishment many of whom take patients in charge during the day to the work in which they are engaged. They are selected with reference to their supposed fitness for their work. They are required to sign a written agreement to abide by, and to follow the rules and regulations of the asylum, which are printed and to be found in the several attendants' rooms. The regulations of the asylum are adopted by the board of trustees and form a code of wholesome rules calculated to point out the spirit in which attendants are to discharge their duties, and to guard against abuses of patients. I am of the opinion the legislature should be requested to enact a stringent law making a willful assault upon an insane person by kicking, maiming or striking with the hand, or an instrument by an attendant or employe in any asylum or county institution of this State, a special misdemeanor to be punished with severe penalties, and requiring the law to be posted in the room of every attendant. The moral effect of such a law, and the certainty of its enforcement by a criminal prosecution, would exercise a restraining influence over such persons as were disposed to do violence and practice cruelty. Such a law would apply only to those who violated it, and would not be objected to by the large majority of attendants, who discharge the duties they are engaged to perform patiently and kindly." –Chapin (29)

7

1880 United States Federal Census - The Inmates Of Willard

In 1880, there were two Enumerators for The Willard Asylum for the Insane; Mr. Charles S. Johnston for Ovid, Seneca County, New York, and Mr. Edmund P. Cole for Romulus, Seneca County, New York. In addition to the regular census, these gentlemen had to complete the 1880 Defective, Dependent & Delinquent Census.

Charles S. Johnston, Enumerator: Under the heading, "Relationship," left these boxes blank but wrote at the top of each sheet "Patients of Willard Asylum." Under the heading "Occupation," Mr. Johnston wrote the words "Occupation Previous To Insanity." Under the heading "Health: Blind, Deaf and Dumb, Idiotic, Insane or Maimed, Crippled, Bedridden or Otherwise Disabled," the inmates of Willard were all marked as "Insane." Under the heading "Education: Cannot Read and

Cannot Write," the enumerator left the boxes blank. Under the heading, "Nativity: Birthplace of Mother and Father," left the boxes blank. This census was taken June 16th through 22nd, 1880, and consisted of twenty-three completed census pages.

Edmund P. Cole, Enumerator: Under the heading, "Relationship," left these boxes blank but wrote at the top of each sheet "Insane Inhabitants" of each particular building. Under the heading "Health: Blind, Deaf and Dumb, Idiotic, Insane or Maimed, Crippled, Bedridden or Otherwise Disabled," the inmates of Willard were all marked as "Insane." Under the heading "Education: Cannot Read and Cannot Write," the enumerator left the boxes blank. Under the heading, "Nativity: Birthplace of Mother and Father," left the boxes blank. This census was taken June 23rd through 25th, 1880, and consisted of eleven completed census pages. It appears that someone else, possibly Mr. Johnston, was checking Mr. Cole's work because there were different dates, which I noted in parenthesis at the top of the spreadsheet, with different hand writing, next to the original dates marked 17th through 21st. Mr. Johnston and Mr. Cole completed the census building by building which is great for us as we can actually see where our ancestors were housed.

Ovid: South Wing Main Building-Women (328), The Branch-Women (226), Detached Building/ Cottage Number 2-Women (272), Detached Building/Cottage Number 3-Men (248).

Romulus: North Wing Main Building-Men (255), Detached Building/Cottage Number 1-Men (238).

Total Males & Females for 1880: 1,567

TOTAL MALES: 741	TOTAL FEMALES: 826
WHITE: 724	WHITE: 811
BLACK: 15	BLACK: 15
MULATTO: 0	MULATTO: 0
CHINESE: 0	CHINESE: 0
INDIAN: 1	INDIAN: 0
SINGLE: 489	SINGLE: 407
MARRIED: 210	MARRIED: 338
WIDOWED: 24	WIDOWED: 73
DIVORCED: 0	DIVORCED: 1
STATUS UNKNOWN: 18	STATUS UNKNOWN: 7

The census spreadsheets for The Inmates of Willard are located at inmatesofwillard.com, under the "Names" tab.

8

1880

In 1880, my great-great-grandmother, Charity, was found living in the home of my great-grandfather and his family; she was 51 and divorced, according to the U.S. Federal Census. Her husband, a tanner and courier by trade, either died on a Civil War battlefield; decided not to come home; or they were legally divorced, which is very rare for that time period. Charity A. Griswold died on February 3, 1886, at the age of 60 and was a domestic at the time of her passing. It is possible that Charity was an inmate of the Yates County poor house for 13 years. An earlier census stated that Charity was a widow, not divorced. If she died at age 60 in 1886, then in 1880, she should have been 54, not 51. As you can see, you can't always be sure that the information on the census is correct. The best way to determine your ancestor's true age is to find an obituary or obtain their death certificate from the state in which they died. NYS began keeping vital records in 1850. The forms for obtaining birth, death, and marriage certificates are available on the NYS Vital Records website but they are not free and it will take a few months before you receive your copy in the mail.

Sadly, I know very little about Maggie's life. The U.S. Federal Census, dated January 6, 1920, Amsterdam, Montgomery County, New York, stated: She was born in Scotland in August 1852; Naturalized; Can Read and Write; Father Born in Scotland; Mother Born in Scotland; Can Speak English; Occupation: Piece Work, Knitting Mill. She was still working at age 68. My grandmother insisted that her mother-in-law was born in Northern Ireland but I can find no evidence of this. On February 4, 1884, Margaret A. Putnam (Putman), my great-grandmother, gave birth to my grandfather; she was thirty-two. Maggie became an inmate of the Willard State Hospital sometime after 1924 and died at the hospital on August 13, 1928, at age 76.

1880

"Medical Observations. The assertion has been made that the increase of the amount of insanity is due, in part, to the fact that the insane in asylums of the present day do not receive the treatment which the advance of science appears to warrant, and as a consequence a greater number of incurables remain now than formerly to be cared for. It has also been asserted on authority as high, and even in an official form, that asylums are no sooner constructed and opened than they are at once filled. As the first statement will be received with considerable doubt and allowance on a comparative examination of the facts, of the correctness of the latter there is no room to question it, for the experience is repeated with the opening of every new asylum. If all the cases which stand ready to enter and occupy the newly prepared wards of an asylum have been the recipients of medical ministrations prior to their admission, then on the assumption that 'insanity is one of the most curable of diseases,' the facts are a sad commentary on the state of the profession at large. These statements, while they show how unsettled is public, and even professional, sentiment on this subject, they deserve a brief mention and notice here. If it is assumed that insanity is one of the most curable of diseases, then from the two statements it may be also correctly inferred that, of the two branches of the profession concerned, neither possesses all the requisite knowledge to furnish the best results attainable, and the responsibility must lie with that branch more intimately associated with those neurotic disorders which culminate in actual insanity, the prevention of which, together with other diseases, all may feel equally called upon to consider.

It may be observed that insanity, in the majority of instances, is the culmination of causes that have been operative for long periods. There are the trials, afflictions, privations, sicknesses and disappointments, which make up the sore experiences of life acting on a mental organization already unbalanced by hereditary predisposition, as well as the deteriorations which result from injudicious and ill-advised marriages, singly or together operating with an irresistible tendency to produce a crisis which no professional or scientific appliances can hope reasonably to avert. The causes are for the most part matters of speculation, not demonstrable, and too intricate for solution by material methods, or scientific instruments after death. The approach and progress of the disordered state is insidious and gradual. When the condition of insanity may be considered established, and the patient brought to the hospital, the damage done already is too often discovered to be irreparable. The cases that may be embraced in this category, together with those marked by organic changes and degenerations of the material substance of the brain, comprise the majority of all that occur.

Erroneous impressions have been drawn undoubtedly, from the earlier asylum statistics and may have been used to the detriment of the existing asylum system. They admitted of deductions relative to the curability of insanity, which experience and analysis may not have confirmed, though they were conscientiously reported at the time. The results presented by the asylum reports, such as they are, however, form the most reliable data, because they are the only ones attainable and must be accepted in the absence of any other, as being more trustworthy than the experiences and opinions of individuals, on the same principle that facts are always more to be relied upon than hypotheses. If it is a fact that physicians of an earlier day did not actually cure as many as they innocently supposed they did, and the cases which they reported as *recovered* were cases which in the light of more experience would appear in the reports of the present day as *improved*, the error which they committed ought to have no weight in lowering the present public estimation of the existing asylums, which with all their alleged defects will be conceded to be infinitely superior to those of a former day, and are rather to be cherished than depreciated, as the expression of the highest philanthropic spirit which a civilized community can exhibit. The legitimate deduction to be drawn is that the disease is not as curable as was at first supposed. The error which has been committed has been the use sometimes made of the earlier and erroneous results as arguments to promote the erection of new hospitals." –Chapin (30)

1881

By 1881, Willard consisted of: the Main Building with North and South Wings; 4 Detached Building Groups or Cottages; Agricultural College Building or The Branch; Two Farm Barns; Cow Barn; Two Piggeries; Hennery; Slaughter House; Coal Pockets and Pump House; Work Shops; Steward's House; Three Farm Dwellings; House for Carpenter, Baker and Gardener; Stable; Straw and Carriage Barn; Two Ice Houses; Gas House; Store House; Dock and Vegetable Cellar.

"Any material reduction of the yearly charge must be attended, with a diminished dietary, more mechanical restraint, lower temperature in the wards, a dirty house and worse odors, dilapidated furniture, and, in time, a shabby, worn-out interior. These conditions mean, in plainer language, a lower standard of care, with all that it implies." –Chapin (31)

"Mechanical Restraint. - There has been a gradual diminution of the use of mechanical restraint; and, we may observe, the assumed occasions for its use have not seemed as numerous. As compared with a period seven years ago, or during the year 1874, with a daily population of 827 patients and an average amount of restraint equal to five per cent, the instances of restraint the past year have not exceeded one-half of one per cent, with a daily population of 1,695. These changes were begun before the so-called agitation of lunacy reform measures, and prompted and suggested by the experience of the asylum.

We then supposed we were using a comparatively moderate amount of restraint. A system of requiring day reports from every ward was introduced six years ago with excellent results. About the same time the rule of charging damage done to the asylum property to the patient by whom it was committed was changed, and the charge made to the general account of furniture and repairs, where it more properly belongs. The individual charges for damages committed were subject to the critical scrutiny of county boards of supervisors, and the complaints occasionally made that patients were permitted to destroy too much clothing and bedding suggested an additional reason for the use of mechanical restraint. While due allowance should be made to the new regulation, the credit is largely due to the assistant physicians and the co-operation of attendants for the reduction of the restraint we have reported.

It may be asked how this much-desired result has been brought about. Certainly not by adhering to the usages and traditions of a former period, nor by aggressively defending the use of restraint. It has been accomplished by the gradual substitution of personal attention and attendance for mechanical methods. Whenever the substitution can be made complete, the problem may be considered settled and solved. When mechanical restraint may be said to be abolished, the new practice becomes a part of a system of management of the insane, the reasonable explanation, or philosophy, of which, is the complete substitution of personal attendance, and improved building plans for all other methods.

While it has appeared in our experience possible to reduce the application of mechanical restraint to a considerable, and perhaps, a minimum degree, it must remain a vexed question whether it is practicable and advisable to abolish it altogether, however strong the desire to do so. Must the abolishment of all restraint come to be regarded a cardinal feature in our practice? There are surgical and medical reasons and certain propensities where its judicious use may seem called for, and there are the recognized peculiarities of our attendants, as well as patients, which differ from those in the English and Scotch asylums where the non-restraint system prevails - their desire for change for various reasons - which remain to embarrass the satisfactory solution of the question. When we recall the great changes that have taken place in the care of the insane, and are going on at this day, no doubt can exist but the time will come when even the record we here present will be regarded by those who will succeed us as one of the relics of a less enlightened system of care. Mechanical restraint will be reduced to the least quantity admissible, and be supplanted by increased personal attendance and attention to that extent." –Chapin (31)

1882

"Discharge of Patients. - The law provides for the discharge of patients by the board when in session, or by a committee of the board acting between the meetings, on the superintendent's certificate of '*complete*' recovery, or that the patient is harmless '*and will probably continue so.*' There are other provisions of the section which appear in full in the appendix of this report. Particular reference is made to the above provisions. The practical operation of this law, if strictly conformed to, is to hinder the discharge of patients. Public sentiment and the action of the courts seem disposed to facilitate and make easy the discharge of patients from the asylums. A little modification of the phraseology of the law could be made that would do away with much of the friction attending its execution. The word 'complete' before recovery, and the words 'and will probably continue so,' might well be omitted. Indeed, the whole section might be expunged with safety and advantage, except that part of it referring to the discharge of the criminal and dangerous insane for whose safe custody and maintenance a bond is provided, and the concurrent action of the courts. The power to regulate discharges might safely be intrusted to boards of trustees and managers to provide for in by-laws. It seems also desirable to provide for the discharge of certain patients on trial, on application of friends, for limited periods, as well as for brief, specified absences without the necessity of the expense and form of a recommitment. As a matter of experience, application is often made by friends who desire to remove a relative to their home with the hope that on trial a return to the asylum may not be necessary. It is desirable to strengthen these relations in every possible manner. The question often occurs whether a change of this nature may not be a desirable one for the patient. It seems no more than just that the responsibility for the discharge of a lunatic who is harmless in the asylum and who is to be removed beyond the supervision of the asylum should be partly shared by the person who petitions for the discharge and the community in which he is to reside." –Chapin (32)

1883

In 1883, the two New York State Asylums for the Chronic Insane were: Willard (Ovid, Seneca County); and Binghamton (Binghamton, Broome County). Binghamton State Asylum opened in

1881 and was the second asylum in the state to care for the chronic insane. It was originally named The New York State Inebriate Asylum, built in 1858, for the treatment of alcoholism. The New York State Asylums for the Acute Insane were: State Lunatic Asylum at Utica (Utica, Oneida County); Hudson River State Hospital (Poughkeepsie, Dutchess County); State Homeopathic Asylum (Middletown, Orange County); and Buffalo State Asylum (Buffalo, Erie County). The Newark Custodial Asylum, located in Newark, Wayne County, New York, was an institution for feeble-minded, childbearing age women that opened in 1878.

"Discharge of Patients. - Patients are discharged by the board of trustees at the regular meetings of the board, held on the first Tuesdays of March, June and September, and at the annual meeting on the second Tuesday of December. During the intervals between the meetings, patients are discharged by a committee of the board of trustees, appointed in pursuance to chapter 190, section 2, Laws of 1881. Patients are not discharged by the superintendent. The power to discharge patients is vested solely in the board of trustees, in pursuance to chapter 446, title 3, section 24, Laws of 1874, as follows: Section 24: The managers, upon the superintendent's certificate of complete recovery, may discharge any patient, except one under a criminal charge, or liable to be remanded to prison; and they may discharge any patient admitted as 'dangerous,' or any patient sent to the asylum by the superintendent or overseers of the poor, or by the (first) judge of the county, upon the superintendent's certificate that he or she is harmless, and will probably continue so, and not likely to be improved by further treatment in the asylum, or when the asylum is full, upon a like certificate that he or she is manifestly incurable, and can probably be rendered comfortable at the poor-house; so that the preference may he given, in the admission of patients, to recent cases, or cases of insanity of not over one year's duration. They may discharge and deliver any patient, except one under criminal charge as aforesaid, to his relatives or friends, who will undertake with good and approved sureties for his peaceable behavior, safe custody and comfortable maintenance, without further public charge. And the bond for such sureties shall be approved by the county judge of the county from which said patient was sent, and filed in the county clerk's office of said county. Upon the presentation of a certified copy thereof, the managers may discharge such patient." (33)

1884

"On the 2d day of August, 1884, Dr. John B. Chapin tendered his resignation as medical superintendent of this asylum. He had held the position from the organization and opening of the institution, in 1869, and had discharged the responsible and arduous duties connected therewith with entire satisfaction to all concerned. He was among the original founders of the asylum, and under his wise care and faithful supervision it had grown to its present dimensions and standing. It was with much regret that we accepted his resignation, to take effect September 1, 1884." (34)

1885

I have never seen the word filthy repeated so many times as I have while researching this book. As I read more and more, I realized that the word *filthy* or the phrase *filthy in their habits*, did not mean not washing one's body and hair, it meant being soiled with human excrement and urine. At the twelfth annual session of the National Conference of Charities and Correction, held in Washington, D.C., June 4 - 10, 1885, Dr. Stephen Smith, State Commissioner of Lunacy, addressed the members with his report, "Care of the Filthy Cases of Insane." After his report was published, the recommendation was made that all state asylums should apply this carefully thought out plan. Between 1886 and 1887, Willard built an infirmary for men, and The Branch for women was reduced to two stories and the first floor was extended, specifically for the purpose to separate and care for this particular class of patients. These were Dr. Smith's recommendations:

"1. State asylums should have separate buildings constructed with special reference to the isolation and care of this class. In no asylum is it possible now to remove the filthy from that contact with the wards of the main building, or with other patients, that is desirable. Wherever they are grouped in a part of a hall, or in separate halls, they so contaminate the atmosphere, through the walls and floors, the beds and bedding, that the dormitories remain, in spite of cleaning, disinfection, and ventilation, so foul and offensive as to be quite uninhabitable by other patients. I have visited single sleeping-rooms of the filthy at mid-day, in summer, which, though scrupulously clean and fully exposed to the external air and strong sunlight, still had an extremely offensive atmosphere. The very presence of these inmates tends, therefore, permanently to damage wards, and render them unfit for future occupation, unless walls and floors are frequently scraped, and thus comparatively renewed. Every State asylum has ample grounds and appropriate sites for the construction of detached buildings for this class. These buildings need not be elaborate or expensive, but certain conditions and conveniences should be supplied. They might be one story in height, with a few single rooms for the more disturbed and an associated dormitory for the quiet. The walls and floors should be impermeable, and susceptible of being thoroughly washed and disinfected daily. There could be a wide veranda constructed completely around the building, where patients could sit or lie in the summer, and, when enclosed, could be so warmed as to be comfortable in winter. The facilities for bathing and cleansing the patients should be immediately at hand, and of the most approved kind. The service should be so organized as to be continuous, day and night, in the raising and bathing of patients. While every State asylum should have its separate building for the filthy classes, the necessity of such provision in the State asylums for the chronic insane is imperative. There is no want of provision for the insane in this State that is to-day so urgent, and that should appeal with greater force to the legislature for suitable appropriations.

2. County asylums should organize, each, a night service for the filthy, and maintain it with well qualified attendants. Already, this service has been instituted in some of the larger and better managed asylums of the counties, with great and immediate benefit to the inmates. In regard to the poorhouses, it is sufficient to state that the filthy insane should never be sent to them, and when found in them should be removed to State asylums for the chronic insane." (35)

1886

"SCHEDULE A. Willard Asylum for the Insane Willard, Seneca Lake, November 27, 1886.

Hon. Oscar Craig, My Dear Sir - It might be stated that the contract for the 'reduction and extension of the branch building,' was made for $23,609, and the contract for construction of the infirmary for men was made for $28,975. The appropriation of $70,000 covers the building, plumbing and heating apparatus, and it is now settled that the whole work will be done within the appropriation. At the present time the buildings are erected and roofed but yet lack completion of the flooring and plastering. The branch will be ready for occupancy about the end of December and the infirmary for men by April 1, 1887. The work done by the asylum in addition to the work contracted for, was the excavation for both buildings, the quarrying of all foundation stone and limestone for the kilns that furnished the lime. This part of the work was effected by the labor of patients and their attendants. With this exception, the cost for building the new infirmary was $180 *per capita*, and the branch about $100 per bed. When it is considered that both buildings are constructed in a first class manner, it must be allowed that this rate for asylum buildings of brick has not been approached before in this country. Very hastily yours, P.M. WISE" (36)

"Public Visitations. Since the opening of this asylum, public visitors have been permitted to see certain wards during the afternoon of all days of the week, except Saturday and Sunday. The asylum being removed from a large town, it is thought to be freed from the curiosity-seeker, but such is not the case. During the summer months we are much annoyed by excursionists, who come in crowds of hundreds, sometimes, over-running the grounds and obliging us to remove patients, who are exercising on the lawns and in the groves, to the wards; thus depriving them of this privilege during the pleasant part of the day. Transportation companies and hotels advertise the asylum as one of the curiosities of the lake region, and, as a consequence, it is 'taken in' by the tourist, as a legitimate curiosity for which he has paid. It is frequently the case that the ordinary business of the asylum is suspended to give proper attention to parties of hundreds, the most of whom may not have reached the age of discretion. On the other hand, discreet visitors to asylum wards do no particular harm. Attendants are stimulated thereby, to a greater pride in the appearance of their wards and patients, and the latter are frequently diverted in a pleasant manner. Discretion, however, in asylum visitors is not a common virtue, and the person who forgets that insanity is the most deplorable ill to which our kind is subject, should never visit an asylum." –Wise (37)

1887

"Training School for Attendants. About a year since a training school for attendants was organized, with forty-five students. Although we have no reason for discouragement in our years' work, we feel that we have still much to acquire in the way of experience before our training school is permanently established. There should be an object created to induce attendants to undertake the special training in addition to that of self-improvement. Without a fair promise of reward it will be found difficult to keep a class together for a sufficient period to cover the two years' course. Then the practical or clinical training of attendants in the performance of their duties - the every-day teaching by persons especially fitted for it - would seem to have even a greater value than the didactic or recitative lessons. The two combined undoubtedly offer the best method. Thus far the lectures and recitations have been the work of some member of the medical staff, and in this connection Dr. Bristol is deserving of especial mention for undertaking the most burdensome part of the work and devoting himself to it with the earnest purpose of making it a success. It cannot be expected that a work of this nature, that may still be called experimental, will present tangible results in the very near future, for, like all educational movements, the benefits arising therefrom may be disseminated, but none the less beneficial to society and to the insane. The State asylum should be an educator in many senses, but in none more than this - teaching the proper personal care of insane persons." –Wise (38)

1888

"Willard Asylum for the Insane. The number of patients October 1, 1888, was 1,962, as against 1,812 October 1, 1887. Of these 945 were men and 1,017 women. The institution has no spare room and some of its wards are crowded. The special appropriation of $33,175 to this institution by the last Legislature has been expended in the manner directed and the work completed. The old steam boilers in the main building have been replaced by new ones; the electric light plant has been perfected for the main building and the detached groups numbers two and four; the improvements in connection with the farm barns, feed mills, etc., have been effected; and the two infirmaries have been fully furnished and equipped. These various improvements have been well made, and the work completed within the appropriation. The institution has now well-appointed hospitals for infirm, feeble and filthy patients of both sexes, with adequate day and night service, which fully meets a long felt and pressing need in this direction." (39)

"The chronic insane only are cared for at this institution; and when visited by the Commissioner July fourteenth, there were 1,940 such inmates; 930 men, and 1,010 women. Of this number 366 women were taking exercise in the grounds and 427 were employed about the building; 440 men were at work on the farm, in the garden and about the house. This asylum might well be called a village for the insane, the groups of buildings for the different classes of patients, with gardens between, being scattered over a large tract of land, with dwellings for officers, barns and out-houses, in many places a mile distant. A narrow-gauge railroad runs to the asylum, and one ignorant of the object of the institution might believe he had come upon some thrifty and prosperous New England settlement. It is here, however, that the most degraded class of patients are cared for; epileptics, the demented, filthy and helpless are sent here, and with buildings especially devoted to their needs, are maintained with the most satisfactory results to both patients and administration. Much patience and forbearance are needed in the care of these classes of the insane, and when visited all appeared as clean and comfortable as possible. The larger proportion of the population are able to help themselves, and also assist in carrying on the labor of the institution." (40)

1889

This excerpt is from the State of New York's First Annual Report of the State Commission in Lunacy that speaks of the conditions in one unnamed county poor house.

"In one of the largest county institutions in the State, one of the only two in which a resident physician is employed, a most deplorable condition of affairs was discovered. This physician was found acting in the place of an attendant; in fact, was attending the male patients or a portion of them at dinner. He was standing over the table giving orders to the patients, his hat on his head and a cigar in his mouth; his tones were rough and brusque in the extreme. His manners and actions were so peculiar that the Commission made some inquiries in regard to his methods. The keeper informed us that he had repeatedly called the attention of the superintendent of the poor to the necessity of having this physician removed; that he was grossly incompetent, and that he himself, would not take a dose of medicine prescribed by him under any circumstances whatever; and yet it appeared that this physician had been in charge of an institution containing nearly 400 patients for a period of sixteen months, and that he was appointed to his present position the day immediately following his graduation. It needed but a slight examination to disclose the fact that the physician was clearly incompetent for the performance of his duties; that he possessed no practical knowledge of mental diseases, and that this, together with his conduct and bearing, clearly indicated his unfitness for the medical charge of such an institution. The institution for the most part, was in a state of extreme disorder and confusion, which, with the conduct and appearance of the patients, presented a most distressing picture, closely resembling that of an ideal madhouse as portrayed in the pages of fiction; patients going about singing and shouting, with disheveled hair, disordered clothing - in fact, typical raving maniacs, seemingly beyond the control of the attendants in charge.

This state of things was only what might naturally be expected from the total lack of proper supervision. In one of the women's wards, in the presence of the commissioners, a woman fell in an epileptic fit, went through all the horrors of convulsions in the presence of the other patients, and, during their stay on the ward, was allowed to lie there with her limbs exposed, and other patients walking about and stepping over her without the slightest concern. It is hardly necessary to state that the commissioners took steps to secure the removal of this incompetent physician. It was weeks, however, before the removal was made. After the physician learned that an effort was being made to displace him, he wrote a letter to the Commission, in which he asked to be retained, and, among other things, described his qualifications as a medical officer for the care and treatment of the insane. This letter is so extraordinary, and gives such a clear insight into the character, training and qualifications of the writer that the Commission deems it advisable to disclose a portion of its contents to the public, especially as the letter concludes as follows:

'...Patients are very rarely inclined to hurt any one. When such a thing happens and the patient is a woman, she is simply shut in her room, and in about three cases, that I recollect, not allowed to go to the next meal. If she is very violent and the fit is one of ugliness, we either put her in the downstairs room or confine her in the crib for five or six hours. If she is persistent, violent and maniacal, we strap her to a chair, put on the muffs or camisole. If the patient is a man, who becomes violent in my presence, I choose to deal with him alone. If an attendant is with me I do not wish his help with such cases as I have had experience with in this institution. I can walk up to any of our men, however violent they may be, and throw them on their backs, without striking or hurting them. After this treatment, three times out of four they are humbled. If they are not, I let them regain their feet and throw them again, and if this does not answer they are confined to a room.' " (41)

9

1880 UNITED STATES FEDERAL CENSUS - THE INMATES OF WILLARD DEFECTIVE, DEPENDENT, AND DELINQUENT CLASSES CENSUS

While I was working on the completion of the 1880 Federal Census for Willard, I noticed what appeared to be a father and son listed one name apart as inmates with the word "son" written next to the father's name. This didn't make sense but keep in mind that the enumerators were probably filling in the information as fast as they could. The inmates' names were Rudolph Harmann, Jr. and Sr. Rudolph junior was listed as 25, imbecile; Rudolph senior, a jeweler, was listed as 58, dementia; both were from Johnstown, Fulton County, New York. In order to verify their relationship, I wanted to see if I could find both their names together on an earlier census, preferably in their own home, but I never found it. What I did find was the 1880 Defective, Dependent, and Delinquent Classes Census. I was unaware that such a census existed. This census also included what city and county the patient was sent from; if they were paying for their care; the history of their attack; if they required restraint or seclusion; if they had been hospitalized before; and if they were an epileptic, suicidal, or homicidal. There were two sets of the same census sheets in different handwriting. Perhaps Mr. Johnson and Mr. Cole compared their censuses to make sure that their information was correct. One set used a rubber stamp with the word "IDIOT" next to some of the inmate's names which was most likely done at the federal level by the workers actually tabulating the censuses; and some sheets from that same set were poorly scanned, folded or unreadable. I believe the reason the federal workers used the stamp was to distinguish the idiot and imbecile class of patients from the insane population. Even though Willard took in many feeble-minded souls, and even though they were all marked as insane on the census, they were not to be counted as insane at the federal level.

Up to this point, I had been focused on finding documents of fact and detail from an impersonal point of view. Although the research was depressing, I still managed to trudge through the documents without getting emotional. And then, I came upon this passage from a surprise inspection of Willard in 1884 and I began to cry: "The patients were seen at dinner; two were eating in the hall, an idiot boy and an old man, the latter taking care of the former under the belief that he was his son." When I read it, I knew that it must be Rudolph Harmann, Jr. and Sr., son and father. They were found in the North Wing of the Main Building, Hall 6, for the demented and feeble class. For the first time in all my research of Willard, I came face to face with love. I will never forget the picture that immediately formed in my brain of these two, long dead souls; eating a meal together, caring for each other, and the love that must have existed between them. It was as if I was being guided by some unknown force to find the answer to my question. It broke my heart.

I was unable to find any other Defective, Dependent, and Delinquent Classes census for any other census year, so I knew that I had to include this important information. The following are the directions to the enumerator, located on the census sheet.

U.S. Federal Census – 1880 Schedules of Defective, Dependent, and Delinquent Classes. (Form 7-321.) SUPPLEMENTAL SCHEDULE NO. 1 – Insane Inhabitants in Willard, in the county of Seneca. State of New York, enumerated by me, June, 1880.

Located at the Top of the Page, above the census:

"The object of this Supplemental Schedule is to furnish material not only for a complete enumeration of the insane, but for an account of their condition. It is important that every inquiry respecting each case be answered as fully as possible. Enumerators will, therefore, *after making the proper entries upon the Population Schedule (No. 1)*, transfer the name (with Schedule page and number) of every insane person found, from Schedule No. 1 to this Special Schedule, and proceed to ask the *additional questions* indicated in the headings of the several columns. Enumerators may obtain valuable hints as to the number of the insane, and their residence, from physicians who practice medicine in their respective districts."

Located at the Bottom of the Page, below the census:

"NOTE A. – An insane person may be found either at his own home or away from it in some institution, such as a hospital, asylum, or poor-house. In the latter case, his residence when at home must be stated, in order that he may be accredited to the State or county to which he properly belongs, and that the county in which the institution is situated may not be charged with more than its due proportion of insane.

NOTE B. – This question can only be answered by physicians. It is not intended that it shall be asked by enumerators, but that it shall be answered by physicians connected with institutions in which insane persons are kept as inmates. *It is not necessary to make minute subdivisions*, but to ascertain the number suffering from certain marked forms of insanity - mania, melancholia, paresis (general paralysis), dementia, epilepsy or dipsomania.

NOTE C. – An insane person may have more than one attack of insanity: he may recover and afterward become again insane. It is important to know at what age the first attack occurred; how many distinct attacks the patient has had; and the duration of the present attack. *If he has not had more than one attack, which still continues, insert the figure '1' in column 9.* The duration of the present attack may be stated in years or months, thus: '1 yr.' or '3 mos.'

NOTE D. – The object of the inquiries in column 11 and 12 is to ascertain approximately the proportion of the insane who cannot be trusted with their personal freedom. In column 11, if the patient is usually or often locked in a room or other apartment in the day-time, say 'yes;' if not, say 'no;' but if locked at night and not by day, say 'night.' In column 12, if usually or often mechanically restrained, state the mode of restraint, thus: straight-jacket, camisole, muff, strap, handcuffs, ball and chain, crib-bed, &c. If, instead of mechanical restraint, the patient has a constant personal attendant, say 'attendant.'

NOTE E. – In column 13 name *all* the hospitals or asylums for the insane (not jails or poor-houses) in which the patient has been for a longer or shorter time an inmate, and in column 14 state the *entire number* of months or years spent in such institutions (whether in one institution or more).

NOTE F. – In making entries in columns 16, 17, and 18, an affirmative mark only will be used, thus: /."

The census spreadsheets for The Inmates of Willard are located at inmatesofwillard.com, under the "Names" tab.

10

1880 Defective, Dependent, and Delinquent Classes Census

"THE DEFECTIVE, DEPENDENT, AND DELINQUENT CLASSES.

Department of the Interior, Census Office, Washington, D.C., December 22, 1882. Hon C.W. Seaton, *Superintendent of Census*. SIR: The most striking result of the effort made in the Tenth Census to obtain a complete and accurate enumeration of the defective, dependent, and delinquent classes of the population of the United States is the apparently great increase in their number, as compared with the figures given in any previous census.

THE AFFLICTED.

If we disregard the census of 1830 (in which the insane and idiotic were not enumerated) and that of 1840 (in which they were enumerated, not separately, but as forming a single class), then the following table exhibits for the four groups included under the term defective the increase referred to; but it must be remembered that this increase is less real than apparent:

Table showing the number of insane, idiotic, blind, and deaf-mutes in the United States, in the years named, respectively, according to the census.

CLASS.	1880	1870	1860	1850
INSANE	91,997	37,432	24,042	15,610
IDIOTS	76,893	24,527	18,930	15,787
BLIND	48,928	20,320	12,658	9,794
DEAF-MUTES	33,878	16,205	12,821	9,803
TOTALS	251,698	98,484	68,451	50,994

The total population for each of the years named was as follows: In 1850 it was 23,191,876; in 1860, 31,443,321; in 1870, 38,558,371; and in 1880, 50,155,783. In other words, although the population has a little more than doubled in thirty years, the number of defective persons returned is nearly five times as great as it was thirty years ago.

During the past decade (or since 1870) the increase in population has been 30 per cent; but the apparent increase in the defective classes has been a little more than 155 per cent.

Table showing the number of insane, idiotic, blind, and deaf-mutes in each million of the population in each of the years named.

CLASS.	1880	1870	1860	1850
INSANE	1,834	971	765	673
IDIOTS	1,533	636	602	681
BLIND	976	527	403	422
DEAF-MUTES	675	420	408	423
TOTALS	5,018	2,554	2,178	2,199

It is not possible to believe that there has, in fact, been any such increase of the defective classes as is indicated by the figures given in the tables above. The inference is irresistible that either the enumeration in 1880 is excessive, or else it was incomplete in 1870 and in the years previous.

The accuracy of the census of these special classes has been from the beginning a matter of doubt on the part of those most conversant with them. Mr. F.B. Sanborn, of Massachusetts, is quoted in the census of 1870 (Compendium, page 626) as having expressed the opinion that 'the number reported in the census, be it state or national, rarely embraces more than 60 or 70 per cent of their respective classes.' But if we accept Mr. Sanborn's estimate, and make it the basis of a calculation; if we increase the number of defectives returned in 1870 by 40 per cent, and make it 137,878, instead of 98,484, even then the increase during the past 10 years, as shown by the census, would appear to have been more than 80 per cent.

The difficulty of enumerating the defective classes with any approach to accuracy is very great. In the first place there are no distinct boundary lines between normal and abnormal conditions of the senses or of the nervous system. How often the sanity or insanity of persons occupying the diffused border line between the two is a matter of furious controversy in newspapers and before the courts. It is almost as hard to say who should be classed as an idiot as it would be to determine at what stage of intemperance one becomes a drunkard. Different observers would form different conclusions. Similarly, it is difficult to say at what stage of impaired vision one becomes blind, or of impaired hearing deaf. Yet the determination of these difficult questions is necessarily left to the untrained judgment either of the enumerator or of the head of the house, or it may be of the servant who comes to the door.

But if there were no obstacle in the way of determining who ought to be included in the defective classes, there would be an almost insurmountable obstacle in the reluctance of friends to publish the infirmities of those dear to them, and the respect felt for this sentiment by enumerators, who hesitate to put disagreeable and, possibly, needless questions." (42)

"Each enumerator was required to transfer to its proper schedule the name of every defective person enumerated by him, and upon that schedule to answer certain definite questions applicable to him as a member of the class to which he was supposed to belong. For this extra service the enumerator was offered additional compensation; and it was impressed upon him that he should make special effort to find these defective persons and make a full report of each case. He was instructed to counsel with physicians upon this point and to make inquiries of neighbors, and to report all defectives, whether the information respecting them should be derived from the families to which they belonged or from other sources, if in his judgment it was worthy of confidence.

With respect to the idiotic and the insane correspondence was had, in addition, with about 100,000 physicians of the United States, who were furnished with blank forms of return, and were requested to report to the Census Office all lunatics and idiots within the sphere of their personal observation and knowledge. Replies were received from four-fifths of those addressed - a result creditable in the highest degree to the public spirit and devotion to science of the medical profession in America - and the names reported by the voluntary observers were, after comparing them with the list returned by the enumerators and carefully purging out duplicates, added to the names already reported.

By the use of the agencies just described it is believed that a much more perfect enumeration of the defective classes, especially of the insane and idiotic, has been secured than ever before in the history of this or perhaps of any other nation.

All possible care has been taken to secure accuracy in the enumeration of the defectives, but it would be claiming too much to assert that the census lists are, even after all the labor bestowed upon them, absolutely accurate. It is certain that names have not been returned to this office which should have been reported; it is also certain that other persons have been improperly reported; but it is thought that these errors must very nearly balance each other. There is, too, a tendency to make duplicate returns of the same person, in the one case at his home and in the other at the institution of which he is an inmate, which has imposed much extra work upon the clerical force in the office, in order to prevent swelling the total number of defectives. One of the great arts of this census of the defective classes is the art of purging out duplicates. Possibly some duplications remain undiscovered; but the percentage of error from this source has been reduced to a minimum. The figures given in the tables are published in the firm conviction that they are as nearly correct as it is possible to make them at the present time with our present facilities for procuring them.

Of these various forms of affliction, the one which causes the most distress, both to the victim and to the circle of his personal friends and acquaintances, is insanity. The interest felt in its ravages leads to the frequent reiteration of an inquiry which is vaguely formulated in the common question: Is insanity increasing in this country relatively to the population? But before this question can be answered, it is essential to know what the inquirer means. If he means nothing more than to ask whether the aggregate number of the insane is increasing, but one reply is possible, and that so obvious as to excite wonder that the question should be put at all. For its solution no census is requisite; it is only necessary to notice the steady growth in the number and capacity of hospitals and asylums for the care of the insane and the utter failure of the provision made to overtake and keep pace with the demand for such provision. If, on the contrary, the inquirer desires to know whether, in the year 1880, the number of new cases - that is, of cases of insanity of less than one year's duration - is larger in proportion to the population than it was in 1870, the reply to this question, so much more precise and penetrating than the other, is a matter of opinion, rather than of statistics, for the reason that the statistical data at our command are not sufficient to enable us to answer it. Yet this is much the more important inquiry of the two; for although the increase of the mass implies an increase of the aggregate amount of sorrow in the world, it does not involve increased liability to insanity on the part of the same, which is probably the peril in the mind of the questioner. An increase in the ratio of new cases to the total population would be an alarming social symptom."

"In dealing with the insane and idiotic population as returned to this office it was found to be necessary to adopt some arbitrary rule for discriminating between the two. In the census of 1840 they were not distinguished, but grouped together as a single class. Since then an attempt has been made in the direction of separation of the two classes, but with what imperfect success will be apparent when attention is directed to the fact that in 1850 the number of idiots reported exceeded that of the insane, but in 1860 the number of insane exceeded that of idiots by twenty-seven per cent, and in 1870 by fifty-two per cent. In the present census the number of insane exceeds that of idiots by only about nineteen per cent, which is still believed to be too high. The reason for the belief here expressed is that insanity in adults is much more readily and surely recognized than is idiocy in infants and very young children; but insanity is for the most part, if not altogether, a disease of mature life, while idiocy, true idiocy, as distinguished from the dementia which results from insanity, is in its origin exclusively a disease of childhood, and is often due to pre-natal conditions. The number of idiots must be, in fact, nearly or quite equal to that of the insane; but the fact does not appear in the census, because so many idiots are unreturned. The distinction between insanity and idiocy is admitted to be subtle; it necessarily eludes the powers of observation and discrimination of the majority of enumerators, and therefore but slight dependence can be placed upon their classification. So little value was believed to attach to it, in the face of any conflicting testimony or evidence, that it was decided to accept it as final wherever uncontradicted, but wherever the answer to the question upon the schedule as to the age at which idiocy or the first attack of insanity occurred was inconsistent with the enumerator's theory of the character of the disability there the original return has been amended in the office. That is to say, if any person whose name was borne upon the list of the insane was reported to have been insane from birth, he has been transferred to the list of idiots; and if any person whose name was borne upon the list of idiots was reported to have become an idiot at the age of forty, he has been transferred to the list of insane, on the ground that the so-called idiocy was actual dementia. Since it was necessary to establish some age as the limit of this rule, the age of puberty was taken; that is twelve in girls and fourteen in boys. This rule was not adopted until after consultation with a number of eminent alienists. It is believed that its adoption has secured upon the whole number of cases a very much more nearly correct result than would have been possible if no such corrections had been made. But its application to individual cases is not always correct, and the risk is taken of errors in the returns made as to the age at which the malady, whatever its nature, overtook its victim. What has now been said will explain the fact that from some hospitals for the insane a few idiots are reported, though they are not returned as such by the officers of the institutions."

"The interest and importance of the inquiry into the number and condition of the defective classes, and of the criminal and pauper population, arises from the fact that these are burdens to be borne - drains upon the vitality of the community. When we consider the growth of our population and of our material resources, we are in danger of forgetting that there is another side to the picture. It is startling to know that of fifty millions of inhabitants, over four hundred thousand are either insane, idiots, deaf-mutes, or blind, or are inmates of prisons, reformatories, or poorhouses. If to these we add the outdoor poor and the inmates of private charitable institutions, the number will swell to nearly or quite half a million, or one per cent of the total population. We cannot begin too soon or prosecute too vigorously the inquiry into the causes of the prevalence of these evils, which are like a canker at the heart of all our prosperity. Nothing can be more important than for us to ascertain at the earliest possible moment the rate at which they are increasing and the means of arresting their growth. The subject is obscure, but in the study of it we may almost be said to have our finger upon the pulse of the nation." (42)

The following excerpt is from the Fourteenth Annual Report of the State Board of Charities for the year 1880 that gives the statistics of the poor and insane in the poor houses, alms houses and state institutions of New York, written and signed by Dr. Charles S. Hoyt, Secretary of the State Board of Charities. It also gives some thought to the people who are always left to fend for themselves and one paycheck away from joining the ranks of pauperism; the middle class.

"Hospitals for the Acute Insane. These State hospitals are designed primarily for the acute insane poor, but they are authorized to receive paying patients, whenever they have room not required by the public exigencies...There is another and numerous class from which a large proportion of the insane burdening the public is derived, in which great neglect of early treatment exists, viz.: persons in moderate circumstances in life. The wealthy are in condition to avail themselves of every needed facility for prompt relief, while the pauper class, as has been seen, is fully provided for by the public. Not so, however, with the middle class whose energies are always heavily taxed in meeting the ordinary conditions of life. When insanity attacks members of families in moderate circumstances, owing to the inability to meet the expense of their treatment and care, at the rate charged for private patients, and from a repugnance to making them burdens upon the public, either as indigent or pauper, resort is had to confinement at home, often in small, ill-ventilated and imperfectly-warmed rooms, and that without medical oversight or care. In this manner they pass the period offering hopes of recovery, and in the end come upon the public as chronic insane, wholly dependent the remainder of their lives. On the contrary, if the attempt be made by such families to maintain their insane members in some State or private hospital, their resources are soon exhausted, and the burden eventually falls upon the public. The effect, however, does not always end here, as not infrequently entire families, in their efforts thus to provide for such insane members, sink into hopeless pauperism. In view therefore, of the extended accommodations of our State hospitals for the acute insane, and of the importance of affording every facility for the prompt treatment of all classes for which they were designed, we believe that sound public policy requires a revision of the system of charges in these institutions."

"Asylums for the Chronic Insane…In the continuance of the policy of the State in the care of the chronic insane, as declared by the act creating the Willard Asylum, the Legislature, by chapter 280 of the Laws of 1879, provided for the conversion of the State Inebriate Asylum at Binghamton, into an asylum for the chronic insane. Appropriations have been made to adapt the building to the purposes intended. These appropriations have been exhausted, and the building is still unfinished. When completed according to the plans designed, it will furnish accommodations for about 300 chronic insane, with central and administrative arrangements for 600 patients."

"County Poor-Houses. According to the returns of the superintendents of the poor, the whole number of inmates of the county poor-houses for the year ending November 30, 1880, was 17,095; the number of out-door poor temporarily relieved was 61,275; total supported and relieved, 78,370. For the year ending November 30, 1879, the number in poor-houses was 18,924; aided outside, 62,673; total 81,597. The sex of those supported the past year was: males, 11,533; females, 5,562; the nativity: United States, 8,523; foreign born, 8,572. The number in the poor-houses at the close of the year was 6,581, as against 6,754 November 30, 1879. Of these, there were insane, 1,741; idiots, 323; epileptics, 169; blind, 127; deaf mutes, 44; children under sixteen years old, 248. The insane were wholly of the chronic class, and the idiots, epileptics, blind and deaf mutes were generally adults. The children over two years of age were mostly feeble-minded, crippled, or otherwise permanently incapacitated."

"City Alms-Houses. The returns of the city alms houses for the year ending November 30, 1880, furnish the following: Whole number of persons supported in-doors, 38,962; relieved outside, 16,317; total, 55,279. Of the indoor cases there were males, 22,239; females, 16,723; of native birth, 13,222; foreign birth, 25,740. At the close of the year there were 9,765 persons under care, in these institutions, of whom 4,146 were insane, 249 idiots, 87 epileptics, 139 blind, 8 deaf mutes, and 721 children under the age of sixteen years. For the preceding year, the number of persons supported in-doors was 39,001; temporarily aided outside, 17,179; total, 56,180."

"Aggregate Results of the Poor-House and Alms-House Returns. The whole number of persons as inmates of the various poor-houses and alms-houses of the State for the year ending November 30, 1880, according to the returns was 56,057; the number of persons temporarily relieved was 77,592; total supported and relieved, 133,649. The sex of those supported was males, 33,772; females, 22,285; the nativity was, United States, 21,744; foreign born, 34,313. The number under care at the close of the year was 16,346; of whom 5,887 were insane, 572 idiots, 256 epileptics, 266 blind, 52 deaf mutes, and 969 children under sixteen years of age. For the preceding year, the returns were as follows: Supported in poor-houses and alms-houses, 57,925; temporarily relieved, 79,852; total, 137,777; under care at the close of the year, 15,870. The expenditures in connection with the poor-houses and alms-houses for the past year summed up as follows: For maintenance and care in-doors, $1,613,581.90; for out-door aid, $695,507.85; total, $2,309,089.75; average *per capita* yearly in-door expenditure, $96.27; weekly average, $1.85; average sum expended for each person aided out-doors, $8.96; estimated value of pauper labor, $74,488.35. The returns for the preceding year were as follows: For in-door support, 1,618,867.63; for outside relief, $692,465.77; total, $2,311,333.40; average annual *per capita* expenditure in-doors, $102.01; weekly *per capita* average, $1.96; average outside expenditure for each person, $8.67; whole value of pauper earnings, $57,419.49." (43)

"Statistics Relating to the Insane. The number of insane in the various institutions of this State, October 1, 1880, reported by the resident officers, was 9,537 as against 9,015 October 1, 1879. Of these, 4,211 were males, and 5,326 females. The increase in institutions during the year was 522, or 5.47 per cent, as against 679, or 9.68 per cent the preceding year. Upon the basis of a population of 5,000,000, the number of insane in institutions October 1, 1880, was equivalent to one to every 524 inhabitants. The following are the several classes of institutions in which the insane of the State were under care, and the number in each, October 1, 1880:

	MALES	FEMALES	TOTAL
IN THE STATE INSTITUTIONS	1,272	1,391	2,663
IN CITY ASYLUMS AND CITY ALMS HOUSES	1,800	2,534	4,334
IN COUNTY POOR HOUSES AND COUNTY ASYLUMS	840	1,152	1,992
IN THE ASYLUM FOR INSANE CRIMINALS	135	11	146
IN PRIVATE ASYLUMS	164	238	402
AGGREGATE	4,211	5,326	9,537

(43)

11

1890

As previously stated, the 1890 U.S. Federal Census was destroyed by a fire in the Commerce Department Building in Washington, D.C., on January 10, 1921. Fragments of the census remain from ten different states which according to NARA (National Archives and Records Administration), include 6,160 persons. The census from Willard State Hospital, Seneca County, New York, did not survive but the official statistics were recorded: "983 men, 1,065 women, 2,048 total; 13, recovered, 46 improved, 20 unimproved, 5 not insane, and 123 died, as of October 1, 1890." (44)

"The total expenditure for the erection of buildings of all kinds, land, furniture, water-works, and all purposes, except salaries and maintenance, has been $1,419,828. The capacity of the asylum is 1,938, and the average cost of construction, equipment, land, etc., has been $732 per patient. The whole number admitted from the opening of the asylum October 12, 1869, to September 30, 1890, was 5,015." (8)

The bright, enthusiastic, naïve outlook in the first report to the Legislature in 1869 by the Trustees of the Willard Asylum for the Insane had changed to one of dismay by the State Commission in Lunacy in 1890. The Defective, Dependent, and Delinquent Classes Census of 1880 had shown a staggering increase of 155 percent of this entire class which included the insane from the previous census of 1870. Whether these statistics are accurate or not, the fact remained that the insane population was increasing throughout the state. Reports about the continual non-compliance of the laws, and the rules and regulations governing the treatment of the insane in the county poorhouses were on the rise. In many cases, the Keeper of the poor house or alms house, who had no qualifications to care for anyone, let alone the insane, was in complete control.

The following excerpt is from The State of New York First Annual Report of the State Commission in Lunacy, 1889, to the Legislature. The enactment of Chapter 283, Laws of 1889, established and organized the State Commission in Lunacy which transferred to them, all the powers that had been formerly given to the State Board of Charities.

"The population in the insane departments of the county alms-houses varies from twenty-five in the smallest to nearly 400 in the largest. The whole number confined in the alms-houses of all these exempted counties is 1,848. The smallest number in custody is greater than the number cared for in many hospitals for ordinary diseases. In none of these hospitals would the proposition to place patients under the immediate control of any class of persons excepting those who had received medical training be seriously considered. Yet in not one of these exempted counties is there an instance of the insane department being in any proper sense under the supervision and control of a medical officer. In only two institutions were resident physicians employed; in only four or five others were physicians required to visit daily. In a majority of these institutions the physicians visit from one to three times weekly, according to the terms of their contract with the superintendent of the poor or other authority. These institutions, are, in most cases in the charge of a 'keeper,' while a few of them are directly controlled by the superintendent of the poor, or, if there be more than one superintendent in a county, by the resident superintendent. It is not pretended that these keepers are in any way qualified, either by training or previous experience, for the care and supervision of insane patients, even assuming that such patients are not sick persons, as they concededly are. The qualifications and capacity of these keepers for this particular work - and here it may be proper to state that there is no disposition on the part of the Commission to unduly criticise the intelligence or the acquirements of the officers in charge of the insane departments of the poor-houses - may be judged when it is stated that their compensation does not on the average amount to more than $600 or $700 per annum. In fairness, however, it should be added that they also receive maintenance for themselves and their families. They have the general oversight and charge of these institutions; their word is law, and they are subject to no control other than the power that appoints them. Even the physicians, who make visits with greater or less regularity, are officially subordinate to these keepers, and in some instances come only when in the latter's judgment a patient requires attention. A letter has been received from one of these physicians, in which he complains that he has no power, that he is subject to and under the control of the keeper. As stated above, in a majority of instances, the physicians appointed to look after the insane are under contract or agreement to visit both the sane and insane paupers a certain number of times weekly - the sane paupers receiving precisely the same visitation as the insane; in other instances they visit only when sent for. The smallest number of people, both sane and insane, that a physician has to care for is not less than fifty, while in some cases it reaches several hundred. When it is understood that the compensation of these physicians averages less than $325 per annum; that in many instances they furnish their own medicines; that in almost every case they reside from one to five miles from the institutions, and that they are engaged in active practice, one can readily imagine how meagre and inadequate the medical treatment must be." (45)

In 1890, nineteen years after the giant step backward in caring for the insane that was caused by the Law of 1871, the State Legislature was forced (largely due to the efforts of Miss Louisa Lee Schuyler and The State Charities Aid Association), to create and enact the *State Care Act*. (Law F) This law would finally remove all insane residents of the state from the county poor houses and from the brutality of the County Superintendents and Keepers of the poor. I am not implying that the superintendents, keepers, physicians, and attendants of the county poor houses were rapists or sexual deviants (although some may have been), but many were cruel and inhumane to the people who they were supposed to be protecting. The male inmates of the county poor houses often took liberties with the women and could not be controlled.

The State Care Act gave extra protection to the transport of women to state mental institutions: "In all cases there shall be provided a female attendant for every female patient, unless she be accompanied by her husband, father, brother or son." (52) This law transferred the care, support and protection of all the insane to the sole custody of the state, at the state's expense. The county was no longer responsible for the support of the insane. Total state care was first suggested on January 12, 1870, by the Trustees of the Willard Asylum but it took twenty years for the New York State legislature to make it happen. This is also the first time that the words pauper and *indigent* insane patients appear together, signaling the expanded breadth of this state system to include people who were not inmates of the county poor houses but who came directly from their homes. Also in 1890, state mental institutions dropped the term "insane asylums" and officially renamed these facilities "state hospitals." The reason being the use of the word hospital signified hope to the patients, relatives, and friends of the inmates as a welcoming place where they would be medically treated and cared for, rather than being removed from society to rot in an insane asylum. The law divided the state into districts and removed the distinction of acute and chronic hospitals. The Willard Asylum for the Insane was now Willard State Hospital; no longer an institution for the chronic insane only.

The Insanity Law of 1896 (Law G) replaced the Law of 1874 which over the course of twenty-two years became obsolete. In 1896, the rule of each hospital board making the decision to release patients as recovered or improved had been abandoned and turned over to the discretion of the Medical Superintendent in charge of each state hospital. Prior to this provision in the law, an inmate who was designated to go back to his or her home by the medical superintendent, often times had to wait several weeks until the next board meeting was held at which time the board members would officially release or deny release of the patient.

For the first time, the alleged insane person or someone in his behalf, had to be notified by the court that a verified petition for an application of commitment, accompanied with the certificate in lunacy of two legally qualified medical examiners, had been filed in a court of record. The "order for a commitment of a person to an institution for the custody and treatment of the insane" or "certified copy of the certificate of a judge of a court of record" was also new and could not be issued unless the previous steps had been carried out. The Insanity Law allowed the judge to hold a hearing "upon the demand of some relative or friend of the alleged insane person" before the order was issued.

12

1900 United States Federal Census - The Inmates Of Willard

In 1900, the Enumerator for Willard State Hospital was Mr. William C. Cooper. Under the heading "Relation," the patients of Willard were listed as "Inmates." Under the heading, "Personal Description," three new questions were asked. The first was: "Number of Years of Present Marriage?" This was filled in for all inmates as "Un" for unknown. Two new questions for women only were: "Mother of How Many Children," and "Number of These Children Living." Where the information was available, it is filled in with a number. In some cases these answers were unknown. From the actual copy of the census, Mr. Cooper wrote "Un" for Unknown, and then went back and filled in the boxes with zeros as this was a number column. If there is a zero next to your ancestor's name, it doesn't necessarily mean that she never gave birth to any children. Of the 861 children recorded; 532 were living, and 329 had died. "Citizenship," in most cases was unknown, so I did not include this information on the spreadsheet. The headings: "Occupation, Trade or Profession," and "Ownership of Home," were left blank by the enumerator. Under the heading "Education," it asked the following questions: "Can read, Can write, Can speak English." These answers were marked with "Y" for Yes; "N" for No; and "U" for Unknown. This census was taken at Willard State Hospital, located in the Towns of Ovid and Romulus, Seneca County, New York, June 4th through 13th, 1900, and consisted of forty-three completed census pages. The thirteen pages in the town of Romulus consisted of men only.

Total Males & Females for 1900: 2,082

TOTAL MALES: 975	TOTAL FEMALES: 1107
WHITE: 964	WHITE: 1092
BLACK: 11	BLACK: 15
SINGLE: 655	SINGLE: 502
MARRIED: 234	MARRIED: 432
WIDOWED: 57	WIDOWED: 162
DIVORCED: 8	DIVORCED: 5
STATUS UNKNOWN: 21	STATUS UNKNOWN: 6

The census spreadsheets for The Inmates of Willard are located at inmatesofwillard.com, under the "Names" tab.

13

1900

After thirty-five years since its inception, 1900 was the end of an era for the first generation of the Inmates of Willard. The name of the institution had changed to Willard State Hospital and accepted both acute and chronic patients. Dr. John B. Chapin, who served as the first Medical Superintendent for fourteen years had resigned in 1884 and was replaced with the following five medical superintendents over a period of sixteen years: Peter M. Wise, 1884 to 1890; Charles W. Pilgrim, February 1, 1890 to 1893; Theodore H. Kellogg, 1893 to November 1, 1895; William Mabon, November 1, 1895 to December 1, 1896; and William Austin Macy, January 1, 1897 to June 1, 1904.

The dream of curing insanity had not come to fruition. The comfort, safety, sympathetic care and better health of the insane had been replaced with overcrowded, warehousing conditions. The beautiful, secluded countryside with clean fresh air and pure water that once made the asylum property a treasured gem of a destination for peace and quiet was now an inconvenient journey. It was too isolated and too far away from large cities. The main building was not fitted with twentieth century accommodations and was in need of constant repair. The percentage of patient labor was 51.69. The inmates worked on the wards, in the kitchen, on the farm, in the garden, in the broom and basket shop, shoe shop, tin shop, sewing room, tailor shop, and they even made their own mattresses. They were also required to make their own clothes. Many of the male patients worked at repairing and maintaining the grounds, cemetery, roads, and buildings. The inmates were not paid for their labor which made this hospital cost effective, saving the state a substantial amount of money.

Willard was also understaffed. The medical staff and employees had to deal with diseases such as Typhoid, Tuberculosis and Diphtheria; provide medical care for over 2,000 inmates; and were expected to perform surgeries and autopsies as necessary. They were under paid and in 1900 alone,

179 employees resigned or were dismissed. One million dollars was finally appropriated by the legislature to be divided among all the state hospitals for updating and improving the facilities, but it wasn't enough.

1900 State Commission in Lunacy, Willard State Hospital – Annual Report

"Hon. S.H. Hammond, *President of the Board of Managers*, etc., Geneva, N.Y. Dear Sir. - I respectfully forward to you herewith, for presentation to the managers of the Willard State Hospital, the annual report of the said institution for the year ending September 30, 1900. The usual statistical tables, together with the other customary reports of the treasurer and steward, are also appended.

The following table shows the movement of population during the past year:

	MEN	WOMEN	TOTAL
REMAINING OCTOBER 1, 1899	1,101	1,152	2,253
ADMITTED DURING THE YEAR	145	124	269
TOTAL NUMBER TREATED DURING THE YEAR	1,246	1,276	2,522
AVERAGE DAILY POPULATION	1,115	1,155	2,270
DISCHARGED DURING THE YEAR	124	132	256

The patients discharged were divided as follows:

	MEN	WOMEN	TOTAL
DISCHARGED AS RECOVERED	23	27	50
DISCHARGED IMPROVED	25	24	49
DISCHARGED UNIMPROVED	7	7	14
DISCHARGED NOT INSANE	5	0	5
DIED	64	74	138
REMAINING OCTOBER 1, 1900	1,122	1,144	2,266

During the year there was an increase of 21 men, a decrease of 8 women, making a total increase of 13. The largest number under treatment on any one day, was 2,295, on August 4th, and the smallest number was 2,252 on October 2d. Of the patients admitted during the year, 188 were brought direct from their homes; 18 were admitted from almshouses; 6 from hotels; 31 from jails; 6 from city hospitals; 11 were transferred from other New York State hospitals, and 9 were received from the Soldiers' Home. All of those admitted were public patients. There were 2 patients admitted who were under 15 years of age; 10 per cent of the whole number were over 70, and of these, 5 were over 80. The largest number admitted were between the years of 50 and 60. The percentage of recoveries, calculated upon the daily average population, was 2.2 per cent. If calculated upon the number of admissions it would be 18.7 per cent. Of the 118 patients discharged, 9 were transferred to other State hospitals in the State; 45 were discharged at the expiration of parole; 56 went direct to their homes and 7 eloped. One of the number who eloped was located after he was discharged and sent to one of the other State hospitals. Five others were found after their discharge to be with their friends, and were getting along sufficiently well to allow their remaining at home. This will show that of the 7 people who eloped, all were satisfactorily accounted for, and their cases closed, except one, who has not been heard of. (A patient who eloped, but who could not be discharged because committed under a criminal order, is included in these figures). The death rate for the year was 6 per cent.

AMUSEMENTS

Such amusements as have been provided for the patients during the past year were much the same as in the immediate preceding year. The Commission has continued to allow us a special fund for the amusement of patients, and this has been expended by having entertainments at the hospital from time to time; by the purchase of one or two new pianos; the purchase of games at different times, music boxes, or such other articles as would conduce to the greatest amount of amusement for the patients. On September 19th, Field Day was observed as usual, and was considered one of the best affairs of the kind known in the history of the hospital. Some two or three thousand or more people were upon the grounds, and many outsiders from some little distance from the hospital were among those viewing the exercises.

OCCUPATION

Such occupations as have been provided for the patients at the hospital during the past year have been very much the same as usual, though in some directions, such industries as have hitherto been started, have been carried out to a greater extent than formerly.

The work on the farm and in the gardens has been very materially interfered with because of the excessive drought, and much less new work in the way of improvements, such as grading, ditching, and many other things of this kind, has been undertaken than usual, partly for the reason that the reduction in the number of employees last year has drawn from our attendants and nurses' force to almost an equivalent degree, for the relief that has had to be provided to meet cases of absence on account of vacations, pass-days and sickness, in different departments that were affected, though in some of the mechanical departments, such as the carpenter and painter's divisions, we have not allowed this to interfere appreciably, but have either had work that was required done by special help allowed by the Commission, or have allowed minor matters to go, because of our not feeling able to meet them. There are quantities, in fact I might almost say, hundreds of small matters during the course of the year, that come up, on the reports, that have to wait, because little alterations to locks, doors, windows, walls, porches and all sorts of things of this kind, have to be attended to, and yet, if we have to put them in an estimate for matters of this kind, they would seem remarkably trivial when asking for additional help by the month. A great many things of this sort accumulate in an institution as large as ours, and particularly when so old, and what I outlined as probable last year, in the matter of accumulation of things of this kind, has already begun, and we find it requires the most constant and painstaking care to prevent this. Of course, as far as we are able and can foresee it, we try to prevent the accumulation of minor repairs and the running down of the hospital, but we find that our former experience still holds, namely, that it is very desirable to have enough permanent men to attend to all of these things, such an arrangement being calculated to do much more towards keeping the hospital in good repair than that which prevails at present, when all repairs or betterments in excess of the capacity of our working force have to be foreseen and separately provided for.

This also affects the employee largely, in not reporting many matters that it is known may have to be waited for indefinitely. I trust that one of these days we will be able to have this matter placed upon a somewhat different footing, and one that will do somewhat more justice to the institution.

I will not burden this report by detailing at length under this caption, the various kinds of employment which our patients have been engaged in, as these are well known to all of the managers, and it is sufficient to say that where possible, our industries have been extended rather than contracted. As to certain matters of new work, I would state that we finished building the breakwater on the lake front and filled in and graded the grounds back of it. We have now almost completed the grading and road building around the exercise field, east of the electric light plant, and a large number of trees were planted on these grounds. We also planted a large number of ornamental trees and shrubs which were allowed us by the Commission, along the main roadside, through the grounds and about the buildings. Such excavation as was necessary at the new building now known as 'Hillside,' and formerly known as the 'Meddick House,' was done and a good cesspool was built and water and sewer pipe put in. A water pipe was also run connecting this building with the main water system, giving fire protection as well.

The water system that had been previously started, for giving us fire protection at the different buildings was completed during this season, and hydrants were conveniently located where necessary. Water was also carried into some of the meadows east of the main road near 'Hillside,' and a cement watering trough was placed there for the stock. Considerable grading was done around the piggeries, and the grounds were otherwise improved. At detached building No. 1, the old driveway was filled in with new shale, and a sidewalk was made to each cottage, and considerable grading was done. Some of the gutters were also repaved to carry off the roof water. With the aid of patients' labor, a cement walk 1,500 to 1,800 feet in length, was built from the main administration building to the railroad depot. The cost of material, considering that we were able, with our sand barge, to get all the sand needed from the hospital sand bank, was only 4 ¾ cents per square foot, and as the paid labor was limited to only one special attendant and an attendant detailed to look after the patients, the total cost of this sidewalk was extremely reasonable.

An excavation was made for a new locomotive house, south of the laundry building, and water and sewer pipes were put in, and such work as was necessary to be done, in connection with the paid labor for building this, was performed by the patients. The grading about the laundry was well started, and in time we hope to have a bleaching ground back of this building, and to very much improve the surroundings at this point on the hospital grounds.

Quite a quantity of rock and shale were placed upon our roads and walks, they being afterwards rolled with a steam roller, and this work we now hope to continue until finished. A dock was built at the sand bank, partly by patients' labor, and a large amount of sand was loaded on the barge and brought to this hospital, as well as a matter of 180 yards or more of gravel. About 10,000 tons of coal were unloaded during the year. We harvested and packed all of the ice used in this institution, gathering during the past winter about 1,800 tons.

During the past year we have introduced into the tailor shop the making of winter caps, mittens, suspenders and fine shirts for men, and ulsters for the women patients. We are employing about one hundred patients regularly in the laundry, and with the new machinery given us by the Commission this last year, we hope in the future to get along better in this division, even than during the past year. We have had much less complaint in our laundry during the past year or two, since the system was inaugurated of checking everything in and out and keeping closer track of the clothing on the wards, except that we have found that our equipment has been hardly great enough to do the work involved, which amounts to about 50,000 pieces per week, or 200,000 pieces per month.

Notwithstanding the conditions which I referred to, from increasing the amount of relief that had to be provided from our ward service, I am glad to state that we have by constant effort, been able to increase the percentage of people employed at some useful occupation. This percentage for the average daily employment for the year, being 51.69 as against 50.49 for the preceding year.

WORK OF THE MEDICAL STAFF

At the first of the year the staff was reduced by two. This obliged us to make a very complete change in the medical organization of the hospital, as laid out prior to this time, and effected a reduction in the number of men working on the acute services. For this reason several methods for the closer study and observation of cases which were being introduced, had either to be modified or abandoned. The reduction of the staff, taken in connection with the large amount of additional work that was thrown upon us during the last year, by reason of the epidemic of diphtheria which we have had to deal with, has, we regret to say, prevented us from making such progress as we would have liked towards the closer study and better individual care of special cases, which we had previously anticipated could have been brought about as time went on. With the present staff, when all are on duty, there are only just about enough men for the ordinary routine work, when done in the way that we would wish, the proportion of physicians to patients being less than 1 to 200, when both the superintendent and woman physician are included in making up the percentage and the special detail, because of having to send physicians to inspect and see patients at a distance; absences because of vacations and sickness; disinfecting and other work of this kind, effect such conditions, that practically it might be considered as equivalent through detailed duty, to having one physician off duty during almost every day of the year. As a matter of fact, during the last year the absences have amounted to over 332 days of twenty-four hours or double the number for twelve hours for one physician, and this, of course, reduces the effective working force, even when the superintendent and woman physician are included in making out the percentage, to very much less than 1 to 200, the standard that it has hitherto been thought necessary to maintain.

Manifestly in an institution as large as this, the superintendent can scarcely be counted in, in making a proportion of this kind, because of any detailed medical work that he is likely to accomplish in giving *individual* care to patients. While the superintendent does have time for a large amount of medical work of every description, still, with 2,200 or 2,300 patients, it can not be expected that he is going to participate very much in the individual care of a great many patients, as there is always an enormous amount of every kind of medical and other work that must pass under his supervision to take his time and attention from such duties.

Even the woman physician must necessarily spend much time in looking after women employees and special cases of women patients, so that the medical service to which she might be assigned, consisting of a definite number of wards, must be comparatively small as compared with that of the men physicians. I merely state these observations, and leave it for time to show which view is the most correct on this subject, well knowing that the views of different individuals vary considerably, but feeling that it is much better to work towards giving the greatest amount of individual care, particularly in acute cases, for the reason that this promises to increase the recovery rate, in these cases while with the chronic cases it tends to make their lives much more endurable, and to very much increase the number who will acquire useful habits, thereby assisting through the work that they accomplish, to maintain themselves and their fellows at a lower per capita rate, and to give them, particularly where large farms and gardens are utilized, a much more liberal diet than would be the case if the same had to be paid for.

Rather less work of a surgical character has been done during the past year, than in the preceding one. This has been particularly because of the prevalence of diphtheria at the hospital. However, twenty-five operations were performed besides minor surgical work, such as the care of wounds, some few fractures, etc. The operations performed included trephining, fixation of kidney, repair of vesico-vaginal fistula, herniotomy, laparotomy, relief of urethral stricture, opening of mastoid process, amputation, etc. This work is much handicapped by lack of facilities and a good operating room, and a special hospital for caring for the sick, separated from all the wards, so as not to have infection of any sort introduced into it, would be very much appreciated.

We are also at somewhat of a disadvantage because of the amount of surgery done not being large, and the inability on this account to have nurses who have received the amount of training in surgical work that we would like to have available in handling operations that we wish to undertake. However, the results from our work have been excellent, and in this we have been fairly well satisfied.

Dr. Wm. B. Jones, of Rochester, N.Y., has gratuitously given his services as surgeon to the hospital when required, virtually acting as consulting surgeon for us. Dr. Jones has been called in cases of a particularly serious nature, when we have felt the need of dividing the responsibility with some one who is doing more surgery than we ordinarily do at the hospital, and he has always very willingly and cheerfully assisted us at all times, and his cooperation has been extremely helpful to the hospital.

I would respectfully recommend to your board that Dr. Jones be made regular consulting surgeon to the hospital. Positions of this kind connected with institutions as large as this, are usually honorary, and Dr. Jones has signified his entire willingness to accept such a position with us, without compensation, providing he is reimbursed to the extent of his actual carfare and expenses in coming to the hospital from Rochester, and if an arrangement of this sort can be arrived at with the

Commission in Lunacy, I think it is only fitting that it should be carried out in recognition of the help already tendered us by Dr. Jones.

No particular disease was especially prevalent during the past year, except diphtheria, and from this we lost no patients. The death rate of the hospital was 5.47% on the whole number treated. There were 165 cases admitted to the sick wards, besides those cared for at the infirmaries for the aged and feeble, and such occasional cases of slight ailments as occurred on the various wards, not severe enough to necessitate removal to the hospital.

TYPHOID

We are very much pleased to state that only two cases of typhoid fever occurred during the year, but on the other hand, at certain seasons of the year an exceptionally large amount of diarrhoeal trouble prevailed at the hospital.

TUBERCULOSIS

The percentage of deaths from this cause is 14.7%. This was less than last year (16%), and the lowest in the history of the hospital since the first three years, although it may be assumed that the diagnosis is now more carefully made than formerly. It would seem, therefore, that the segregation and more systematic and thorough treatment were having some effect. Isolation is still, however, very imperfectly accomplished, owing to the location of the isolation wards and their limited capacity. In the case of the ward for women, the exposure is toward the north, and it does not receive sufficient sunshine.

The facilities for getting the patient out of doors are also insufficient. It would be very desirable if, following the reduction in the death rate thus far obtained, and the improvement in a great many cases which has resulted because of segregating and giving special care to tuberculosis cases, we could add to our equipment a special building, with sun rooms and other facilities for combating disease. There are at present in the hospital 42 patients, in whom the diagnosis of pulmonary tuberculosis has been made, 26 being women and 16 men.

DIPHTHERIA

Twenty-five cases of this disease have occurred during the year, nine of whom were men and sixteen women; nineteen of the number were employees, among whom the disease has prevailed more extensively than among the patients, whenever it has appeared at the hospital. The disease was distributed as follows: Two in the main building; two at D.B. 1; two at D.B. 3; four at D.B. 4; four at the infirmary; ten at the branch, and one at 'Hillside.' The number of cases mentioned in this paragraph include only cases of membranous diphtheria, and no mention is made of the large number of germ cases, from many of which we found infection spread.

Counting from early in the summer of 1899 through to the end of this fiscal year, but, of course taking a few more months, the number of cases of diphtheria that we have had to contend with was between seventy and eighty, and, aside from the large number of people showing germ infection that we have had to isolate and quarantine, during the recurrent outbreaks during the development of the twenty-five cases referred to, the principal difficulty that we have had here in the year mentioned, has come through the strain of meeting these conditions, and the fright occasioned by it among the employees and consequent changes in the service, etc.

Still, I desire to record in connection with what I said about the diphtheria, that the majority of the employees have all met this matter in a very self-sacrificing spirit, and that they have very earnestly cooperated with us in carrying out the methods taken to stamp out the infection. Considerable has been written about the outbreak of diphtheria at this hospital, and we have noticed similar accounts of epidemics of this sort in other institutions and places, but it would burden the report considerably to detail all that has been done at this place. It would probably be sufficient to state that in addition to the very large number of cultures, aggregating over 21,225, which have been taken and examined during the year, and the immense amount of laboratory work which this has occasioned, we have immunized patients and employees at each outbreak very extensively, hundreds of people having been treated in this way, with few, if any cases of alarming reaction from the remedy. We have also disinfected as far as this seems possible, with formaldehyde, sulphur and disinfecting solutions of various kinds, and have made a series of laboratory tests to see whether the disinfection of clothing, bedding and all sorts of articles which required disinfection was thorough, etc. Narration of these details might properly belong to a medical article, but such steps are so constantly taken nowadays, that I hesitate to introduce an account of them into this report. No absolute way of eradicating infection of this kind seems thus far to have been found. When introduced into a very crowded institution, infection does not seem to be confined to the human being involved, but extends to the bedding, walls, wall paper, and many other things which apparently carry infection for a very long time, and surroundings thus infected may be dangerous for months, outbreaks occurring sometimes long after it had been supposed that places previously disinfected were free from germs. There is thus always a question whether this outbreak is from an old or a new infection. Some data, of course, have been collected by the bacteriologists concerning the life of the Klebs-Loeffler in the air, and under ordinary conditions, but time will probably tell whether all of the conclusions thus far drawn have been correct. Massachusetts is drawing marked attention to the necessity of finding some way of absolutely stamping out diphtheria infection, and the attention of all bacteriologists interested in this has been directed to this matter for a long time. While we do not claim that we have discovered any positive way of guaranteeing the stamping out of diphtheria infection, we have found great aid both from immunizing and antitoxin and also from culture taking.

If we had to-day to depend on one or the other, I think there is no doubt that we would entirely prefer to fall back upon the immunization method, but at the same time, culture taking in our experience, has enabled us to determine, to some considerable extent, what individuals carry infection, and thus to keep some track of its spread through the hospital, and so valuable has this been that we feel it is almost entirely because of the culture taking methods that we have pursued, that, with the combined use of antitoxin as an immunizing agent, we have been able to keep informed of the infection and to virtually keep it under control, while it has seemed from time to time and week to week as if we were almost on the point of absolutely stamping it out. That we have not actually stamped out the infection at these times would seem to be due to the saturation of the surroundings with the germs, and it has been a great satisfaction for us to keep it as well in check as we have been able to, and also to be able to record that in spite of many cases of considerable severity, some of which were among the children of the officers or employees as well as among the adult population, we have been fortunate enough not to lose a single case by death in the past two years among over eighty cases of membranous diphtheria treated. It may be interesting in this connection to mention one of the limits that we place in the culture taking, to determine as far as possible the absence of infection from the throats, etc., of those previously showing bacilli.

Early in the investigation we found that some limit had to be fixed upon, so as to enable us to decide when to discharge people from quarantine, and, believing that all cases carrying the Klebs-Loeffler germ were undoubtedly dangerous and a menace to our community, we readily isolated and quarantined all those showing such germs, continuing to take culture until we succeeded in getting at least three successive negative cultures on alternate days from both nose and throat. A number of instances occurred where patients showed germs in the nasal secretions long after they disappeared from the throat, and one reason why we have tried to guard against these cases, was our conviction, based on the work of others (and particularly because of our own experience in the outbreaks that we have suffered here in the past), that germs left in the human system upon the mucous membrane, etc., even though degenerated and incapable of reproduction, may regain their virility, and again become capable of spreading the disease. We have thus far found no case of germ infection reappearing in the same case, except from new infection, after the disappearance of the germs from both throat and nose was established by the method referred to. I do not mean to claim that this test is absolute and that there may not be exceptions to this, as I can conceive that germs might exist in very small colonies isolated upon inaccessible portions of the mucous membrane, which might develop activity after the six days mentioned in connection with this culture taking method. Still, as this is the best result that we have been able to arrive at within comparatively narrow limits, it is given for the benefit of those who may wish to try it.

THYROID TREATMENT

The use of thyroid extract as a remedial agent in the treatment of insanity, has been continued in a few cases. Four women, who were becoming chronic and were regarded as very unfavorable cases for mental improvement, were given thyroid in increasing doses until the usual reaction was obtained. Two of the patients became much brighter, more active mentally and progressed favorably for two or three weeks, but after that time relapsed into the previous stuporous and indifferent state. The remaining two were not appreciably improved at any time.

PAINT

One of the matters that has been most firmly impressed upon us by reason of our having to contend with diphtheria at the hospitals for so long, is the necessity of abandoning the use of cheap preparations for the walls, and relying for wall coverings entirely upon paint. In fact, it would seem as if it was almost as necessary to have the same smooth surface as is obtained by the so-called porcelain paints that is always insisted upon for general hospitals. Our different investigations into the methods of disinfection show that wall paper and wall coverings of any kind which are partly porous are absolutely dangerous, and cases of infection have started up immediately after the use of rooms the walls and ceilings of which were covered with material of this nature, upon the first use of these rooms, after having, as we thought, been freed from infection, and although we had resorted to every known method of disinfection. Further confirmation of this lies also in the experience that we have had here in relation to the subsidence of erysipelas in wards where we had previously used kalsomine or other wall dressings. Here we have found a history, upon careful investigation among older employees, of cases of erysipelas appearing with quite a great deal of regularity over considerable extent of time. Probably when the matter was first looked into there had been an interval during which some protection had been afforded by something which had been placed upon the walls, but, upon having them carefully scraped and painted, all the seams being thoroughly filled, the base-boards removed, the walls plastered behind these boards to the floor, the floor itself being carefully dressed, etc., there has seldom been any reappearance in the rooms treated in this way; though, up to the time that we finally abandoned all dressings except paint, we had quite a number of cases recur in these rooms, without there being apparently any ascribable cause. My own experience has always been in favor of paint and of surfaces that were just as smooth as they could well be made on side walls and ceilings, but in the tendency to economize in order that institutions like ours can be maintained at the very lowest per capita, there is always a tendency for the different superintendents to become pitted against each other, in seeing how far they can go in different directions to reduce expenses. Some of the older institutions in this country show a very plain record of results of such tendencies in their annual reports.

MEDICAL MEETINGS

During the past year the same custom was pursued of having the medical staff met daily by either the first assistant physician or the medical superintendent, and bringing up the discussion of such medical or other matters as affected the welfare of the patients directly or indirectly, the discussion of special cases, and many other matters that would be of constant interest to us in the care of our cases, and we have also continued to maintain our medical society, meeting as a rule once a month, and having a certain number of especially prepared papers read and discussed. This past year our meetings were somewhat interfered with by various matters, still several regular meetings were held at which 20 papers were read and discussed and a number of cases presented. The medical meetings, though not at all largely attended by outsiders, were of great value, and many of the papers prepared were well up to the average of such papers, as are usually read at the meetings of other medical societies. The Journal Club of the hospital staff has continued to meet each two weeks, as in the past, and different members have at these occasions been assigned regular work in the culling over of the current medical journals, and the review of such special subjects, as they take, or are assigned to them so as to keep the different members in this way in close touch with what is being done in the various lines of interest to them.

AUTOPSIES

There were 28 autopsies made, and in many of these interesting and valuable observations were made, but we would have liked to have made more systematic and closer study and collection of data in some of these cases than has been entirely possible with the great amount of work that our medical staff has had in hand during the past year.

LABORATORY

The usual clinical work has been carried on, though in rather an incomplete way, because of the large amount of cultures and other work made necessary by the presence of diphtheria in the hospital, which has largely absorbed the energies of the laboratory assistants. Two, and for a time, three extra assistants were employed in this laboratory work by permission of the Lunacy Commission, two of them being physicians, and the others medical students.

MEDICAL LIBRARY

Seventy-seven volumes were added during the year, and the number of journals subscribed for was increased by three.

TRAINING SCHOOL FOR NURSES

During the past year 25 applicants were admitted to the school, and 8 were graduated. The school for nurses at this hospital has been handicapped considerably because of the amount of detailed work that it has been necessary to throw upon our ward attendants, and the constant changing in service that this has occasioned. Then, too, owing to commercial relations in the general community and other matters of this sort, there have been a large number of changes in the employees during the past year, there having been 179 resignations and dismissals.

The number of changes has even caused difficulty to us in filling the higher positions among the employees with those who have had sufficiently good and thorough training. While I believe that outside conditions have contributed quite a little to these results, still it is certain that the isolated condition of this institution and the lack of facilities for recreation and change, in the surroundings of the hospital, because of the lack of pleasant and healthful quarters for the nurses, or opportunities for diversion and amusement, except by going to some considerable distance from the hospital by cars, have had a great deal to do in producing this result. Some of the best nurses that we have had have very frankly told us when leaving that they had nothing whatever to complain of as far as the hospital was concerned, and were grateful for the opportunity which they had for studying and training themselves in nursing, etc., but the one plea we invariably do have, is that it was too lonely here for them to remain in such quiet surroundings. We must necessarily cope with this because of the peculiar location of the institution, but, it is to be hoped, that as time goes on, attractive attendants' homes with recreation rooms and sufficiently ample quarters, fitted up well enough to be pleasant and attractive will do much to offset this feeling.

The nurse's life, as everyone knows, is one round of tiring routine and the monotony of such existence is all the more marked when it is among the insane. We have done the most that was possible with the facilities at hand, to make the surroundings of the nurses as attractive as possible, and have done whatever seemed practicable in encouraging a proper interest in their work. A special library of books pertaining to nursing and allied subjects has been established during the past year, and now contains thirty-three volumes and has been very extensively used.

IMPROVEMENTS

In reporting on the matters that come under this caption, I wish to take advantage of the opportunity to state that during the past year, as in the year preceding, we have had to feel that as far as the resources of the Lunacy Commission are concerned, they have willingly cooperated, and the remarks that we have made concerning the necessary improvements which should be taken up, have not been intended to be taken as coming from the superintendent in any hypercritical spirit, but merely as a matter of record to draw attention to matters that much need attention at this hospital.

In an old institution like the Willard State Hospital, there is much that was built up on a standard that was ideal many years ago, but that does not now conform to modern ideas. Then, too, there are things which progressive institutions try to secure from year to year to increase their facilities or equipment that must be mentioned in lists of needs though it is not always expected that they can be obtained at once. All hospitals, as a rule, furnish data of this kind, and then try to follow them up as years go on, in order that the resulting institution, after the lapse of considerable time, may have such betterments and additional facilities as have from time to time been asked for, and the necessity of which has been made apparent. In this hospital the most trying necessities are a better supply of drinking water, better plumbing and improved sanitary conditions in general. After these are finally provided for, we come to minor improvements that it would be desirable to secure, and as large appropriations are often harder to obtain than smaller ones, an institution frequently succeeds in gradually getting small allotments, when it is very difficult to get large ones.

I would state in regard to the change in the water supply, that it has been our hope that we would be able to find water in this section which we could utilize in place of the lake water, and at one of the meetings of the board of managers a committee consisting of Managers Morris, Osborne and the superintendent were appointed to begin a study of the resources of the surrounding country, to see what could be done in this line. This work has been pursued uninterruptedly up to the present, and the work done by the committee was very materially enhanced by the assistance of the State geologist, Prof. Frederick J.H. Merrill, and one of the gentlemen connected with his department, Mr. E.C. Eckels, the State geologist very kindly allowing his assistant to come to the hospital on several different occasions, and make a careful survey of the geology of the section, with particular regard to its water carrying capacity. Our relations with these gentlemen have been of the pleasantest kind, and we desire to acknowledge the very ready cooperation that we have met from them.

The work of the water committee has tended to show that for a temporary source of water, comparatively shallow wells driven on the uplands would probably give us a supply during about nine months out of the twelve in the dryer seasons, but that in an exceedingly dry year or great drought, such as we have had this year, even these wells would be likely to fail because of the demand upon them, on account of the size of the institution, and that the only prospect of obtaining a supply other than by putting in a filtration system, would probably be met with by driving a deep well and going down through the different strata and testing each stream of water as it was met with, in order to see if a good supply of pure water might be obtained at considerable depth. To do this would be a very expensive experiment, but the necessities of the case entirely justify quite a considerable expense, with any possibility in view of getting good water. At the last meeting of the board of managers a resolution was passed requesting that the Lunacy Commission set aside for the digging of a test well, and the other work in connection with it, at least $5,000, the details of the method of digging, etc., being left for further consideration. It is thought that the proper way to do would be to sink either a 12-inch well, so as to have ample space for testing different supplies of water met with, or a 6-inch and going down and pumping at each level, carrying the casing by bad water, and stopping at sweet water wherever it is met with, this size pipe being considered amply large enough for all the immediate needs of the institution.

It is not necessary to refer to the lists of desirable additions to, or changes in the facilities and equipment of this hospital, as they have appeared in our reports of late years. They speak for themselves, and some of these matters have gradually been attended to, while many others remain to be done. To place this institution on the basis of a thoroughly modern institution in every respect would probably cost a good many thousand dollars, and it is to be hoped that the effort in this direction that has been persevered in the past will still be continued until this and all the institutions in this State stand among the best of their respective type in the land.

HOSPITAL REPORT

Early in the spring when the time came for us to take up the needs of the hospital, we had some small matters in hand which had been carried over from the preceding fall. The Lunacy Commission then called upon us for a list of such needs as it might be possible to attend to at that time, and at the time of their visit to the hospital, such a list was presented and gone over, and provisional allotments were made as far as they were willing to grant us funds. Under the arrangements in effect at that time, and those which were presented by reason of our having the provisional allotments referred to, the following named sums of money were expended for the purpose described opposite the expenditure, as follows:

SAND DOCK	268.54
REPAIRS TO MEDDICK AND VANVLEET HOUSES	159.96
CHANGE IN WATER SUPPLY	882.97
REBUILDING LOCOMOTIVE HOUSE	1,093.22
SCREENS FOR LABORATORY AND SHOPS	113.00
REPAIRS TO EMPLOYEES' HOME	452.68
NEW GUTTERS ON STORE AND REAR EAST BUILDINGS	242.04
ADDITIONAL LAUNDRY MACHINERY	1,197.20
STEAM CARVING TABLES	221.95
ADDITION TO 'HILLSIDE' FOR BOOTS, CLOTHING AND BATH ROOM	625.90
CEMENT WALK, MAIN BUILDING TO RAILROAD STATION	536.20
PAINTING OUTSIDE BUILDINGS	868.80
FOOD CAR, TRAINWAY TO KITCHEN	60.00
RESHINGLING GRAIN BARN AT 'HILLSIDE'	80.00
SPRAY BATH AT BRANCH AND INFIRMARY	31.80
FARM FENCE	244.40
STEAM HEATING PLANT AT HOTEL	72.95
SWITCHES TO LOCOMOTIVE HOUSE AND SCALES	32.90
TOTAL	$7,179.51

The list practically speaks for itself, but I draw attention to just a few matters. The sand dock has already been of a very great value to us, and four or five hundred cubic yards of sand, and quite a large supply of gravel, have been brought across the lake during the season for use at the hospital. The repairs to the Meddick house, which is now known as 'Hillside' enabled us, together with other appropriations which have since been made, to provide accommodations for twenty-five farm workers, outside of the regular buildings of the hospital. It had been hoped that we could have provided accommodations at the lake farm for between 30 or 40 patients additional, who could be utilized in the small fruit orchard and gardens that we have been establishing there, and had hoped to extend, but this work was brought to a standstill, and in all probability will not now be pushed for some time to come. We would not advocate these extensions as a matter of increasing the size of the hospital but rather in giving additional facilities in caring for the insane in a better and more profitable way, and reducing overcrowding in our main buildings.

Changes in the water supply as far as fire protection was concerned, were finally accomplished by putting in a very effective outside hydrant system, giving us 100 to 150 pounds pressure at the hydrants at most of our buildings. The old locomotive house was taken down and a new one has been built with the sum of money specified. The house is of brick and is 75 feet long by about 40 feet wide, and the reason for the small expenditure is that we had a great deal of old material that we used in the construction of the building. The building is now placed where it is not unsightly, and the old site will gradually be cleaned up and improved. The facilities for laundry work will be very materially improved by the addition of two machine washers and one new centrifugal wringer. The cement walk from the administration building to the railroad station has been a very much needed improvement, and we have apparently obtained a very fine piece of work, and visitors can now come dry shod from the station directly to our office.

The painting of the outside buildings, other than the main building, was begun, but this work will still take some time to complete. We found, on going over these old buildings, that some twelve years had elapsed since anything had been done upon them in the way of painting, and much more labor and material was necessary on this account then would otherwise have been the case, and various repairs were also necessitated by reason of rotten wood, etc. This work is still in progress and excellent headway is being made, although it is very slow, particularly by reason of the large number of windows that have to be gone over and the constant changing of swing scaffolds, etc. Repairs were made to the roofs of the buildings during the period specified, to the amount of about $400. We also built two silos and intend trying the use of silage for the dairy of the hospital. A new floor was placed in the ironing room of the laundry.

In the spring the question came up as to what we should do with the hotel near the lake, and this matter was referred to the president of the Lunacy Commission, who advised that inasmuch as there was no guarantee of there being sufficient business to pay any regular hotel keeper to keep the hotel open at his own expense and pay rent, we should make whatever terms we could with the party to whom we should give the hotel, and either employ him to run it for the hospital in order that the friends of patients from such a wide district as this hospital has, should have proper accommodations when they came here to visit their relatives, or else that we should remit all rent and make some kind of an arrangement to have the hotel run by some hotel proprietor on his own account. The hospital was very unwilling to make any provision which would make it responsible for the actual arrangements, and therefore an offer was made to the party having the hotel during the previous year to take the hotel and run it, and he agreed to do this if all the rent was remitted or waived to him, and if the hospital should make some arrangements during the season to heat the hotel properly so that when winter came this could be done by burning coal at one point and thus allowing him to save help. These matters were all brought before the board of managers, and such arrangements meeting with their approval, they were also brought before the Commission in Lunacy who also approved of them, and since the time referred to we have been working under this agreement which has thus far been fairly satisfactory.

I wish to say that I am particularly pleased to report one small matter, but one worthy of some attention, and that is, that during the past year we were able to get the Lehigh Valley railroad to change the name of the station formerly known as 'Willard' by naming it 'Gilbert,' after Captain Gilbert, who has been for so many years connected with the hospital. The name of the station at the hospital proper is also changed from 'Asylum' to 'Willard.' This change obviates a very annoying complication that has previously come from the wrong ideas that people got who wanted to come to the hospital from a distance, because of the peculiar name of these stations. Generally outsiders expected that the station known as 'Willard' was right at the hospital, and many of them would go there, not knowing it was over a mile away from the hospital, while the name 'Asylum' clinging to the locality years after the name of the institution itself had been changed to hospital, was something that we had long wished to have changed. The railroad has finally made the substitution in the name as described, and now those coming to Willard arrive at a little station that the railroad people built upon the grounds, only a short distance from the hospital, to which a cement walk leads directly.

NEEDS OF THE HOSPITAL

This fall the Commission notified the superintendent that when they visited the hospital they wished to have presented to them a list of such needs as the hospital would like to have considered by them during the coming year, and after careful consideration, and having referred the subject to one of the Board of Managers (almost all of these items have been before the Board itself at one time or another, either upon the direct representation of the superintendent at the meetings of the Board, or in the annual reports), a list was drawn incorporating some of the items that had previously been presented in the annual report, and this list was divided under the two heading of 'Needed' and 'Desirable.'

At the time of the visit of the said Commission these matters were all gone over with them carefully in detail, and the two members of the Commission who were present at the visitation agreed to incorporate such items as they were willing to endorse in the list of needs that would be presented to the Legislature this fall. It would seem to the superintendent that the bringing up of such matters in the fall, in anticipation of a session of the Legislature (instead of in the spring) was much more desirable than the method which has hitherto been followed, and, if these matters are brought in itemized form before the finance committee at the coming session, it is to be hoped that this hospital will receive substantial aid in getting some of the betterments that it has waited for a good many years to obtain. When these have been given us some of the other matters which have figured in previous lists, and which would be considered as desirable, can be brought forward.

As the minutes of the visitation of the Commissioners referred to immediately before will probably best give an idea of the matters that were brought to their attention and their view of the same, we will include the same hereafter in full. The remarks of the Commission which are placed opposite the items in the different lists will be printed immediately beneath each item as it occurs, and the full minutes of the visits of the Commissioners in the visiting book will be included as an appendix at the end of the report.

OVERCROWDING

There is very little to be said under this caption, other than what has appeared in previous reports. The conditions are virtually the same as they have been for the past two years, and, relatively, I suppose must continue as now, until the general condition of the State, as far as overcrowding is concerned in the State hospitals, is improved sufficiently to allow of materially lessening the numbers that are cared for in our principal wards. This overcrowding of the institution is probably more appreciated in the dining rooms and serving rooms than it is when one walks through the wards and sees them as they are usually made up and a few or none of the patients in bed. In four of our detached buildings we still continue to have to place tables in the day wards between the sleeping rooms and comparatively close to the water section, to avoid the most pernicious kind of overcrowding in the dining rooms, overcrowding that would mean the placing of the patients back to back, so that it would be utterly impossible for an attendant to pass between in order to serve the patients. This method of arrangement gives us quite tolerable results, but of course is not desirable when it can be overcome. Proper pantries and serving rooms were not planned for when the buildings were originally constructed, and apparently little attention was given to this subject in the way that it is now arranged for in any modern institution.

One of the worst ways in which overcrowding makes itself felt in institutions for the insane is in rendering it very difficult to separate from close contact with the well, those patients suffering from diseases of contagious or infectious character. We have met with great difficulties in fighting diphtheria at this hospital, on this account particularly as it was necessary to free one or two wards from the patients who ordinarily resided there, doubling them up in other wards, and thus giving room for detention wards in order to care for those whom it was necessary to isolate from the others, as no ordinary building built for infectious cases would be likely to be elastic enough to meet all of the requirements of an institution of this size. We have been fortunate in having a small quarantine station where membrane cases have been treated. This will accommodate in a pinch 12 or 15 beds.

Another extremely important matter in an institution of this kind to be considered in this connection is the presence of tuberculosis cases, and the facilities required for their proper care. This subject has already been touched upon in connection with remarks concerning the work of the medical staff, etc. For the sick and particularly for all such cases, proper facilities are always required, and with the tuberculosis patient, not only are ordinary comfortable surroundings necessary, but I think as much as anything, these surroundings should be such that they would have ample solarium space, which could be enclosed in summertime with screens to prevent flies and other insects from getting on them and possibly spreading the trouble. This matter has attracted our attention, particularly during the last very warm summer or two that we have had, and especially since much has been noted regarding the possibility of flies carrying disease germs.

MEDICAL STAFF

The following changes have occurred in the medical staff during the past year: Erving Holley, M.D., transferred from Manhattan State Hospital October 1st, to the position of junior assistant physician; William Steinach, M.D., resigned October 20th, Donald L. Ross, M.D., promoted to assistant physician October 21st, Albert G. Rising, M.D., appointed medical interne October 26th, Louis T. Waldo, M.D., appointed junior assistant physician at Hudson River State Hospital September 1st, Robert M. Andrews, M.D., appointed medical interne September 19th.

EMPLOYEES

The following changes have occurred among the employees during the past year: F.M. Hamlin, M.D., died March 19, 1900; W.J. McKee appointed Steward at Central Islip, left June 30th; J.X. Williams, transferred from Buffalo State Hospital to the position of bookkeeper.

ACKNOWLEDGMENTS

Religious services of visitation have been performed during the past year, and we desire to tender our thanks to Rev. H.A. Porter, Rev. C.W. McNish, Rev. Wesley Mason, Rev. Joseph W. Hendrick and Rev. J.A. Kennedy, all of Ovid.

During the latter portion of this year we were officially notified by the Assistant Secretary of the State Charities Aid Association of the appointment to this hospital as regular visitors for the said Association of Mrs. Clara E. Field of North Hector, N.Y., and the Rev. Robert Ellis Jones, President of Hobart College, Geneva, N.Y. Both Mrs. Field and Dr. Jones have already made several visits, and the relations sustained with them have been extremely pleasant. Several of the surgical operations have been performed by Dr. William B. Jones, of Rochester, N.Y., to whom the hospital is indebted for skillful service freely rendered.

SPECIAL ACKNOWLEDGMENTS

I desire again to particularly acknowledge the assistance and help that has been given to us by the New York city board of health, in connection with the work that we have done in fighting the epidemic of diphtheria at this hospital, and in particular to recognize the courtesy and kindness received, both for the institution and in a personal way, in this matter from Dr. Hermann M. Biggs and Dr. William H. Park.

OFFICIAL VISITS

The members of your Board and members of the State Commission in Lunacy have visited the hospital from time to time during the past year. Although a great many people visit the hospital first and last, and it hardly seems possible to make a record of visitors that would be of special importance because of this fact, and for the reason that many people come to the hospital without always making themselves known to us, we deem it well to follow the old custom of acknowledging the visits of the following: Hon. Otto Kelsey. Dr. Everett Flood, Epileptic Hospital, Palmer, Mass. Dr. Ernest Scribner, Superintendent, Worcester, Mass., insane asylum. Dr. H.E. Allison.

In conclusion I wish to express to your Board and through your Board to the Lunacy Commission, my appreciation of the treatment that has been accorded to me in this work during the past year. Very respectfully yours, WM. AUSTIN MACY *Medical Superintendent*" (46)

1901

By 1901, there were thirteen state hospitals for the insane in the State of New York.

"State Hospitals for the Insane. The State Hospitals for the care and custody of the insane are mainly supported from the proceeds of a general State tax for the maintenance and treatment of the insane, supplemented by moneys received for the maintenance of private patients. The managers of the several institutions are appointed by the Governor, by and with the advice and consent of the Senate."

"State Hospital Districts. By the provisions of chapter 126, Laws of 1890, as amended by chapter 545, Laws of 1896, the State Commission in Lunacy was given power to divide the State into State hospital districts.

Utica State Hospital District - Counties of Fulton, Hamilton, Herkimer, Montgomery, Oneida, Saratoga, Schenectady and Warren.

Hudson River State Hospital District - Counties of Albany, Columbia, Dutchess, Greene, Putnam, Richmond, Rensselaer, Washington and Westchester.

Middletown State Hospital District - Counties of Orange, Rockland, Sullivan and Ulster.

Buffalo State Hospital District - Counties of Erie and Niagara.

Willard State Hospital District - Counties of Allegany, Cayuga, Genesee, Ontario, Orleans, Schuyler, Seneca, Steuben, Tompkins, Wayne and Yates.

Binghamton State Hospital District - Counties of Broome, Chemung, Chenango, Cortland, Delaware, Madison, Otsego, Schoharie and Tioga.

St. Lawrence State Hospital District - Counties of Clinton, Essex, Franklin, Jefferson, Lewis, Onondaga, Oswego and St. Lawrence.

Rochester State Hospital District - Counties of Monroe and Livingston.

Long Island State Hospital District (Kings Park and Flatbush) - Counties of Kings, Queens, Nassau and Suffolk.

Manhattan State Hospital District (Manhattan East, Manhattan West, and Central Islip) - Counties of New York and Richmond.

Gowanda State Homoeopathic Hospital District - Counties of Cattaraugus, Chautauqua and Wyoming. (57)

1902

The Survey, Charity Organization Society of the City of New York

"It is difficult to understand how the expenditure for the insane can be reduced below what it was in 1900. As a matter of fact, the expense of maintaining the insane that year reached the lowest rate in the history of state care, a rate so low that the State Commission in Lunacy acknowledged that 'it must admit that economy has gone too far in some instances, notably in those supplies which are essential to the maintenance of a high sanitary condition of the hospitals.' In other words, economy had been carried to such an extreme that the health of the patients was endangered. An instance of this is seen in the case of the Willard State Hospital, where, during the past five and a half years, there have been 160 cases of diphtheria, supposed to be due largely to a defective water supply, poor plumbing, drainage and ventilation."

"One of the directions in which economy has been carried too far is the reduction of the working force of the state hospitals...Another example of excessive economy is to be found in the food supply... During the past year there have been periods when potatoes were considered too expensive to be allowed, and it was hard to convince patients who had been accustomed all their lives to eating potatoes every day that other articles of diet, because they contained similar nutritive values, would answer the purpose. Some hospitals bought 'culls' – little potatoes, ordinarily fed by farmers to their pigs, and in hard times sold in the market to the very poor. So with milk and eggs and meat. High market prices have meant deprivation to the patients in our state hospitals."

"The cost of the insane to the state is much discussed, but the income to the state from the insane is seldom mentioned. It is perhaps not generally known that the state hospitals do not derive any benefit from the money received from the board of reimbursing patients, from the sale of farm products, or from other sources of income. All this money goes into the state treasury for the benefit of the state at large. The receipts from private and reimbursing patients amount to nearly a quarter of a million dollars a year. About sixty per cent of the patients are engaged in some useful occupation. The estimated value of farm and garden products is over a quarter of a million dollars a year, while the estimated value of articles made or manufactured by patients is about the same amount." (47)

1904:

"With the approval of the State Commission in Lunacy, the names of the various buildings at Willard have been changed as follows:

Branch = Grand View; Meddick House = Hillside; Infirmary = Hermitage; DB 1 = The Maples; DB 2 = The Pines; DB 3 = Sunnycroft; DB 4 = Edgemere; North Cottage = Lake Farm; South Cottage = Vinelands; Main Building = Chapin House; Superintendent's House = Brookside; Farm House = The Grange; Steward's House = Bleak House; Isolation Hospital = The Rookery." (48)

LAWS

Law A: 1824 – An Act To Provide For The Establishment Of County Poorhouses.

Chapter 331, Laws of 1824, Passed 27th November 1824.

I. *Be it enacted by the People of the State of New York, represented in Senate and Assembly,* That it shall be the duty of the board of supervisors of each county in this State (the counties of Genesee, Yates, Greene, Washington, Rensselaer, Queens, Essex, New York, Montgomery, Suffolk, Schoharie, Chautauqua, Cortland, Dutchess, Orange, Allegany, Richmond, Monroe, Sullivan, Cattaraugus, Kings, Putnam, Delaware, Franklin, Oswego, Otsego, Columbia, St. Lawrence, Rockland, Albany, Tompkins, Tioga, Schenectady, Seneca, Madison, Onondaga, Oneida and Ulster, excepted), at their next meeting after the passing of this act, to direct the purchase of one or more tracts of land, not exceeding the quantity of two hundred acres, and thereon build and erect for the accommodation, employment and use of the said county, one or more suitable buildings, to be denominated the poorhouse of the county of _____ and to defray the expense of such purchase and building, raise by tax on estates real and personal, of the freeholders and inhabitants of the same county, a sum not exceeding the sum of seven thousand dollars, by such installments and at such times as may be ordered by the board of supervisors, to be assessed and collected in the same manner as the other county charges are assessed and collected, which money, when collected, shall be paid over by the treasurer of said county to said supervisors, or such persons as they shall for that purpose designate, to be applied to defraying the expenses aforesaid.

II. *And be it further enacted,* That it shall be the duty of the supervisors of said county, at their meeting on the first Tuesday of October, annually, to choose and appoint, by plurality of votes, not less than five persons, who shall be denominated superintendents of the poorhouse of the county of who shall, until the first Tuesday of October next thereafter, take upon themselves, and have the exclusive charge, management, direction and superintendence of said poorhouse, and of everything relating to the same: and shall and may, from time to time, with the approbation and consent of a majority of the judges of the county courts of such county, make, ordain and establish such prudential rules, regulations and by-laws, for the well ordering of the same, and the employment, relief, management and government of the persons therein placed, and the officers and servants therein employed, and the correction of the refractory, disobedient and disorderly, by solitary confinement therein, and feeding them on bread and water only, as they shall deem expedient for the good government of the same; and shall and may, from time to time, appoint and employ a suitable person to be keeper of the same house, and necessary servants under him, and the same keeper and servants remove at pleasure, or otherwise, if they shall deem it more advisable; and it shall be lawful for the said superintendents to contract with some suitable person for the support of those persons who are placed in said poor house, who shall give a bond to said superintendents, with sufficient sureties, for the faithful performance of his contract, and who shall and may be authorized to employ the persons so committed to his charge, in like manner as if he was appointed keeper of said poorhouse.

III. *And be it further enacted*, That whenever, after the said poorhouse shall be completed, any poor person in any city or town of the same county shall apply for relief, the said overseer of the poor of such city or town shall make application to a justice of the peace of said county, which said justice and overseer shall enquire into the state and circumstances of the person so applying for relief as aforesaid; and if it shall appear to the said justice and overseer of the poor, that such person is in such indigent circumstances as to require relief, it shall be their duty (unless the sickness of the pauper prevent) instead of ordering relief in the manner directed in and by the twenty-fifth section of the act entitled "An act for the relief and settlement of the poor," to issue his warrant under his hand, directed to any constable of such city or town, whose duty it shall be to execute the same, thereby requiring said constable forthwith to take such poor person so applying for relief, and remove him or her to said poorhouse, and there deliver him or her to the care of the keeper of the same house, to be relieved and provided for as his or her necessities shall require; and he or she shall be discharged therefrom by order of the superintendents of the same house, or some one of them. *And further*, That in case the said superintendent, by a resolution to be passed by a majority of the board, shall give permission, and so long and no longer, as such permission shall be continued, it shall and may be lawful for any justice of the peace of said county, whenever a disorderly person, under or within the meaning of the act entitled "An act for apprehending and punishing disorderly persons," instead of the punishment directed by the same act, by warrant under his hand and seal, to commit such disorderly person or persons to said poorhouse, into the custody of the keeper thereof, there to be kept at hard labor for any time not exceeding six months, unless sooner discharged therefrom by order of such superintendents or a majority of them; in which warrant it shall be sufficient to state and set forth generally, that such person has been duly convicted of being a disorderly person, without more particular specification of the offence.

IV. *And be it further enacted*, That it shall and may be lawful for the overseers of the poor of any town or city in said county, to take up any child under the age of fifteen years, who shall be permitted to beg or solicit charity from door to door, or in any street or highway of such city or town, and carry or send him or her to said poorhouse, there to be kept and employed, and instructed in such useful labor as he or she shall be able to perform, and supported until discharged therefrom by order of said superintendents, whose duty it shall be to discharge such child as soon as he or she shall be able to provide for himself or herself.

V. *And be it further enacted*, That it shall be lawful for the keeper of said poorhouse, to require and compel all persons committed to his care or custody in the same by virtue of this act, to perform such work, labor and service, towards defraying the expense of their maintenance and support, as they shall severally be able to perform, or said superintendent shall from time to time direct; and in case any such person shall neglect or refuse to perform the work, labor and service required of him or her, or shall at any time refuse or neglect any rule, regulation or by-law which, shall as aforesaid be made and established by said superintendents, for the well ordering and government of the persons committed or placed in said poorhouse, or shall at any time depart therefrom, until he or she shall be regularly and duly dismissed and discharged therefrom; in each and every such case, it shall and may be lawful for the keeper of the same house, to place and keep each and every such person in solitary confinement in some part of the same house, and feed him, her or them, with bread and water only, until he or she shall submit to perform the same labor, work and service, and obey, conform and observe the rules, regulations and by-laws aforesaid; or for such time as said keeper shall judge proportioned to his or her respective offence or offences: *Provided however*, That every such person who shall think himself or herself aggrieved by the conduct of such keeper towards them, may and shall be permitted to make his or her complaint to said superintendents, or any one of them, who shall immediately examine into the grounds of such complaint, and make such order and direction in the case as to him or them shall appear fit and proper; which order shall be final and conclusive in the case.

VI. *And be it further enacted*, That the expense of supporting and maintaining such persons as shall or may be sent to or placed in said poorhouse pursuant to the provisions of this act, and all expenses incident to keeping, maintaining and governing said poorhouse, shall be a charge upon said county; and it shall and may be lawful for the supervisors of said county, to cause such sum as shall remain unpaid at the end of each year, and may be necessary to defray the same expenses, to be annually assessed and collected by a tax on the estates, real and personal, of the freeholders and inhabitants of the same county, in the proportion to the number and expenses of paupers the several towns respectively shall have in the said poorhouse; which monies, when collected, shall be paid by the collectors of the several cities and towns in the said county, into the hands of the treasurer of such county, subject to the orders of said superintendents, to be by them applied to the paying and defraying of the same expenses.

VII. *And be it further enacted*, That the said superintendent may, at the expense of said county, from time to time, purchase and procure such raw materials to be wrought and manufactured by the persons in said poorhouse; and shall and may at all times sell and dispose of the produce of the labor of the same persons, in such manner as they shall judge conducive to the interests of said county; and it shall be the duty of the said superintendents annually, at the meeting of the supervisors of said county, on the first Tuesday of October in each year, to account with the board of supervisors of the said county, for all monies by them received and expended as such superintendents, and pay over any such monies remaining in their hands, as such superintendents, unexpended, to the superintendents who shall then be chosen and appointed in their stead.

VIII. *And be it further enacted*, That no person shall be removed as a pauper, out of any city or town, to any other city, town or county, by any order of removal and settlement; but the county where such person shall become sick, infirm and poor, shall support him; and if he be in sufficient health to gain a livelihood, and still become a beggar or vagrant, then he shall be treated as a disorderly person: *Provided*, That nothing herein contained shall prevent the removal of any pauper from one city or town to any other city or town in the same county.

IX. *And be it further enacted*, That if any person or persons shall hereafter send, carry or transport, or cause to be sent, carried or transported, any pauper or paupers, or other poor and indigent person or persons, from and out of any town in any county of this State, into any town in any other county, with intent to charge such other town or county with the maintenance and support of such pauper or paupers, poor and indigent persons, such offense shall be deemed and adjudged a misdemeanor; and such person or persons so offending, on conviction thereof before any court of competent jurisdiction, be punished, by fine in a sum not exceeding one hundred dollars, or imprisonment for a term not exceeding six months, or both, in the discretion of said court.

X. *And be it further enacted*, That if any board of supervisors, or a majority of them, in any of those counties heretofore excepted, shall, at any of their annual meetings hereafter, determine that it will be beneficial to their county to erect a county poorhouse, that by filing such determination with the clerk of said county, they shall be at liberty to avail themselves of the provisions of this act. (49)

Law B: 1865 - Laws Relating To The Willard Asylum For The Insane.

Chapter 342, Session Laws of 1865. Passed April 8, 1865. An Act to authorize the establishment of a State asylum for the chronic insane, and for the better care of the insane poor, to be known as 'The Willard Asylum for the Insane.' The trustees of the Willard Asylum for the Insane shall have all the rights and powers, and be subject to the same duties in said asylum, as are now possessed by and imposed upon the board of managers of the State Lunatic Asylum at Utica. Said trustees shall also fix the rate per week, not exceeding two dollars, for the board of patients. It shall further be the duty of said trustees, as soon as portions of said asylum are completed and ready for the reception of the insane, to designate, in a just and equitable manner, and with the approval of the Governor, the counties from which the chronic pauper insane shall be sent to said asylum, as part of the room shall be ready, from time to time, for the reception of patients. (50)

Law C: 1871 – Chapter 713 - An Act In Relation To The Chronic Pauper Insane.

Passed April 25, 1871; three-fifths being present. *The People of the State of New York represented in Senate and Assembly do enact as follows:*

SECTION 1. The board of State Commissioners of Public Charities are hereby authorized to hear and determine all applications which may be made to them in writing, by the county superintendents of the poor of the several counties of this State, for exemption from the operation of the tenth section of the act entitled "An act to authorize the establishment of a State asylum for the chronic insane, and for the better care of the insane poor," to be known as "The Willard Asylum for the Insane," passed April eighth, eighteen hundred and sixty-five. And whenever said board on such application shall determine that the buildings and means employed to take care of the chronic pauper insane of such county are sufficient and proper for the time being for such purpose, and shall file the same in the office of the clerk of the county making such application, then and in that case, and until such determination shall be revoked as hereinafter mentioned and provided, the county superintendents of the poor of such county shall be relieved from sending the chronic pauper insane of such county to the Willard Asylum for the Insane, as now provided by law. Said board may at any time revoke such determination, but such revocation must be made in writing, and filed in the county clerk's office of the county making such application, and notice thereof shall be given in writing to the county superintendents of the poor of such county, and upon the filing of the same the said county superintendents of the poor of such county shall from thenceforward be again subject to the provisions and operations of the said act.

SECTION 2. The board of State Commissioners of Public Charities are hereby authorized and required, whenever they shall be satisfied that the provisions made for the chronic insane in any county poor-house is inadequate and unsuitable, to direct the superintendents of the poor of such county to remove the chronic insane of that county to the Willard Asylum for the Insane within ten days after receiving a written or printed notice to make such removal.

SECTION 3. This act shall take effect immediately. (51)

Law D: 1874 – Laws Relating To The Insane, Chapter 446, Laws of 1874; Commitment of the

Insane, Title First, Article First.

Section 1. No person shall be committed to or confined as a patient in any asylum, public or private, or in any institution, home or retreat for the care and treatment of the insane, except upon the certificate of two physicians under oath, setting forth the insanity of such person. But no person shall be held in confinement in any such asylum for more than five days, unless within that time such certificate be approved by a judge or justice of a court of record of the county or district in which the alleged lunatic resides, and said judge or justice may institute inquiry and take proofs as to any alleged lunacy before approving or disapproving of such certificate, and said judge or justice may, in his discretion, call a jury in each case to determine the question of lunacy.

Section 2. It shall not be lawful for any physician to certify to the insanity of any person for the purpose of securing his commitment to an asylum, unless said physician be of reputable character, a graduate of some incorporated medical college, permanent resident of the State, and shall have been in the actual practice of his profession for at least three years, and such qualifications shall be certified to by a judge of any court of record. No certificate of insanity shall be made, except after a personal examination of the party alleged to be insane, and according to forms prescribed by the State Commissioner of Lunacy, and every such certificate shall bear date of not more than ten days prior to such commitment.

Section 5. The county superintendents of the poor of any county or town, to which any person shall be chargeable, who shall be, or shall become a lunatic, may send any such person to any State lunatic asylum by an order under their hands, and in compliance with the provisions of this act. (50)

Relating To The Willard Asylum For The Insane. Title IV, Article Third, Chapter 446, Laws of

1874.

Section 2. Said trustees shall have all the rights, privileges and powers, and be subject to the same duties, in said asylum, as are now possessed by and imposed upon the board of managers of the State Lunatic Asylum at Utica. Said trustees shall also fix the rate per week, not exceeding the actual cost of support and attendance, exclusive of officers' salaries, for the board of patients. It shall further be the duty of said trustees, as portions of said asylum are completed and ready for the reception of the insane, to designate, in a just and equitable manner, and with the approval of the Governor, the counties from which the chronic pauper insane shall be sent to said asylum, as parts of the room shall be ready, from time to time, for the reception of patients except as hereinafter provided.

Section 10. The chronic pauper insane from the poor-houses of the counties that shall be designated, as provided in section two, of this article, shall be sent to the said asylum by the county superintendents of the poor, and all chronic insane pauper patients who may be discharged not recovered from State lunatic asylums, and who continue a public charge, shall be sent to the Asylum for the Insane hereby created; and all such patients shall be a charge upon the respective counties from which they are sent. And all the chronic insane paupers of the several counties of the State shall be sent to said asylum by the superintendents of the poor, except from those counties having asylums for the insane, to which they are now authorized to send such insane patients by special legislative enactments, or such counties as have been, or may hereafter be exempted by the State Board of Charities. (50)

Law E: 1877 - EXHIBIT M.

Rules and Regulations Established by the State Board of Charities for the Government of County Insane Asylums Exempt From the Operation of the Tenth Section of The Willard Asylum Act, As Provided by Chapter 713 of The Laws of 1871. Adopted October 16, 1877.

1. Medical Supervision. The proper authorities of each and every such county insane asylum, in which the number of insane persons detained therein shall be less than one hundred, shall appoint a physician to such asylum, acceptable to the Commissioner of the State Board of Charities of the district in which the asylum is situated, who shall be designated the visiting physician of such asylum, and who shall visit the wards and rooms occupied by the insane of the institution, daily, and as much oftener as in his judgment the welfare and comfort of the insane may require. In every such county insane asylum, where there are more than one hundred insane persons detained therein, the proper authorities of such county shall appoint a physician to such asylum, acceptable to the commissioner of the district in which the asylum is situated, who shall be designated the resident physician of such asylum, and who shall not only visit the wards and rooms occupied by the insane, daily, but whose whole time shall be at the service of said authorities as may be required. Said authorities are hereby required to erect or provide, as soon as the same can conveniently be done, suitable dwelling and office accommodations, in order that the resident physician can reside with his family, either in or contiguous to the asylum for the insane. The commissioner of the district has power to waive the requirement of the physician residing in said asylum, for one current year, in case he is of the opinion that the visiting physician, so appointed, can satisfactorily perform the duty required. The visiting physician, or the resident physician so appointed, shall be the chief medical officer of such asylum, and shall have the medical supervision and treatment of all insane persons committed thereto, and he shall make requisition for, and have the control and distribution of the medical supplies, hospital stores and other appliances, for the treatment of the insane in such asylum.

2. Attendants. The proper authorities of each and every such county asylum shall appoint a properly educated chief male attendant, and a chief female attendant, to be acceptable to the visiting or resident physician thereof, and commissioner of the district, and the number of attendants in each and every such county insane asylum, for either sex, shall equal one to every twenty insane persons or fractional part thereof, exceeding one-half that number, in any ward of such asylum; provided that no pauper or other inmate of any poor-house or alms-house shall be appointed such attendant, and provided also that the appointment of such attendants shall be approved of by the visiting or resident physician of such asylum, and that they shall subscribe and agree to maintain the rules and regulations thereof.

3. Diet, Clothing, Classification, Restraint, Amusement, Occupation, etc., for the Insane. The proper authorities for each and every such county asylum shall, within three months, with the approval of the visiting or resident physician thereof, and the written concurrence of the commissioner of the district in which the asylum is situated, establish rules and regulations, upon the following and such other points as they may deem advisable relating to such asylum, which rules and regulations so for as practicable, shall conform to the rules and regulations now in force at the State Lunatic Asylum at Utica, or the Willard Asylum for the Insane at Ovid, viz.:

1. As to the diet of the insane.
2. As to the special diet for the sick and infirm.
3. As to the clothing of the insane.
4. As to classification.
5. As to the means of restraint, by whom and when to be employed, how long continued, etc.
6. As to amusements for the insane.
7. As to the occupation of the insane.
8 As to the duties of the attendants.
9. As to the duties of the chief male attendant, which are intended to include those now performed by the supervisors and third physician at said State asylum; and he shall also keep such record of the number, condition and treatment of the insane, under the direction of the visiting or resident physician, or proper authorities of the asylum, as the board of supervisors, or the State Board of Charities may require.
10. As to the duties of the chief female attendant, which are intended to include those of the matron in said State asylum, and such other duties as may be required.
11. As to the sanitary condition of the asylum buildings and grounds. (39)

Law F: The State Care Act

AN ACT to promote the care and curative treatment of the pauper and indigent insane in the counties of this state, except New York, Kings and Monroe counties, and to permit said excepted counties or either of them, in accordance with the action of their respective local authorities, to avail themselves or any one or more of them, of the provisions of this act. Approved by the Governor April 15, 1890. Passed three-fifths being present. *The People of the State of New York, represented in Senate and Assembly, do enact as follows:*

Section 1. The state shall be divided into as many asylum districts as hereinafter defined as there are state insane asylums in this state, and the state commissioners in lunacy, the president of the state board of charities, and the comptroller of the state, and their successors in office, shall constitute a board to be known and designated as the "board for the establishment of state insane asylum districts and other purposes," said board is hereby empowered and directed to proceed without unnecessary delay to define the boundaries of the several districts into which the state shall be divided provided; however, that no county shall be divided in such classification, and that not more than one of the existing state asylums be embraced in any one district...

Section 2. ... Whenever a new state asylum is established a number of pauper or indigent patients or both shall be assigned to it, such number to be determined by the state commission in lunacy, whereupon said asylum shall be deemed to be embraced within and governed by the provisions of this act in all respects so far as the same may be applicable; and whenever any new state asylum shall be established, the said board is hereby required to divide the state again into districts in compliance with the provisions of this act.

Section 3. In order to carry out the intention of this act, the state commission in lunacy is directed to ascertain from time to time, what vacancies, if any, exist in any one or more of the state insane asylums, and said commission is hereby authorized and required to forthwith cause the removal to such asylum or asylums, from some one or more of the counties of the district to which said asylum has been assigned, under the provisions of this act, as many of the pauper and indigent insane patients as can be accommodated. Such removal to be made pursuant to the provisions of section six of this act.

Section 4. To provide for the pauper and indigent insane of the district in which each state asylum is situated, should the existing accommodations not be sufficient for this purpose, there shall be erected on the grounds of such asylum a sufficient number of buildings of a moderate size, each being designed to accommodate not less than ten nor more than one hundred and fifty patients...

Section 5. After receiving such certificate from said managers or trustees, the said chairman of the state commission in lunacy shall ascertain whether the buildings are ready for occupancy, and if he finds them to be ready, he shall forthwith direct the superintendents of the poor in each county within the district, in which said state asylum so certified is situated, to send such number of pauper or indigent insane patients to said state asylum as can be therein accommodated. Each of the state asylums for the insane shall receive patients, whether in an acute or chronic condition of insanity, from the district in which the asylum is situated, subject to the power of removal from one state asylum to another under the provisions of section eight of this act.

Section 6. All county superintendents of the poor, or town, county or city authorities, sending a patient to any asylum under the provisions of this act shall, before sending him, see that he is in a state of bodily cleanliness, and is comfortably clothed in accordance with regulations to be prescribed by the chairman of the state commission of lunacy. The said patients shall be sent by said county superintendents of the poor, or town, county or city authorities, in a manner prescribed by said chairman, to the state asylum within the district embracing said county at the expense of the state, and any state asylum to which said patient is to be sent may be required, by and under the regulations made by said chairman, to send a trained attendant to bring the patient to the asylum. In all cases there shall be provided a female attendant for every female patient, unless she be accompanied by her husband, father, brother or son. After said patient or patients has or have been delivered to the managers or trustees of said asylum, the care and custody of the county authorities over said insane persons cease. The bills for the reasonable expenses incurred in the transportation of patients to the state asylums, after they have been approved in writing by the state commission in lunacy, shall be paid by the treasurer of the state on the warrant of the comptroller from funds provided for the support of the state asylums.

Section 7. After sufficient accommodations shall have been provided in state institutions for all the pauper and indigent insane of all the counties of the state, the expense of the custody, care, maintenance, treatment and clothing of pauper and indigent insane patients in state insane asylums shall not be a charge upon any county after first of October next ensuing, but the cost of the same shall be out of the funds provided by the state for the support of the insane.

Section 8. In case the buildings of any state asylum shall at any time become overcrowded in carrying out the provisions of this act, or number of said buildings be reduced by fire or other casualty, the chairman of the state commission in lunacy is hereby empowered in his discretion to cause the transfer of patients therefrom to another state asylum, where they can be conveniently received, or to make, in special emergencies, temporary provision for their care, and all expenditures under this section shall be chargeable to the state, and paid out of any appropriation made to carry out the provisions of this act.

Section 9. Whenever in any district, established under the provisions of this act, the buildings now existing and erected as herein provided for the use of the pauper or indigent insane shall be filled with patients to their full capacity, the managers or trustees thereof shall not receive further patients until vacancies occur, or new or additional accommodations are provided, and then only to the extent of the accommodation supplied... The expenses of the transfer of said pauper patients to said asylum beyond the limits of the district where the patient is regularly to be cared for, shall be chargeable to the state, and the bills for the same, when approved by the state commission in lunacy, shall be paid by the treasurer of the state on the warrant of the comptroller out of any moneys appropriated to carry out the provisions of this act. In case any insane person, his relatives, guardians or friends may desire that he may become an inmate of any state asylum situated beyond the limits of the district where he resides, and there be sufficient accommodation there to receive him, he may be received there in the discretion of the chairman of the state commission in lunacy and the superintendent of such asylum. Any expense of removal, in such case, must be borne by the insane person's guardians, relatives or friends, as the case may be.

Section 10. The state commission in lunacy, whenever it shall deem it necessary and expedient, by reason of overcrowding, or in order to prevent the same shall, in its annual report to the governor, recommend the erection of such additional buildings on the grounds of any or all state asylums then existing as shall, in the judgment of said commission, provide sufficient accommodations for the immediate prospective wants of the insane of this state; or, if said commission deem it more expedient, it shall recommend the establishment of another state asylum or asylums in such part of the state as in its judgment will best meet the requirement of the pauper and indigent insane.

Section 11. It is the intent and meaning of this act that, when and after the state shall have been divided into districts, as herein provided, and sufficient accommodations in state institutions shall have been provided for all the pauper and indigent insane of all the counties of the state, and certified, as set forth in the seventh section of this act, no insane person shall be permitted to remain under county care, but that all the insane who are now, or may hereafter become a public charge, shall be transferred to the respective state asylums without unnecessary delay, there to be regarded and known as the wards of the state, and to be wholly supported by the state.

Section 12. The state commission in lunacy shall hereafter furnish the comptroller, on or before the fifteenth day of September in each year, an estimate of the probable number of patients who will become inmates of the respective state asylums during the year beginning October first next ensuing, and the cost of the additional buildings and equipment, if any, which will be required to carry out the provisions of this act...

Section 13. The foregoing provisions of this act shall not apply to or include the counties of New York, Kings or Monroe, nor embrace the state asylum for insane criminals at Auburn, nor the state asylum for insane criminals at Matteawan, nor the state asylum for insane emigrants, on Ward's Island, in New York city, or any of them, except as provided in the succeeding section of this act, nor shall it be construed to affect those provisions of existing statutes by which the three counties aforesaid are now permitted to send their acute and chronic insane to state asylums.

Section 14. Whenever the counties of New York, Kings and Monroe, or any one of them, desire to be included in the provisions of this act, application may be made in writing to the governor, by the respective county or local authorities in either of said counties, to transfer any or all of such buildings, land, appurtenances and equipment as are used by them as county insane asylums to the state for the same purpose, upon such terms and conditions as may be specified in such application...

Section 15. The word "insane," as used in this act, shall be construed to include all persons of unsound mind except idiots.

Section 16. When this act goes into effect, no county shall be exempted either by the state board of charities or the state commission in lunacy from the provisions of this act under any existing law; and all exemptions heretofore granted by said board or said state commission in lunacy, under the provisions of chapter seven hundred and thirteen of the laws of eighteen hundred and seventy-one, or of acts amendatory of the same, or under any existing law, and exemptions granted by chapter three hundred and sixty of the laws of eighteen hundred and seventy-seven, and by chapter three hundred and sixty of the laws of eighteen hundred and eighty-eight shall be revoked and cease.

Section 17. No insane person now or hereafter under the care of any state asylum in this state shall be returned or committed to the care of the superintendent of the poor of any county, or to any other county, town or city authorities; and the said county superintendents, and county, town and city authorities, are hereby forbidden to receive any such patient who may be returned or committed to them in violation of this section. The foregoing provisions of this section shall not apply to the superintendents of the poor, or the county, town or city authorities, of the counties named in section thirteen of this act.

Section 18. None of the provisions of this act shall restrain or abridge the power and authority of the supreme court of the state over the persona and property of the insane.

Section 19. The reasonable expenses of the board created by this act and of the state commission in lunacy for necessary clerical assistance, traveling and other incidental expenses incurred by said board and said commission in carrying out the provisions of this act shall be paid by the treasurer of the state on the warrant of the comptroller out of any moneys appropriated for the purposes of this act.

Section 20. All acts and parts of acts inconsistent with this act are hereby repealed.

Section 21. This act shall take effect immediately. (52)

Law G – The Insanity Law.

This bill became chapter 545 of the Laws of 1896. Revisers' Note Explanatory Of The Insanity Law. This chapter of the revision prescribes the powers of the State Commission in Lunacy; the organization, management and control of State hospitals for the insane; the commitment, care and treatment of the insane; the management of the State hospitals for insane criminals; and the transfer of such criminals thereto and their discharge therefrom.

The last general revision of the laws relating to the custody, care and treatment of the insane was contained in chapter 446 of the Laws of 1874. This act provided for the commitment of the insane to State asylums and their support therein at the expense of relatives or the municipality from which they were committed. The laws relating to the management of the Utica State Asylum were incorporated in article 3 of this act. Other articles provided respectively for the management of the Willard Asylum, the Hudson River State Hospital, the Buffalo State Asylum and the State Homeopathic Asylum for the Insane at Middletown, and many of the provisions of the article regulating the control of the Utica State Asylum were made applicable to such institutions. Since the passage of that act, the Binghamton asylum has been established by chapter 280 of the Laws of 1879; St. Lawrence State Asylum, by chapter 375 of the Laws of 1887; Rochester State Hospital, by chapter 338 of the Laws of 1891; Collins Farm State Hospital, by chapter 777 of the Laws of 1894; Long Island State Hospital, by chapter 628 of the Laws of 1895.

All these acts are similar. The number of the managers and their terms of office vary in the several State hospitals, but such managers and the superintendents and other officers possess like powers. In article 3 of the revision, we have inserted a section making the number of managers uniform for all the State hospitals, with a uniform term of office. In such article we have also included general provisions relating to all State hospitals and to the powers and duties of the managers and officers, their salaries, the purchase of supplies, and all other matters pertaining to the control of these institutions.

Very many of the requirements contained in the general act of 1874 supplementary thereto, are obsolete, because of more recent legislation. By chapter 132 of the Laws of 1890, the names of the several State asylums were changed to State hospitals. By chapter 126 of the Laws of 1890, all indigent insane persons are to be supported by the State in the several State hospitals. This act, known as the 'State Care Act,' revolutionized the method of caring for the insane. Prior thereto the counties were chargeable with the cost of the maintenance of such insane persons as became public charges. They were confined in the several country almshouses, or in the State asylums, if the condition of the insane person warranted his treatment therein.

The present State Commission in Lunacy was created by chapter 283 of the Laws of 1889, which act was amended as a whole by chapter 273 of the Laws of 1890. The commission superseded the commissioner appointed by the act of 1874. The assumption by the State of the care of insane persons made it necessary to greatly extend the powers of the commissions. They became a supervising body, vested with the power to direct the method of caring for and treating all insane persons.

In view of the great amount of money annually expended by the State for the support of the insane, the Legislature, by chapter 214 of the Laws of 1893, provided a system for the careful supervision of expenditures by the Commission in Lunacy and the Comptroller. The superintendents of the several State hospitals are thereby required to make monthly itemized estimates to the commission, of the amount of money required for the purchase of supplies and payment of salaries, wages, etc., for the ensuing month, which are revised by the commission, and warrants are drawn by the Comptroller upon the State Treasurer in accordance with such revised estimates. All the essentials of this system are re-enacted in this revision.

Additional powers have been imposed upon the State Commission in Lunacy, many of them contained in laws making appropriations for the support of the State hospitals, notably chapter 358 of the Laws of 1894, page 719, and chapter 693 of the Laws of 1895. The general provisions contained in these acts applicable to the subject-matter of this chapter of the revision have been inserted in the proper places.

The acts of 1890, and the acts passed since that time, do not specifically repeal any part of the consolidated law of 1874, but all inconsistent provisions are doubtless superseded. It is difficult to determine the precise effect of the later development of the law upon the former legislation. The changes wrought by the later acts justify a complete revision of the laws relating to the care and treatment of the insane.

In this chapter we have endeavored to preserve the law as it is; striking out all inconsistent provisions, and all matter which the recently adopted system of caring for the insane has made nugatory. Changes have been made, which are noted with reasons therefor, at the end of the sections thereby affected.

The following are the material changes made in the revision:

1. State hospital districts are to be established by the Commission in Lunacy, instead of by the commissioners, State Board of Charities and Comptroller. (See note to Section 10.)
2. The number of managers of the State hospitals and their terms of office are made uniform. (See note to Section 31.)
3. The requirement of a 'commissioner's visiting book' to be kept by the authorities of the several institutions, is omitted. (See note to Section 47.)
4. No person is to be committed to an institution for the care and treatment of the insane, except upon an order of a judge of a court of record. Such order is to be granted upon a verified petition, and a certificate of lunacy, signed by two medical examiners, after notice to the alleged insane person, or some person in his behalf, to be designated by the court. A hearing may be had by the judge to whom the application is made, in his discretion, or upon the demand of some relative or friend of the alleged insane person. (See Sections 60-63 and notes thereto.)
5. It is proposed that no insane person shall be confined in a prison, jail or lockup, unless he is dangerous and no other suitable place for his confinement can be had. (See note to Section 69.)
6. A change is made in the method of transfer of an insane criminal from penal institutions to the State hospital for insane criminals. By the present law the transfer is made upon the certificate of the physician of the institution. It is proposed that the question of insanity be determined by legally qualified medical examiners in a manner similar to that required in the commitment of insane persons to State hospitals. (See note to Section 97.)

The table at the end hereof shows the disposition of the sections of the present laws which are to be repealed by this chapter.

THE INSANITY LAW. AN ACT in relation to the insane, constituting chapter twenty-eight of the general laws. Became a law May 12, 1896, with the approval of the Governor. Passed, three fifths being present.

THE INSANITY LAW. ARTICLE I.

State Commission in Lunacy. (Sections 1 - 16)

Section 1. Short title. - This chapter shall be known as the insanity law.

Section 2. Definitions. - When used in this chapter, the term poor person means a person who is unable to maintain himself and having no one legally liable and able to maintain him; the term, an indigent person, means one who has not sufficient property to support himself while insane, and the members of his family lawfully dependent upon him for support; the term institution means any hospital, asylum, building, buildings, house or retreat, authorized by law to have the care, treatment or custody of the insane; the term commission means the state commission in lunacy; the term patient means an insane person committed to an institution according to the provisions of this chapter. (New.)

Section 3. Appointment, qualifications, terms of office and salaries of commissioners. - There shall continue to be a state commission in lunacy, consisting of three commissioners, all of whom shall be citizens of this state. One of them, who shall be president of the commission, shall be a reputable physician, a graduate of an incorporated medical college, of at least ten years' experience in the actual practice of his profession, who has had five years' actual experience in the care and treatment of the insane and who has had experience in the management of institutions for the insane. He shall receive an annual salary of five thousand dollars. One of such commissioners shall be a reputable attorney and counselor-at-law of the courts of this state of not less than ten years' standing, who shall receive an annual salary of three thousand dollars. The third commissioner shall be a reputable citizen, and shall receive ten dollars per day for actual services rendered as a member of the commission. Such salaries may be fixed by the governor, secretary of state and comptroller, at different amounts than those prescribed in this section, whenever in their discretion such amounts should be changed. Each commissioner shall receive annually twelve hundred dollars, payable monthly, in lieu of his traveling and incidental expenses. The full term of office of a commissioner shall be six years. Where the term of office of a commissioner expires at a time other than the last day of December, the term of office of his successor is abridged so as to expire on the last day of December, preceding the time when such term would otherwise expire, and the term of office of each commissioner thereafter appointed shall begin on the first day of January. The commissioners shall be appointed by the governor, by and with the advice and consent of the senate.

(L. 1889, ch. 283, Sections 1 - 5, as amended by L. 1890, ch. 273, There have been omitted from Section 1 the temporary provisions relating to the creation of the first commission. The matter relating to the filling of vacancies, and the taking and filing of oaths of office is omitted since it is amply covered by Pub. Off. L., Sections 10 and 28. The sentence providing that the salaries of the commissioners may be fixed by the governor, secretary of state and comptroller was not included in the bill as originally submitted to the legislature by this commission. It was inserted in the committee of the assembly.)

Section 4. Office and clerical force of commission. - The commission shall be provided by the proper authorities with a suitably furnished office in the state capitol, where it shall hold stated meetings at least once in three months. It may hold other meetings, at such office or elsewhere, as it may deem necessary. It may employ a secretary, a stenographer, and such other employes as may be necessary. The salaries and reasonable expenses of the commission and of the necessary clerical assistants shall be paid by the treasurer of the state on the warrant of the comptroller, out of any moneys appropriated for the support of the insane.

(L. 1889, ch. 283, Section 6, as amended by L. 1890, ch. 273, without material change. The limit to be appropriated for salaries is omitted. Since the passage of the act creating the commission, their powers and duties have been increased and consequently the legislature has disregarded the limit by this section. The part relating to the power of the secretary to attest papers is re-enacted in the next section).

Section 5. Official seal and execution of papers. - The commission shall have an official seal. Every process, order or other paper issued or executed by the commission, may, by the direction of the commission, be attested, under its seal, by its secretary or by any member of the commission, and when so attested shall be deemed to be duly executed by the commission.

(L. 1889, ch. 283, Sections 6 and 14, as amended by L. 1890, ch. 273, The commission, by Section 843 of the code of civil procedure, has the power to administer oaths in all matters which they are required to investigate. By Section 933 of the code copies of all papers filed in a public office, having an official seal, may be introduced as evidence upon a proper certification by the officer having charge of such papers. It is then only necessary to re enact the part of this section relating to the official seal).

Section 6. General powers. - The commission is charged with the execution of the laws relating to the custody, care and treatment of the insane, as provided in this act, not including feeble-minded persons and epileptics as such and idiots. They shall examine all institutions, public and private, authorized by law to receive and care for the insane, and inquire into their methods of government and the management of all such persons therein. They shall examine into the condition of all buildings, grounds and other property connected with any such institution, and into all matters relating to its management. For such purpose each commissioner shall have free access to the grounds, buildings and all books and papers relating to any such institution. All persons connected with any such institution shall give such information, and afford such facilities for any such examination or inquiry as the commissioners may require. The commission may, by order, appoint a competent person to examine the books, papers and accounts, and also into the general condition and management of any institution to the extent deemed necessary and specified in the order.

(L. 1889, ch. 283, Section 10, as amended by L. 1890, ch. 273, without change in substance. The last sentence is new. By Section 11 of article 8 of the constitution, the state commission in lunacy is made a constitutional body and the power conferred upon them to visit and inspect institutions for the insane, not including institutions for epileptics and idiots).

Section 7. Official visits. - The commission, or a majority thereof, shall visit every such institution at least twice in each calendar year. Such visits shall be made jointly or by a majority of the commission on such days and at such hours of the day or night, and for such length of time, as the visiting commissioners may choose. But each commissioner may make such other visits as he or the commission may deem necessary. Each visit shall include, to the fullest extent deemed necessary, an inspection of every part of each institution, and all the out-houses, places, buildings and grounds belonging thereto or used in connection therewith. The commissioners shall, from time to time, make an examination of all the records and methods of administration, the general and special dietary, the stores and methods of supply, and, as far as circumstances may permit, of every patient confined therein, especially those admitted since the preceding visit, giving such as may require it suitable opportunity to converse with the commissioners apart from the officers and attendants. They shall, as far as they deem necessary, examine the officers, attendants and other employes, and make such inquiries as will determine their fitness for their respective duties. At the next regular or special meeting of the commission, after any such visit, the visiting commissioners shall report the result thereof, with such recommendations for the better management or improvement of any such institution, as they may deem necessary. But such recommendations shall not be contrary to the doctrines of the particular school of medicine adopted by such institutions. The commissioners shall, from time to time, meet the managers or responsible authorities of such institutions, or as many of the number as practicable, in conference, and consider, in detail, all questions of management and improvement of the institution, and shall also send to them, in writing, if approved by a majority of the commissioners, such recommendation in regard to the management and improvement of the institution as they may deem necessary or desirable.

(L. 1889, ch. 283, section 11, as amended by L. 1890, ch. 273, without change in substance. The part relating to recommendations is new. It is not required here as in the old law to enter at length the result of the inspection in the 'commissioner's visiting book.' This has been proved by experience to be of no practical value.)

Section 8. Regulations and forms. - The commission shall make such regulations in regard to the correspondence of the insane in custody as in its judgment will promote their interests, and it shall be the duty of the proper authorities of each institution to comply with and enforce such rules and regulations. All such insane shall be allowed to correspond without restriction with the county judge and district attorney of the county from which they were committed. The books of record and blank forms for the official use of the hospitals shall be uniform and shall be approved by the commission.

(L. 1889, ch. 283, Section 19, as amended by L. 1890, ch. 273, without change in substance. L. 1895, ch. 693. The last two sentences are new in the statute although the commission in lunacy have formerly made similar requirements by means of rules and regulations.)

Section 9. Annual report. - The commission shall, annually, report to the legislature its acts and proceedings for the year ending September thirtieth last preceding, with such facts in regard to the management of the institutions for the insane as it may deem necessary for the information of the legislature, including estimates of the amounts required for the use of the state hospitals and the reasons therefor; and also the annual reports made to the commission by the board of managers of each state hospital and by the State Charities Aid association.

(L. 1889, ch. 283, Section 18, as amended by L. 1890, ch. 273, without change in substance. The part relating to the including of the annual reports of the boards of managers and of the State Charities Aid Association is new. The report formerly required did not contain estimates of amounts required for the use of state hospitals. This change is made because of the estimate system adopted in 1893).

Section 10. State hospital districts; how defined. - The state commission in lunacy shall divide the state into as many state hospital districts as there are state hospitals. No county shall be divided in such classification, unless more than one of the existing state hospitals be situated within such county. Whenever the commission shall deem it necessary to more conveniently care for the insane, in the various hospitals, it may change the limits of such hospital districts. When a new state hospital shall be established, they shall again divide the state into hospital districts. Before any such change or re-establishment of hospital districts shall be made, the board of managers of each such hospital shall be notified by the commission that they may be heard in regard thereto at a specified time and place. Such hospital districts shall be so defined that the number of patients in each district shall be in proportion, as nearly as practicable, to the accommodations which are or may be provided by the state hospital or hospitals within such district.

(L. 1890, ch. 126, Section 1. This act created a board for the establishment of state insane asylum districts and gave them the power to divide the state into districts. Such board consisted of the president of the state board of charities, the comptroller of the state and the commissioners in lunacy. Since the passage of that act, the power of the state board of charities has been materially changed, and their supervision over state hospitals has been placed with the commission in lunacy. We have, therefore, provided by the revision that the commission in lunacy be given the power formerly vested in such state board of charities. We have omitted the temporary provision contained in Section 1, and only preserved such part as is now in force.)

Section 11. Change of hospital districts and reassignment of patients. - When a change or re-establishment of state hospital districts shall be made, or a new state hospital district created, the commission shall make a report thereof, designating the counties included within each district affected thereby, and file the same with the secretary of state, and send a copy to the managers and superintendent of each state hospital, and to each judge of a court of record, each county superintendent of the poor, and each county clerk in the state, to be filed in his office.

(L. 1890, ch. 126, Section 2, with such changes as were necessary in striking out the temporary matter.)

Section 12. Record of medical examiners. - Any physician who receives a certificate as a medical examiner in lunacy shall file such original certificate in the office of the clerk of the county where he resides, and forward a certified copy thereof to the office of the commission within ten days after such certificate is granted. The commission shall keep in its office a record showing the name, residence and certificate of each duly qualified medical examiner, and shall immediately file in its office, when received, each duly certified copy of a medical examiner's certificate, and advise the examiner of its receipt and filing. No examiner shall be qualified until he has received from the commission an acknowledgment of the receipt and filing of his certificate.

(This section is a part of L. 1889, ch. 283, Section 7, as amended by L. 1890, ch. 273.)

Section 13. Record of patients. - The commission shall keep in its office, and accessible only to the commissioners, their secretary and clerk, except by the consent of the commission or one of its members, or an order of a judge of a court of record, a record showing:

1. The name, residence, sex, age, nativity, occupation, civil condition and date of commitment of every patient in custody in the several institutions for the care and treatment of insane persons in the state, and the name and residence of the person making the petition for commitment, and of the persons signing such medical certificate, and of the judge making the order of commitment.
2. The name of the institution where each patient is confined, the date of admission, and whether brought from home or another institution, and if from another institution, the name of such institution, by whom brought, and the patient's condition.
3. The date of the discharge of each patient from such institution since the fifteenth day of May, eighteen hundred and eighty nine, and whether recovered, improved or unimproved, and to whose care committed.
4. If transferred, for what cause, and to what institution; and if dead, the date and cause of death.
(L. 1889, ch. 283, Section 8, as amended by L. 1890, ch. 273, without change in substance.)

Section 14. Institutions to furnish information to commission. - The authorities of the several institutions for the insane shall furnish to the commission the facts mentioned in the last preceding section, and such other obtainable facts relating thereto as the commission, may from time to time, in the just and reasonable discharge of its duties, require of them, with the opinion of the superintendent thereon, if requested. The superintendent or person in charge of such institutions, whether public or private, must, within ten days after the admission of an insane person thereto, cause a true copy of the medical certificate and order on which such person shall have been received, to be made and forwarded to the office of the commission; and when a patient shall be discharged, transferred or shall die therein, such superintendent or person in charge shall, within three days thereafter, send the information to the office of the commission, in accordance with the forms prescribed by it.

(L. 1889, ch. 283, Section 9, as amended by L. 1890, ch. 273, without material change in substance.)

Section 15. Commission to provide for the prospective wants of the insane. - The commission shall provide sufficient accommodations for the prospective wants of the poor and indigent insane of the state. To prevent overcrowding in the state hospitals, it shall recommend to the legislature the establishment of other state hospitals, in such parts of the state as in their judgment will best meet the requirements of such insane. It shall also furnish to the legislature in each year, an estimate of the probable number of patients who will become inmates of the respective state hospitals during the year beginning October first next ensuing, and the cost of all the additional buildings and equipments, if any, which will be required to carry out the provisions of this chapter relating to the care, custody and treatment of the poor and indigent insane of the state. No money shall be expended by the managers of a state hospital for the erection of additional buildings, or for unusual repairs or improvements of state hospitals, except upon plans and specifications to be approved by the commission. The cost of such buildings as are to be occupied by patients erected on the grounds of existing state hospitals, including the necessary equipment for heating, lighting, ventilating, fixtures and furniture, shall, in no case exceed the proportion of five hundred and fifty dollars per capita for the patients to be accommodated therein. No municipality of the state shall have the power to modify or change plans or specifications for the erection, repair or improvement of state hospital buildings or the plumbing or sewerage connected therewith.

(L. 1890, ch. 126, Sections 10 – 12, without change, except in form and phraseology. The sentence relating to the approval of plans by the commission is taken from L. 1894, ch. 358, p. 719, par. 1. The provision relating to the cost of buildings is new, as is also the last sentence.)

Section 16. Director of the pathological institute. - The commission shall, after a special civil service examination therefor, appoint a director of the pathological institute, who shall perform, under the direction of the commission, such duties relating to pathological research as may be required for all of the state hospitals for the insane. His office and laboratory shall be in the city of New York. He shall receive an annual salary to be fixed by the commission, subject to the approval of the governor.

(New, but see L. 1895, ch. 693, and L. 1874, ch. 446, tit Ill, Section 4, R.S., 8th ed., p. 2163.)

THE INSANITY LAW. ARTICLE II.

Institutions for the Care Treatment and Custody of the Insane. (Sections 30 - 49).

Section 30. State hospitals for the poor and indigent insane. - There shall continue to be the following hospitals for the care and treatment of the poor and indigent insane of the state which are hereby declared to be corporations; but other insane persons, who are residents of the state, may be admitted when there is room therein for them:

1. Utica State hospital, at the city of Utica, in the county of Oneida.
2. Willard State hospital, in the town of Ovid, county of Seneca.
3. Hudson River State hospital, near the city of Poughkeepsie, in the county of Dutchess.
4. Buffalo State hospital, in the city of Buffalo, county of Erie.
5. Middletown State Homeopathic hospital, at Middletown, in the county of Orange.
6. Binghamton State hospital, at Binghamton, in the county of Broome.
7. Rochester State hospital, at the city of Rochester, in the county of Monroe.
8. Saint Lawrence State hospital, near the city of Ogdensburg, in the county of Saint Lawrence.
9. Collins State Homeopathic hospital for the insane, in the town of Collins, county of Erie.
10. Long Island State hospital, at Kings Park, Suffolk county, Long Island.
11. Manhattan State hospital, in New York city and at Central Islip, Suffolk county. (348,349)

(L. 1890, ch. 132, Sections 1 – 7, L. 1891, ch. 335, Section 1, L. 1894, ch. 707, Section 1, L. 1895, ch. 628, Section 1, L. 1896, ch. 2, Section 1. The act of 1890 changed the names of the insane asylums then existing; the act of 1894 established the Collins State Homeopathic hospital; that of 1895, the Long Island State hospital, and that of 1896, the Manhattan State hospital.)

Section 31. Managers of state hospitals and their terms of office. - Each state hospital shall be under the control and management of its present board of managers or trustees, subject to the statutory powers of the commission, and to the provisions of this section as to the modification of their terms of office and the number of such trustees. Such trustees or managers shall hereafter be termed managers. On or before the thirty-first of December, after this chapter takes effect, and at which time the terms of the managers then in office shall expire, the governor shall appoint a board consisting of seven members for each state hospital by so arranging terms of one, two, three, four, five, six and seven years, that a term shall expire on the thirty-first day of December in each year, beginning with the year eighteen hundred and ninety-seven. If a vacancy occur otherwise than by expiration of term, the appointment of a manager to fill such vacancy shall be for the unexpired term of the manager whose office became vacant; but the provisions of this section shall not apply to the Middletown State Homeopathic hospital at Middletown, in the county of Orange, where the number of managers shall be thirteen.

(This section is new. By the statutes now in force, the number of managers and their terms of office varies in the different hospitals. Utica hospital is controlled by nine managers, appointed for three years (L. 1874, ch. 446, tit Ill, Section1); Willard hospital by eight trustees for eight years (L. 1874, ch. 446, tit IV, Section 1); Hudson River State hospital by nine managers for six years (L. 1874, ch. 446, tit V, Section 1); Buffalo State hospital by ten managers for six years (L. 1874, ch. 446, tit VI, Sections 1, 2); Middletown State hospital by thirteen managers for six years (L. 1875, ch. 634, p. 808); Binghamton State hospital by eleven managers for six years (L. 1879, ch. 8280, Section 1; L. 1880, ch. 61, Section 1); St. Lawrence State hospital, ten managers for six years (L. 1887, ch. 575, Section 1); Rochester State hospital, nine managers for nine years (L. 1891, ch. 338, Section 2); Long Island State hospital, seven managers for seven years (L. 1895, ch. 628, Section 4); Collins Farm State hospital, three managers for six years (L. 1894, ch. 707).

Section 32. Appointment and removal of managers. - The managers and their successors appointed after the appointment and classification made pursuant to the preceding section, shall severally be appointed by the governor, by and with the advice and consent of the senate, as often as a vacancy shall occur by expiration of term, or otherwise; and they may severally continue in office until their successors are appointed and have qualified; and they shall be subject to removal by the governor upon cause shown and an opportunity to be heard. All managers hereafter appointed shall reside in the hospital district in which the hospital is situated for which they are respectively appointed, but no person shall be eligible to the office of manager who is either an elective state officer or a member of the legislature, and if any such manager shall become a member of the legislature or such elective state officer, his office as manager shall be vacant. All the managers of the Middletown State Homeopathic hospital and of the Collins State Homeopathic hospital may be appointed from any portion of the state and shall be adherents of homeopathy. If any manager fails for one year to attend the regular meetings of the board of which he is a member, his office shall be vacant, and the board by resolution shall so declare, and a certified copy of every such resolution shall forthwith be transmitted by the board to the governor.

(L. 1874, ch. 446, tit. III, Section 1; tit. IV, Section 1; tit. V, Section 1; tit. VI, Section 1,2; tit. VII, Section 1; R.S., 8th ed., pp. 2162-2172, L. 1876, ch. 121, R.S. 8th ed., p. 2177, L. 1879, ch. 280, Section 1, as amended by L. 1889, ch. 427; R.S. 8th ed., p. 2178, L. 1887, ch. 375, Section 1, R.S. 8th ed. P. 2189, L. 1895, ch. 628, Section 4. The provisions of these acts relating to the appointment and removal of managers are here re-enacted and made uniformly applicable to all the state hospitals. There is no material change made as the same provisions are somewhere contained in the acts establishing the several hospitals.) (333 – 352)

Additional Sections of Article II:

33. General powers and duties of boards of managers. 34. Appointments of resident officers by managers. 35. General powers and duties of superintendent. 36. The general and medical superintendents of the Long Island and Manhattan State hospital. 37. Monthly meetings of superintendents. 38. Salaries of officers and wages of employes. 39. Monthly estimates of expenses; contingent fund. 40. Powers and duties of treasurer. 41. Monthly statement of receipts and expenditures; vouchers. 42. Actions to recover moneys due the hospital. 43. General powers and duties of the steward. 44. Purchases. 45. Official oath. 46. Actions against commissioners in lunacy, or officers or employes of state hospitals. 47. Private institutions for the insane. 48. Recommendations of commission. 49. Visitors to state hospitals.

THE INSANITY LAW. ARTICLE III.

Commitment, Custody and Discharge of the Insane. (Sections 60 - 77)

Section 60. Order for commitment of an insane person. - A person alleged to be insane and who is not in confinement on a criminal charge, may be committed to and confined in an institution for the custody and treatment of the insane, upon an order made by a judge of a court of record of the city or county, or a justice of the supreme court of the judicial district, in which the alleged insane person resides or may be, adjudging such person to be insane, upon a certificate of lunacy made by two qualified medical examiners in lunacy, accompanied by a verified petition therefor, or upon such certificate and petition, and after a hearing to determine such question, as provided in this article. The commission shall prescribe and furnish blanks for such certificates, and petitions which shall be made only upon such blanks. An insane person shall be committed only to a state hospital, a duly licensed institution for the insane, or the Matteawan State hospital, or to the care and custody of a relative or committee, as hereinafter provided. No idiot shall be committed to or confined in a state hospital. But any epileptic or feeble-minded person becoming insane may be committed as an insane person to a state hospital for custody and treatment therein.

(Substitute for L. 1874, ch. 446, tit. I, Section 1 in part; R.S. 8th ed. p. 2155. Under the law as it now is, a person may be confined in an asylum upon the certificate of two physicians, under oath, setting forth the insanity of such person, which certificate is to be approved by the court within five days after the confinement of such person. Under the proposed revision the order of the court must issue upon the certificate of two physicians and the petition of the applicant before the insane person can be confined. The following section contains the proceedings for determining the insanity of a person.)

Section 61. Medical examiners in lunacy; certificates of lunacy. - The certificate of lunacy must show that such person is insane and must be made by two reputable physicians, graduates of an incorporated medical college, who have been in the actual practice of their profession at least three years, and have filed with the commission a certified copy of the certificate of a judge of a court of record, showing such qualifications in accordance with forms prescribed by the commission. Such physicians shall jointly make a final examination of the person alleged to be insane within ten days next before the granting of the order. The date of the certificate of lunacy shall be the date of such joint examination.

Such certificate of lunacy shall be in the form prescribed by the commission, and shall contain the facts and circumstances upon which the judgment of the physicians is based and show that the condition of the person examined is such as to require care and treatment in an institution for the care, custody and treatment of the insane.

Neither of such physicians shall be a relative of the person applying for the order or of the person alleged to be insane, or a manager, superintendent, proprietor, officer, stockholder, or have any pecuniary interest, directly or indirectly, or be an attending physician in the institution to which it is proposed to commit such person.

(L. 1894, ch. 446, tit. I, Sections 1, 2: R.S. 8th ed. p. 2155, L. 1890, ch. 273, Section 7; R.S., 8th ed. (supp.) p. 3437, with such change as is necessary because of the suggested method of commitment. The order of the court issues after the certificate of lunacy is made. The present law requires no order. The provision that the certifying physicians shall not be relatives of either party is new. The examination made by the two physicians is to be joint, and the date of the certificate is to be the date of the joint examination.)

Section 62. Proceedings to determine the question of insanity. - Any person with whom an alleged insane person may reside or at whose house he may be, or the father or mother, husband or wife, brother or sister, or the child of any such person, and any overseer of the poor of the town, and superintendent of the poor of the county in which any such person may be, may apply for such order, by presenting a verified petition containing a statement of the facts upon which the allegation of insanity is based, and because of which the application for the order is made. Such petition shall be accompanied by the certificate of lunacy of the medical examiners, as prescribed in the preceding section. Notice of such application shall be served personally, at least one day before making such application, upon the person alleged to be insane, and if made by an overseer or superintendent of the poor, also upon the husband or wife, father or mother or next of kin of such alleged insane person, if there be any such known to be residing within the county, and if not, upon the person with whom such alleged insane person may reside, or at whose house he may be. The judge to whom the application is to be made may dispense with such personal service, or may direct substituted service to be made upon some person to be designated by him. He shall state in a certificate to be attached to the petition his reason for dispensing with personal service of such notice, and if substituted service is directed, the name of the person to be served therewith.

The judge to whom such application is made may, if no demand is made for a hearing in behalf of the alleged insane person, proceed forthwith to determine the question of insanity, and if satisfied that the alleged insane person is insane, may immediately issue an order for the commitment of such person to an institution for the custody and treatment of the insane. If, however, it appears that such insane person is harmless and his relatives or a committee of his person are willing and able to properly care for him, at some place other than such institution, upon their written consent, the judge may order that he be placed in the care and custody of such relatives or such committee. Such judge may, in his discretion, require other proofs in addition to the petition and certificate of the medical examiners.

Upon the demand of any relative or near friend in behalf of such alleged insane person, the judge shall, or he may upon his own motion, issue an order directing the hearing of such application before him at a time not more than five days from the date of such order, which shall be served upon the parties interested in the application and upon such other persons as the judge, in his discretion, may name. Upon such day, or upon such other day to which the proceeding shall be regularly adjourned, he shall hear the testimony introduced by the parties and examine the alleged insane person if deemed advisable, in or out of court, and render a decision in writing as to such person's insanity. If it be determined that such person is insane, the judge shall forthwith issue his order committing him to an institution for the custody and treatment of the insane, or make such other order as is provided in this section. If such judge can not hear the application he may, in his order directing the hearing, name some referee, who shall hear the testimony and report the same forthwith, with his opinion thereon, to such judge, who shall, if satisfied with such report, thereon judge shall report render his decision accordingly. If the commitment be made to a state hospital, the order shall be accompanied by a written statement of the judge as to the financial condition of the insane person and of the persons legally liable for his maintenance as far as can be ascertained. The superintendent of such state hospital shall be immediately notified of such commitment, and he shall, at once, make provisions for the transfer of such insane person to such hospital.

The petition of the applicant, the certificate in lunacy of the medical examiners, the order directing a further hearing as provided in this section, if one be issued, and the decision of the judge or referee, and the order of commitment shall be presented at the time of the commitment to the superintendent or person in charge of the institution to which the insane person is committed, and verbatim copies shall be forwarded by such superintendent or person in charge and filed in the office of the state commission in lunacy. The relative, or committee, to whose care and custody any insane person is committed, shall forthwith file the petition, certificate and order, in the office of the clerk of the county where such order is made, and transmit a certified copy of such papers, to the commission in lunacy, and procure and retain another such certified copy.

The superintendent or person in charge of any institution for the care and treatment of the insane may refuse to receive any person upon any such order, if the papers required to be presented shall not comply with the provisions of this section, or if in his judgment, such person is not insane within the meaning of this statute, or if received, such person may be discharged by the commission. No person shall be admitted to any such institution under such order after the expiration of five days from and inclusive of the date thereof.

(This section is a substitute for the method of commitment now contained in the statute. See L. 1874, ch. 446, tit. I, Sections 1-4, 12; R.S. 8th ed. p. 2155. L. 1890, ch. 273, Section 7; R.S. 8th ed. (supp.) p. 3437. A person is now committed upon the certificate of two medical examiners, approved by a judge of a court of record. The alleged insane person may be confined upon the certificate in lunacy for five days preceding the approval of the judge. The judge may, in his discretion, take proofs as to any alleged lunacy before approving the certificate, or he may call a jury to determine the question.

By the proposed proceedings application is to be made to a court of record by verified petition, stating the facts upon which the allegation of insanity is based. Such petition is to be accompanied by the certificate in lunacy of two medical examiners.

Provision is made for the service of a notice of the application upon the alleged insane person and his relatives. Upon the petition and certificate the judge may issue his order of commitment.

If a relative or friend of an alleged insane person demand a hearing and a trial of the issue, or if the judge deem a trial necessary for complete justice, he must issue an order directing a hearing before him or a referee appointed by him, at which all the parties interested may be present and testify as to the condition of the alleged insane person.

It is not intended by this change to provide a trial of the issue in every case of alleged insanity. In a majority of the cases the insanity of the person is clearly apparent, and there is no occasion for an extended hearing. In such cases it is for the material advantage of all parties interested that the person be confined in an institution for the custody and treatment of the insane. There may be cases, however, where the insanity of the person may be in doubt, or where the applicants for the order of commitment are pecuniarily or otherwise interested in securing the confinement of the alleged lunatic. These cases should be carefully scrutinized and every opportunity be given to the alleged lunatic or to other persons interested in his welfare, to be heard if they so desire.

The provision that the judge issuing the order of commitment of an insane person to a state hospital shall make a statement, in writing, to accompany the order, of the financial condition of the person committed is new. It is presumed that the judge will ascertain such condition, and the information acquired will be of use to the hospital authorities and the commission in lunacy in securing from the estate of the person committed, or his relatives legally liable for his support, compensation for his maintenance at the hospital.)

Section 63. Appeal from order of commitment. - If a person ordered to be committed, pursuant to this chapter, or any friend in his behalf, is dissatisfied with the final order of a judge or justice committing him, he may, within ten days after the making of such order appeal therefrom to a justice of the supreme court other than the justice making the order, who shall cause a jury to be summoned as in case of proceedings for the appointment of a committee for an insane person, and shall try the question of such insanity in the same manner as in proceedings for the appointment of a committee. Before such appeal shall be heard, such person shall make a deposit or give a bond, to be approved by a justice of the supreme court, for the payment of the costs of the appeal, if the order of commitment is sustained. If the verdict of the jury be that such person is insane, the justice shall certify that fact and make an order of commitment as upon the original hearing. Such order shall be presented, at the time of the commitment of such insane person, to the superintendent or person in charge of the institution to which the insane person is committed, and a copy thereof shall be forwarded to the commission by such superintendent or person in charge and filed in the office thereof. Proceedings under the order shall not be stayed pending an appeal therefrom, except upon an order of a justice of the supreme court, and made upon a notice, and after a hearing, with provisions made therein for such temporary care or confinement of the alleged insane person as may be deemed necessary.

If a judge shall refuse to grant an application for an order of commitment of an insane person proved to be dangerous to himself or others, if at large, he shall state his reasons for such refusal in writing, and any person aggrieved thereby may appeal therefrom in the same manner and under like conditions as from an order of commitment.

(L. 1874, ch. 446, tit. I, Section 11; R.S. 8th ed. p. 2157, It is proposed in this section to provide an appeal from an order of commitment in the same manner as is provided for appeals in cases of appointment of committees for insane persons. The present method of a rehearing is not materially changed. (See Code of Civil Procedure, Section 2307f.) The requirement of a bond or deposit by the person appealing is new.)

Section 64. Costs of commitment. - The costs necessarily incurred in determining the question of the insanity of a poor or indigent person and in securing his admission into a state hospital, and the expense of providing proper clothing for such person, in accordance with the rules and regulations adopted by the commission, shall be a charge upon the town, city or county securing the commitment. Such costs shall include the fees allowed by the judge or justice ordering the commitment to the medical examiners. If the person sought to be committed is not a poor or indigent person, the costs of the proceedings to determine his insanity and to secure his commitment, as provided in this article, shall be a charge upon his estate, or shall be paid by the persons legally liable for his maintenance. If in such proceedings, the alleged insane person is determined not to be insane, the judge or justice may, in his discretion, charge the costs of the proceedings to the person making the application for an order of commitment, and judgment may be entered for the amount thereof and enforced by execution against such person.

(This section is new. The amount of the costs are in the discretion of the court. See Code Civil Procedure, Section 3240.)

Section 65. Liability for care and support of poor and indigent insane. - All poor and indigent insane persons not in confinement under criminal proceedings, shall, without unnecessary delay, be transferred to a state hospital and there wholly supported by the state. The costs necessarily incurred in the transfer of patients to state hospitals shall be a charge upon the state. The commission shall secure from relatives or friends who are liable or may be willing to assume the costs of support of inmates of state hospitals supported by the state, reimbursement, in whole or in part, of the money thus expended.

(L. 1890, ch. 126, Section 11; R.S. 8th ed. (supp.) p. 3419. By this section all poor and indigent insane were made a state charge; to this extent it is re-enacted in this section. The last sentence imposes a power upon the commission in lunacy not formerly possessed. A similar power is vested in the treasurers of the state hospitals by Section 42 ante, and in superintendents and overseers of the poor by Sections 914-915 of the Code of Criminal Procedure.)

Section 66. Liability for the care and support of the insane other than the poor and indigent. - The father, mother, husband, wife and children of an insane person, if of sufficient ability, and the committee or guardian of his person and estate, if his estate is sufficient for the purpose, shall cause him to be properly and suitably cared for and maintained.

The commission and the superintendent of the poor of the county, and the overseer of the poor of the town where any such insane person may be, or in the city of New York, the commissioners of public charities, and in Brooklyn, the commissioners of charities and correction, may inquire into the manner in which any such person is cared for and maintained; and if, in the judgment of any of them, he is not properly or suitably cared for, may apply to a judge of a court of record for an order to commit him to a state hospital under the provisions of this article, but such order shall not be made unless the judge finds and certifies in the order that such insane person is not properly or suitably cared for by such relative or committee, or that it is dangerous to the public to allow him to be cared for and maintained by such relative or committee.

The costs and charges of the commitment and transfer of such insane person to a state hospital shall be paid by the committee, or the father, mother, husband, wife or children of such person, to be recovered in an action brought in the name of the people by the commission, the superintendent of the poor of the county, or the overseer of the poor of the town where such insane person may be, or in the city of New York in the name of the commissioners of public charities, and in the city of Brooklyn in the name of the commissioners of charities and correction.

(L. 1874, ch. 446, tit. I, Sections 12, 13; R.S. 8th ed., p. 2157, are included in the first paragraph of this section. The second paragraph is new. The power of poor officers to institute proceedings for the commitment of insane persons is also granted by Section 62, ante. The procedure is to be regulated by that section, and if such proceedings are instituted by such officers under this section the order of commitment should include a statement that it is dangerous for the alleged lunatic to be at large, etc.)

Section 67. Duties of local officers in regard to their insane. - All county superintendents of the poor, overseers of the poor and other city, town or county authorities, having duties to perform relating to the insane poor, are charged with the duty of seeing that all poor and indigent insane persons within their respective municipalities, are timely granted the necessary relief conferred by this chapter, and when so ordered by a judge, as herein provided, or by the commission, shall see that they are, without unnecessary delay, transferred to the proper institutions provided for their care and treatment as the wards of the state. Before sending a person to any such institution, they shall see that he is in a state of bodily cleanliness and comfortably clothed with new clothing, in accordance with the regulations prescribed by the commission. The commission may, by order, direct that any person it deems unsuitable therefor shall not be so employed or act as such attendant.

Each patient shall be sent to the state hospital, within the district embracing the county from which he is committed, except that the commission may, in their discretion, direct otherwise, but private or public insane patients, for whom homeopathic care and treatment may be desired by their relatives, friends or guardians, may be committed to the Middletown State Homeopathic hospital, or to the Collins State Homeopathic hospital from any of the counties of the state, in the discretion of the judge granting the order of commitment; and the hospital to which any patient is ordered to be sent shall, by and under the regulations made by such commission, send a trained attendant to bring the patient to the hospital. Each female committed to any institution for the insane shall be accompanied by a female attendant, unless accompanied by her father, brother, husband, or son. After the patient has been delivered to the proper officers of the hospital, the care and custody of the municipality from which he is sent shall cease.

(L. 1874, ch. 446, tit. III, Section 23, R.S. 8th ed., p. 2166, L. 1890, ch. 126, Section 6, R.S. 8th ed. (supp.) p. 3419, L. 1893, ch. 214, Section 5 is here enacted without change. The provision allowing the commission to direct that unsuitable persons shall not act as attendants is new. The theory of ch. 126 of L. 1890, is that the patients of each district be committed to the hospital situated therein. By L. 1893, ch. 323, amending L. 1890, ch. 126, Section 13, it was provided that nothing in such act should prevent the sending of public patients to the State Homeopathic hospital, if homeopathic treatment was desired. This privilege is retained in this section with such changes as seem necessary because of the proposed method of commitment.)

Section 68. Duty of committee and others to care for the insane; apprehension and confinement of a dangerous insane person. - When an insane person is possessed of sufficient property to maintain himself, or his father, mother, husband, wife or children are of sufficient ability to maintain him, and his insanity is such as to endanger his own person, or the person and property of others, the committee of his person and estate, or such father, mother, husband, wife, or children must provide a suitable place for his confinement, and there maintain him in such manner as shall be approved by the proper legal authority. The county superintendent of the poor and the overseers of the poor of towns and cities, the commissioners of public charities in the city of New York, and the commissioners of charities and correction in the city of Brooklyn, are required to see that the provisions of this section are carried into effect in the most humane and speedy manner.

Upon the refusal or neglect of a committee, guardian or relative of an insane person to cause him to be confined, as required in this chapter, the officers named in this section shall apply to a judge of a court of record of the city or county, or to a justice of the supreme court of the judicial district in which such insane person may reside or be found, who, upon being satisfied, upon proper proofs, that such person is dangerously insane and improperly at large, shall issue a precept to one or more of the officers named, commanding them to apprehend and confine such insane person in some comfortable and safe place; and such officers in apprehending such insane person shall possess all the powers of a peace officer executing a warrant of arrest in a criminal proceeding. Unless an order of commitment has been previously granted, such officers shall forthwith make application for the proper order for his commitment to the proper institution for the care, custody and treatment of the insane, as authorized by this chapter, and if such order is granted, such officer shall take the necessary legal steps to have him transferred to such institution. In no case shall any such insane person be confined in any other place than a state hospital or duly licensed institution for the insane, for a period longer than ten days, nor shall such person be committed as a disorderly person to any prison, jail or lockup for criminals, unless he be violent and dangerous, and there is no other suitable place for his confinement, nor shall he be confined in the same room with a person charged with or convicted of crime.

Any person apparently insane, and conducting himself in a manner which in a sane person would be disorderly, may be arrested by any peace officer and confined in some safe and comfortable place until the question of his sanity be determined, as prescribed by this chapter. The officer making such arrest shall immediately notify the superintendent of the poor of the county, or the overseers of the poor of the town or city, or, in the city of New York, the commissioners of public charities, or, in the city of Brooklyn, the commissioners of charities and correction, who shall forthwith take proper measures for the determination of the question of the insanity of such person.

(Pt. I, ch. 20, tit. III, Sections 1-6; R.S. 8th ed., p. 2153, L. 1874, ch. 446, tit. I, Sections 6, 8, 9, 37; R.S. 8th ed., p. 2157, are here re-enacted with such changes as are necessary to conform the inconsistent provisions of such sections. The only material change is that before confining the lunatic in an institution, the proper order of the court should be obtained. It is proposed that no insane person should be confined in a prison, jail or lockup, unless he is dangerous and no other suitable place for his confinement can be had. It is also provided that any peace officer may arrest an insane person conducting himself in a disorderly manner.)

Section 69. Patients admitted under special agreement. - The managers of a state hospital may authorize the superintendent to admit thereto, under special agreement, insane patients, who are residents of the state, other than poor and indigent insane persons, when there is room for such insane therein. But no patient shall be permitted to occupy more than one room in any state hospital, nor shall any patient, his friends or relatives, be permitted to pay for his care and treatment therein a sum greater than ten dollars a week. Such patients, when so received, shall be subject to the general rules and regulations of the hospital. The amount agreed upon for the maintenance of such insane persons in a state hospital, shall be secured by a properly executed bond, and bills therefor shall be collected monthly. The commission may appoint agents, whose duty it shall be to secure from relatives and friends who are liable therefor, or who may be willing to assume the cost of support of any of the inmates of state hospitals as are being supported by the state, reimbursement in whole or in part of the money so expended. The compensation of each agent shall not exceed five dollars a day, and the necessary traveling and other incidental expenses incurred by him, to be approved by the comptroller.

(L. 1874, ch. 440, tit. III, Section 22; R.S. 8th ed., p. 2166, L. 1887, ch. 375, Section 12, R.S. 8th ed., p. 2193, L. 1893, ch. 214, Section 7, L. 1895, ch. 693, Section 1, are contained herein without material change.)

Section 70. Entries in case book. - Every superintendent or other person in charge of an institution for the care and treatment of the insane, shall, within three days after the reception of a patient, make, or cause to be made, a descriptive entry of such case in a book exclusively set apart for that purpose. He shall also make or cause to be made entries from time to time, of the mental state, bodily condition and medical treatment of such patient during the time such patient remains under his care, and in the event of the discharge or death of such person, he shall state in such case book the circumstances thereof, and make such other entries at such intervals of time and in such form as may be required by the commission.

(L. 1874, ch. 446, tit I, Section 4; R.S. 8th ed., p. 2156, without change of substance.)

Section 71. Transfer of patients when hospital is overcrowded. - When the building of any state hospital shall become overcrowded with patients, or the number of buildings shall be reduced by fire, or other casualties, or for other cause, the commission may, in its discretion, cause the transfer of patients therefrom, or direct that patients required to be sent thereto, be transferred to another state hospital, where they can be conveniently received, or make, in special emergencies, temporary provision for their care, preference to be given in such transfers to a hospital in an adjoining rather than in a remote district. The expenses of such transfer shall be chargeable to the state, and the bills for the same, when approved by the commission, shall be paid by the treasurer of the state, on the warrant of the comptroller, out of any moneys provided for the support of the insane.

(L. 1890, ch. 126, Sections 8, 9; R.S. 8th ed., (supp.) p. 3419, consolidated and the unnecessary parts omitted. A part of Section 9 is covered by Section 65 of the revision.)

Section 72. Investigation into the care and treatment of the insane. - When the commission has reason to believe that any person adjudged insane is wrongfully deprived of his liberty, or is cruelly, negligently or improperly treated, or inadequate provision is made for his skillful medical care, proper supervision and safe keeping, it may ascertain the facts, or may order an investigation of the facts by one of its members. It, or the commissioner conducting the proceeding, may issue compulsory process for the attendance of witnesses and the production of papers, and exercise the powers conferred upon a referee in the supreme court. If the commission deem it proper, it may issue an order directed to any or all institutions, directing and providing for such remedy or treatment, or both, as shall be therein specified. If such order be just and reasonable, and be approved by a justice of the supreme court, who may require notice to be given of the application for such approval, it shall be binding upon any and all institutions and persons to which it is directed, and any willful disobedience of such order shall be a criminal contempt and punishable as such. Whenever the commission shall undertake an investigation into the general management and administration of any institution for the insane, it may give notice to the attorney general of any such investigation, and the attorney general shall appear personally or by deputy and examine witnesses who may be in attendance. The commission, or any member thereof, may at any time visit and examine the inmates of any county or city alms-house, to ascertain if insane persons are kept therein.

(L. 1890, ch. 273, Section 13, amending L. 1889, ch. 283, without material change.)

Section 73. Habeas corpus. - Any one in custody as an insane person is entitled to a writ of habeas corpus, upon a proper application made by him or some friend in his behalf. Upon the return of such writ, the fact of his insanity shall be inquired into and determined. The medical history of the patient, as it appears in the case book, shall be given in evidence, and the superintendent or medical officer in charge of the institution wherein such person is held in custody, and any proper person, shall be sworn touching the mental condition of such person.

(This section is new. See Code of Civil Procedure, Section 2015ff.)

Section 74. Discharge of patients. - The superintendent of a state hospital, on filing his written certificate with the secretary of the board of managers, may discharge any patient, except one held upon an order of a court or judge having criminal jurisdiction in an action or proceeding arising out of a criminal offense at any time, as follows:

1. A patient who, in his judgment, is recovered.

2. Any patient who is not recovered but whose discharge, in the judgment of the superintendent, will not be detrimental to the public welfare, or injurious to the patient; provided, however, that before making such certificate, the superintendent shall satisfy himself, by sufficient proof, that friends or relatives of the patient are willing and financially able to receive and properly care for such patient after his discharge.

When the superintendent is unwilling to certify to the discharge of an unrecovered patient upon request, and so certifies in writing, giving his reasons therefor, any judge of a court of record in the judicial district in which the hospital is situated may, upon such certificate and an opportunity of a hearing thereon being accorded the superintendent, and upon such other proofs as may be produced before him, direct, by order, the discharge of such patient, upon such security to the people of the state as he may require, for the good behavior and maintenance of the patient. The certificate and the proof and the order granted thereon shall be filed in the clerk's office of the county in which the hospital is situated, and a certified copy of the order in the hospital from which the patient is discharged. The superintendent may grant a parole to a patient not exceeding thirty days, under general conditions prescribed by the commission.

The commission may, by order, discharge any patient in its judgment improperly detained in any institution. A poor and indigent patient discharged by the superintendent, because he is an idiot, or an epileptic, not insane, or because he is not a proper case for treatment within the meaning of this chapter, shall be received and cared for, by the superintendent of the poor or other authority having similar powers, in the county from which he was committed. A patient, held upon an order of a court or judge having criminal jurisdiction, in an action or proceeding arising from a criminal offense, may be discharged upon the superintendent's certificate of recovery, approved by any such court or judge. (The authority to grant a parole and the right of the commission to grant discharges are new provisions).

(L. 1874, ch. 446, tit. III, Section 24, as amended by L. 1895, ch. 172, L. 1889, ch. 280, Section 21, as amended by L. 1889, ch. 427, with some changes. The authority to grant a parole and the right of the commission to grant discharges are new provisions.)

Section 75. Clothing and money to be furnished discharged patients. - No patient shall be discharged from a state hospital without suitable clothing adapted to the season in which he is discharged; and if it can not be otherwise obtained, the steward shall, upon the order of the superintendent, furnish the same, and money not exceeding twenty-five dollars, to defray his necessary expenses until he can reach his relatives or friends, or find employment to earn a subsistence.

(L. 1874, ch. 446, tit. III, Section26; R.S. 8th ed., p. 2166, with no change in substance.)

Section 76. Transfer of nonresident patients. - If an order be issued by any judge, committing to a state hospital a poor or indigent person, who has not acquired a legal settlement in this state, the commission in lunacy shall return such insane person, either before or after his admission to a state hospital, to the country or state to which he belongs, and for such purpose may expend so much of the money appropriated for the care of the insane as may be necessary, subject to the audit of the comptroller.

(L. 1893, ch. 214, Section 6, without material change.)

Section 77. Insane Indians. - Poor and indigent insane Indians living within this state or upon any of the Indian reservations shall be committed to, confined in, and discharged from the state hospitals for the insane in the same manner and under the same rules and regulations as other poor and indigent insane persons; and all the provisions of this chapter shall apply to the Indians residing within this state the same as to other persons.

(Substitute for L. 1888, ch. 451, Section 4; R.S. 8th ed., p. 2146, The powers of the state board of charities, relating to the care of the insane, were by ch. 283 of L. 1889, transferred to the state commission in lunacy. By ch. 126 of L. 1890, the care of the indigent insane was made a state charge. There can, then, in view of these changes made since 1888, be no impropriety in providing that the indigent insane Indians be maintained in the same manner as other insane.)

ARTICLE IV. State Hospital for Insane Criminals. (Sections 90 - 104).

Section 90. Establishment and purposes of the Matteawan State hospital, 91. Medical superintendent, 92. Medical superintendent as treasurer of the hospital, 93. Salaries of resident officers, 94. Powers and duties of medical superintendent and assistants, 95. Monthly estimates, 96. Power of removal, 97. Transfer of insane convicts to the Matteawan State hospital, 98. Disposal of insane convicts after expiration of term of imprisonment, 99. Convicts on recovery to be transferred to prison, 100. Certificate of conviction to be delivered to medical superintendent and copy filed, 101. Transfer from state hospital to Matteawan State hospital, 102. Authority to recover for the support of patients, 103. Tenure of office, 104. Communications with patients.

ARTICLE V. Laws Repealed; When to Take Effect. (Sections 110 - 111).

Section 110 Laws repealed. - Of the laws enumerated in the schedule hereto annexed, that portion specified in the last column is repealed.

Section 111. When to take effect. - This chapter shall take effect on July first, eighteen hundred and ninety-six.

SCHEDULE OF LAWS REPEALED.

Revised Statutes, pt. 1, ch. 20, tit. 3.....ALL

Laws of-	Chapter	Sections.
1838	218	All
1874	446	All, except title 1, Sections 21, 22, 26." (53)

BIBLIOGRAPHY

Cover Photo:

Anonymous Grave Marker - Willard State Hospital Cemetery by Roger Luther at www.nysAsylum. com.

Dedication Page:

1. Fourth Annual Report Of The Trustees Of The Willard Asylum For The Insane For The Year 1872, Transmitted to the Legislature January 28, 1873, Albany: The Argus Company, Printers, 1873. <http://books.google.com/>

Preface:

2. Penney, Darby & Stastny, Peter, *The Lives They Left Behind, Suitcases From A State Hospital Attic,* Photographs by Lisa Rinzler, Bellevue Literary Press, New York, 2008, Page 32.

3. Salem Village Witchcraft Victims' Memorial at Danvers at <http://salem.lib.virginia.edu/ Commemoration.html>

Chapter 1:

4. Documents of the State of New-York, Eightieth Session, 1857, Volume I, No. 1 to No. 40, Albany: C. Van Benthuysen, Printer to the Legislature, 1857, Pages 1-4, 9-12, 94, 95. <http:// books.google.com/>

5. Excerpt from *The Dundee Record, Welfare Edition Recalls Evolution of Yates County's Home – Esperanza.* A document from the Yates County Historian's Office, no date, no author. (This article was about the original poor house, not the Esperanza Mansion, which did not become the Yates County Poor House until it was purchased by the county on July 8, 1922.)

6. Schedule, Comparative Statements of the Condition of the Various County Poor Houses of the State of New York in the Years 1868, 1878 and 1888, Pages 517, 518. <http://books.google.com/>

Chapter 2:

7. Third Annual Report of The Board of State Commissioners of Public Charities of the State of New York to which is Appended the Report of the Secretary of the Board, Transmitted to the Legislature March 28, 1870, Albany: The Argus Company Printers 1870, Pages 6,7. <http://books. google.com/>

8. Twenty-Second Annual Report of the Trustees of the Willard State Hospital for the Year 1890, Transmitted to the Legislature January, 1891, Albany: James B. Lyon, State Printer, 1891, Page 10. <http://books.google.com/>

9. *History of Seneca County*, New York, Philadelphia: Everts, Ensign & Everts, 716 Filbert Street, 1876, Press of J.B. Lippincott & Company, Philadelphia, Page 49. <http://books.google.com/>

10. "Transactions of the International Medical Congress," Ninth Session, Edited for the Executive Committee by John B. Hamilton, M.D., Secretary General, Volume V., Washington, D.C, U.S.A., 1887, Page 229. <http://books.google.com/>

11. *The National Cyclopedia of American Biography,* Volume IX. New York: James T. White Company, 1899, page 329. <http://books.google.com/>

12. Documents of Senate of the State of New York. Ninetieth Session. – 1867. Volume I, Nos. 1 to 28. Albany: Van Benthuysen & Sons Printing House, 1867, Page 405.

13. State of New York, Fifty-Second Annual Report of the State Board of Charities For the Year 1918, Volume Two, Albany, 1919, Page 2. <http://books.google.com/>

14. "Medical and Surgical Reporter," May 22, 1869, Volume 20, Edited by Harold Havelock Kynett, D.G. Brinton, Samuel Worcester Butler, Page 397. <http://books.google.com/>

15. First Annual Report of The State Charities Aid Association to The State Commission in Lunacy, December 1, 1893, Albany, James B. Lyon, State Printer, 1894, Page 23. <http://books.google. com/>

16. Fifth Annual Report Of The Trustees Of The Willard Asylum For The Insane For The Year 1873, Transmitted to the Legislature January 14, 1874, Albany: Weed, Parsons And Company, Printers, 1874, Page 26. <http://books.google.com/>

17. First Annual Report of the Trustees of the Willard Asylum for the Insane, for the year 1869, Transmitted to the Legislature, January 12, 1870, Albany, The Argus Company, Printers, 1870, Pages 5-21, 31, 36. <http://books.google.com/>

Chapter 3:

18. Eighteenth Annual Report of the State Board of Charities, Transmitted to the Legislature, January 27, 1885, Albany, N.Y., Weed, Parsons & Company Printers, 1885, Pages 120, 121, 163-179, 180. <http://books.google.com/>

Chapter 4:

19. Merriam-Webster On Line Dictionary. <http://www.merriam-webster.com/>

20. Reprinted from Chapin, John B., *A Compendium of Insanity*, (John B. Chapin, M.D., L.L.D., Physician in Chief, Pennsylvania Hospital for the Insane; Late Physician Superintendent of Willard State Hospital, New York; Honorary Member of The Medico-Psychological Society of Great Britain and The Society of Mental Medicine Belgium, etc.), Illustrated, Philadelphia: W.B. Saunders, 925 Walnut Street, 1898, Pages 29, 30, 31, 32-35, 36-43, 59-65, 101-109, 110, 117-125, 135, 138, 139, 140-143, 145, 147-149, 153, 154-159, 166-172, 174-176, 177-180, 181-186, 187, 188. <http://books.google.com/>

21. Reprinted from Tuke, D. Hack, *A Dictionary of Psychological Medicine Giving The Definition, Etymology, And Synonyms Of The Terms Used In Medical Psychology, with the Symptoms, Treatment, And Pathology Of Insanity And The Law Of Lunacy In Great Britain And Ireland.* (Edited by D. Hack Tuke, M.D., LL.D., Examiner in Mental Physiology in the University of London; Lecturer on Psychological Medicine At The Charing Cross Hospital Medical School; Co-Editor Of The "Journal Of Mental Science"), Volume I, London, J. & A. Churchill, 11 New Burlington Street, 1892, Pages 389-391, 393-395. <http://books.google.com/>

Chapter 5:

1870 United States Federal Census interpreted by L.S. Stuhler.

Chapter 6:

1870:

17. First Annual Report Of The Trustees Of The Willard Asylum For The Insane For The Year 1869, Transmitted to the Legislature January 12, 1870, Albany: The Argus Company, Printers, 1870, Pages 29,30. <http://books.google.com/>

22. Second Annual Report Of The Trustees Of The Willard Asylum For The Insane For The Year 1870, Transmitted to the Legislature January 24, 1871, Albany: The Argus Company, Printers, 1871, Pages 15,16. <http://books.google.com/>

1871:

23. Third Annual Report of the Trustees of the Willard Asylum for the Insane for the Year 1871, Transmitted to the Legislature January 16, 1872, Albany: The Argus Company Printers, 1872, Page 13. <http://books.google.com/>

1872:

1. Fourth Annual Report of the Trustees of the Willard Asylum for the Insane for the Year 1872, Transmitted to the Legislature January 28, 1873, Albany: The Argus Company Printers, 1873, Pages 6, 7, 9, 10, 28, 29, 30, 31, 33, 34, 35. <http://books.google.com/>

1873:

24. Fifth Annual Report Of The Trustees Of The Willard Asylum For The Insane For The Year 1873, Transmitted to the Legislature January 14, 1874, Albany: Weed, Parsons And Company, Printers, 1874, Page 11, 12, 28. <http://books.google.com/>

1874:

25. Sixth Annual Report of the Trustees of the Willard Asylum for the Insane for the Year 1874, Transmitted to the Legislature January 14, 1875, Albany: Weed, Parsons and Company, Printers, Pages 9, 10, 16, 17, 30, 32, 33, 35. <http://books.google.com/>

1875:

26. Seventh Annual Report of the Trustees of the Willard Asylum for the Insane 1875, Transmitted to the Legislature January 14, 1876, Albany: Weed, Parsons & Company, Printers, 1876, Pages 9, 33, 34. <http://books.google.com/>

25. Sixth Annual Report of the Trustees of the Willard Asylum for the Insane for the Year 1874, Transmitted to the Legislature January 14, 1875, Albany: Weed, Parsons and Company, Printers, Pages 40, 41. <http://books.google.com/>

1876:

26. Eighth Annual Report of the Trustees of the Willard Asylum for the Insane for the Year 1876, Transmitted to the Legislature January 12, 1877, Albany: Jerome B. Parmenter, State Printer, 1877, Pages 27, 30, 31. <http://books.google.com/>

1877:

27. Ninth Annual Report of the Trustees of the Willard Asylum for the Insane for the Year 1877, Transmitted to the Legislature January 14, 1878, Albany: Jerome B. Parmenter, State Printer, 1878, Page 7. <http://books.google.com/>

1878:

28. Tenth Annual Report of the Trustees of the Willard Asylum for the Insane for the Year 1878, Transmitted to the Legislature January 15, 1879, Charles Van Benthuysen & Sons, 1879, Pages 10, 11, 22, 23. <http://books.google.com/>

1879:

29. Eleventh Annual Report of the Trustees of the Willard Asylum for the Insane 1879, Transmitted to the Legislature January 14, 1880, Albany: Weed, Parsons & Company, Printers, 1880, Pages 12, 14, 15, 34, 35. <http://books.google.com/>

Chapter 7:

1880 United States Federal Census interpreted by L.S. Stuhler.

Chapter 8:

1880:

30. Twelfth Annual Report of The Trustees of the Willard Asylum of the Insane for the Year 1880, Transmitted to the Legislature January 14, 1881, Albany: Weed, Parsons & Company, 1881, Pages 30, 31. <http://books.google.com/>

1881:

31. Thirteenth Annual Report of the Trustees of the Willard Asylum for the Insane 1881, Transmitted to the Legislature January 12, 1882, Albany: Weed, Parsons & Company, 1882, Pages 26, 28, 29. <http://books.google.com/>

1882:

32. Fourteenth Annual Report of the Trustees of the Willard Asylum for the Insane 1882, Albany: Weed, Parsons & Company 1883, Page 74. <http://books.google.com/>

1883:

33. Fifteenth Annual Report of the Trustees of the Willard Asylum for the Insane 1883, Transmitted to the Legislature January 8, 1884, Albany: Weed, Parsons & Company 1884, Page 36. <http://books.google.com/>

1884:

34. Sixteenth Annual Report of the Trustees of the Willard Asylum for the Insane, September 30, 1884, Page 6. <http://books.google.com/>

1885:

35. "Care of the Filthy Cases of Insane," Stephen Smith, M.D., State Commissioner of Lunacy, New York City. Proceedings of the National Conference of Charities and Correction, at the Twelfth Annual Session Held in Washington, D.C., June 4 – 10, 1885, Edited by Isabel C. Barrows, Official Reporter of the Conference, Boston: Press of George H. Ellis, 141 Franklin Street, 1885, Pages 148-153. <http://books.google.com/>

1886:

36. Twentieth Annual Report for the State Board of Charities for the Year Ending September 30, 1886, Transmitted to the Legislature January 4, 1887, Weed, Parsons and Company, 1887, Page 144. <http://books.google.com/>

37. Eighteenth Annual Report of the Trustees of the Willard Asylum for the Insane for the Year 1886, Willard, N.Y., Asylum Press Print, 1886, Pages 22, 23. <http://books.google.com/>

1887:

38. Documents of the Assembly of the State of New York, One Hundred and Eleventh Session, 1888, Volume IV., Part 2, Nos. 25-29, Nineteenth Annual Report of the Trustees of the Willard Asylum for the Insane for the Year 1887, Transmitted to the Legislature January 16, 1888, The Troy Press Company, Printers, 1888, Pages 23, 24. <http://books.google.com/>

1888:

39. Twenty-Second Annual Report of the State Board of Charities for the Year 1888, Transmitted to the Legislature January 30, 1889, Albany: The Troy Press Company Printers, 1889, Page 25. <http://books.google.com/>

40. Sixteenth Annual Report of the State Commissioner in Lunacy for the Year 1888, Transmitted to the Legislature January 15, 1889, State of New York, No. 24., Albany: The Troy Press Company, Printers, 1889, Pages 39, 40. <http://books.google.com/>

1889:

41. First Annual Report of the State Commission in Lunacy for the Year 1889, Transmitted to the Legislature January 1890, Albany: James B. Lyon, State Printer, 1890, Pages 67-69. <http://books.google.com/>

Chapter 9:

1880 United States Federal Census, Defective, Dependent and Delinquent Classes, interpreted by L.S. Stuhler.

Chapter 10:

1880 Defective, Delinquent and Dependent Classes

42. Compendium of the Tenth Census (June 1, 1880), Compiled Pursuant to An Act of Congress Approved August 7, 1882, Part II, Washington: Government Printing Office, 1883, Pages 1659 – 1665. <http://books.google.com/>

43. State of New York Fourteenth Annual Report of the State Board of Charities, Transmitted to the Legislature January 20, 1881, For the Year 1880, Albany: Weed, Parsons and Company, Printers, 1881, Pages 15, 16, 17, 23, 24, 25, 26, 27. <http://books.google.com/>

Chapter 11:

1890

44. Twenty-Fourth Annual Report of the State Board of Charities for the Year 1890, Volume 24, Transmitted to the Legislature January 5, 1891, Albany: James B. Lyon, State Printer 1891, Page 22. <http://books.google.com/>

8. Twenty-Second Annual Report of the Trustees of the Willard State Hospital for the Year 1890, Transmitted to the Legislature January, 1891, Albany: James B. Lyon, State Printer, 1891, Page 14. <http://books.google.com/>

45. Chapter 39, State of New York First Annual Report of the State Commission in Lunacy, 1889, Pages 787, 788. <http://books.google.com/>

53. Reprinted from Annual Report of the Commissioners of Statutory Revision of the State of New York, Transmitted to the Legislature, April 21, 1896, No. 87, In Assembly, Wynkoop, Hallenbeck Crawford Co., State Printers, Albany and New York, 1896, Pages 333-396. <http://books.google.com/>

Chapter 12:

1900 United States Federal Census interpreted by L.S. Stuhler.

Chapter 13:

1900:

46. Thirty Second Annual Report of the Board of Managers of the Willard State Hospital to the State Commission in Lunacy for the Year 1900, Chapter 20 Report of the Board of Managers of the Willard State Hospital, Pages 257-286. <http://books.google.com/>

1901:

57. Manual for the use of the Legislature of the State of New York, 1901, Prepared pursuant to the provisions of Chapter 683, Laws of 1892 by John T. McDonough, Secretary of State, Albany, Brandow Printing Company, 1901, pages 412,416. <http://books.google.com/>

1902:

47. "The Survey, Charity Organization Society of the City of New York," Survey Associates, Charities – A Weekly Review of Local and General Philanthropy, Vol. IX, July – December, 1902, New York, 105 East 22D Street, Pages 79, 80, 81. <http://books.google.com/>

1904:

48. Twelfth Annual Report of the State Charities Aid Association to the State Commission in Lunacy, November 1, 1904, New York City, United Charities Building, 105 East 22d Street, Pages 46, 47. <http://books.google.com/>

Additional Sources:

54. First Annual Report of The State Charities Aid Association To The State Commissioners Of Public Charities Of The State Of New York, March 1, 1873, New York: Cushing, Bardua & Co., Steam Book and Job Printers, Nos. 644 and 646 Broadway, Page 6,12. <http://books.google.com/>

55. The Organization of Charities, Being a Report of The Sixth Section Of The International Congress Of Charities, Corrections, And Philanthropy, Chicago, June 1893, Baltimore: The John Hopkins Press; London: The Scientific Press, 428 Strand W.C., 1894, Pages 62-65. <http://books.google.com/>

Laws:

Law A - An Act To Provide For The Establishment Of County Poorhouses.

49. Documents of The Senate of the State of New York, One Hundred and Twenty Seventh Session, 1904, Vol. XIV. No. 22, Part 4, Annual Report of the State Board of Charities for the Year 1903, In Three Volumes with Statistical Appendix to Volume One bound separately. Volume Three Charity Legislation in New York 1609 to 1900. Transmitted to the Legislature February 1, 1904, Pages 241-245. <http://books.google.com/>

Law B - Laws Relating To The Willard Asylum For The Insane.

50. Thirty-First Annual Report of the Board of Managers of the Willard State Hospital to the State Commission in Lunacy, Reprints of Reports for the years 1867 1868 1872 1873 1874 1875 1877 1878 1879 1880 and 1898, Albany: James B. Lyon, State Printer, 1900. Annual Report of the Board of Managers of the Willard State Hospital for the Year 1898, Page 65. <http://books.google.com/>

Law C - Chapter 713. An Act In Relation To The Chronic Pauper Insane.

51. Laws of the State of New York, Passed at the Ninety-Fourth Session of the Legislature, Begun January Third, and Ended April Twenty-First 1871. In the City of Albany. Volume II. Albany: The Argus Company Printers 1871, Pages 1541,1542. <http://books.google.com/>

Law D – Laws Relating To The Insane, Chapter 446, Laws of 1874.

50. Thirty-First Annual Report of the Board of Managers of the Willard State Hospital to the State Commission in Lunacy, Reprints of Reports for the years 1867 1868 1872 1873 1874 1875 1877 1878 1879 1880 and 1898, Albany: James B. Lyon, State Printer, 1900. Annual Report of the Board of Managers of the Willard State Hospital for the Year 1898, Page 140. <http://books.google.com/>

Law E – Exhibit M.

39. Twenty-Second Annual Report of the State Board of Charities for the Year 1888, Transmitted to the Legislature January 30, 1899, Albany: The Troy Press Company Printers, 1889, Pages 288-290. <http://books.google.com/>

Law F – The State Care Act.

52. The Revised Statutes of the State of New York, Fifth and Sixth Supplemental Volumes, To the Eighth Edition of the Revised Statutes and to Birdseye's Revised Statutes, Comprising The General Statutes of 1889-1892, both inclusive, As Amended to the Commencement of the Session 1893, Ninth Edition, Volume V, Edited by Charles A. Collin, 1892, Banks and Brothers Law Book Publishers, Albany, New York, Pages 3417-3422. <http://books.google.com/>

Law G – The Insanity Law.

53. Annual Report of the Commissioners of Statutory Revision of the State of New York, Transmitted to the Legislature, April 21, 1896, No. 87, In Assembly, Wynkoop, Hallenbeck Crawford Co., State Printers, Albany and New York, 1896, Pages 333-396. <http://books.google.com/>

Law H – An Act further to define the powers and duties of the board of State commissioners of public charities, and to change the name of the board to The State Board of Charities.

56. Second Annual Report Of The State Charities Aid Association, March 1, 1874, New York: Slote & Janes, Stationers and Printers, 93 Fulton Street, 1874, Page 21. <http://books.google.com/>

Acknowledgements

I wish to thank my husband, Don, for believing in me. Without his encouragement, patience, love, and support, throughout the creation of this book, I would have given up.

I wish to thank John Garger for his help, advice, insights, support, and creative ideas that helped me pull the book and blog together. Without him, *The Inmates of Willard 1870 to 1900* would still be sitting in a folder on my computer.

CPSIA information can be obtained at www.ICGtesting.com
Printed in the USA
LVOW050313130412

277451LV00003B/37/P